Where's My Free Lunch?

Be a better leader - of yourself, and other people.

Thoughts, observations and useful ideas about life, leadership and change, taken from a lifetime of listening.

"The only thing we control is ourselves"

By

Eddie Ross

131 Finsbury Pavement, London EC2A 1NT

https://www.theempirepublishers.co.uk/

Our books may be purchased in bulk for promotional, educational, or business use.

Please contact The Empire Publishers at +44 20 4579 8116, or by email at support@theempirepublishers.co.uk

First Edition November 2024

About the Author

Edward Paterson Ross, owner and founder of *EPR Business International Coaching & Consulting*, is a certified executive leadership coach based in Madrid, Spain.

Eddie specializes in business strategy and transformation through team and executive coaching.

He has had a career spanning a number of industries and has extensive senior leadership experience in international strategy, marketing, communication, and eCommerce. He works with business leaders to optimize leadership, personal impact, and communication skills via an action-oriented approach.

During his career, Eddie worked in advertising for *Saatchi & Saatchi, WCRS*, and the *EURO RSCG Group*. In travel technology for *Amadeus IT Group* and *Rumbo.com*. In the UK legal sector for *QualitySolicitors*.

Already a published business author, Eddie has an MSc Masters degree in *Consulting & Coaching for Change* from Oxford University, UK & HEC Paris, France, and a BSc undergraduate degree in *Systems Management* from City University, London. He was trained by the *Coach Training Institute* and *FocalPoint Business Coaching*.

Eddie is a joint US/UK citizen who was raised in the UK and has lived most of his adult life in Madrid, Spain, and Dallas, Texas. He is married and has four children. He is a fluent Spanish speaker.

Dedication

This book is dedicated, with grateful thanks, to all of the friends, colleagues, bosses and clients who I have listened to, and observed, over the years. You have all taught me so much.

Some of you may perhaps think you recognize yourself somewhere in these pages. If you feel I am describing you in a highly positive light then yes, it is probably you. If you feel I am being in any way critical or negative. Then no, it isn't you.

Blank page left intentionally

Contents

Foreword

by David Wheldon OBE

I have known Eddie Ross for almost 40 years, we met back in the halcyon days of Saatchi & Saatchi in 1986. So, I am biased as I read and comment on this wonderful testament to Eddie's listening skills.

A beautifully written mixture of personal anecdote, observations and musings with deep intellectual and academic thought to underpin the lessons for us all to learn.

From a lifetime of working with great people in all sorts of challenging situations Eddie extracts the key moments of personal development and growth. Always with humility, humor and kindness, laughing with people, not at them.

Eddie's eye for the learning opportunity has developed from those early days of working together. Now a fully trained and qualified Coach, he highlights that change must always come from within. He offers a very cogent argument for the absolute need for what he calls me-pathy: understanding ourselves and our strengths and weaknesses, and how others react to us.

The current president of the World Bank and former CEO of Mastercard, Ajay Banga recently suggested another key metric DQ, for 'decency quotient' to complement IQ, and EQ. In the same way Eddie's new me-pathy metric MQ can be added to the human skills necessary to be a great leader.

Eddie has IQ, EQ, DQ and MQ in abundance and it is very generous of him to share it with us all.

From my perspective, reminding us that there is no such thing as a free lunch is very apt, given how many great lunchtime discussions Eddie and I have enjoyed over the years. Indeed, the lunch was never free, but it was always valuable.

David Wheldon OBE (for services to advertising and marketing), President Emeritus of the World Federation of Advertisers. Fellow of the Marketing Society, Fellow of the IPA. Consultant, coach, mentor and speaker.

Introduction

It does feel like we live in times of volatility, uncertainty, complexity, and ambiguity - a *'VUCA world'*- as it was first described by someone in about 1987[1]. That means we've had over 35 years of it already, so we ought really to be getting quite good at dealing with it.

In truth, the world has always been pretty VUCA - we have just gradually invented better acronyms. We all constantly face challenges that are both personal and professional. Our work and business lives are intertwined, and we can often feel the VUCA-ness affecting us in different ways as we try to navigate relationships, family, and career.

---

[1] VUCA acronym first appeared in 1987, drawing on the leadership theories of Warren Bennis and Burt Nanus – to describe or to reflect on the volatility, uncertainty, complexity and ambiguity of general conditions and situations. Initially used in military education following the cold war.

Challenges also bring opportunities. Whatever we are up against, we still need to work out how to advance and be successful, and to define what success means for each of us.

We need to anticipate, understand the consequences of our decisions or actions, prepare well, and be good at identifying ideas and possibilities that will move us forward to something better.

Whatever may be happening, history has shown that we need leaders. To inspire us, to enthuse us, to move us to action, and to help us on our way. There will always be leaders, and they will not always be great, but they will always be there.

History does repeat itself, and we can all learn from past mistakes and successes. Our own, and those of others.

If you are in a leadership position, then you will probably (hopefully…) feel you have taken on an important responsibility, to guide and support others towards greater success - however that might be measured in your own particular situation. I expect you think a lot about how to do that better.

I reflect on all the countless conversations I have had with colleagues, clients, leaders, and friends over the years. Coaching sessions, brainstormings, strategy meetings, or late-night chats in hotel bars with a glass of whisky after the sensible people have all gone up to bed.

I've noticed that the same subjects and challenges come up over and over again. The same old stuff keeps us all awake at night.

The idea of this book is to share what I have heard, observed, and learned in many years of work, coaching, and life about handling all that stuff.

My thoughts after listening to leaders who want or need to transform or improve something - themselves, their lives, their impact, their team, their relationships, or their business.

You, as a leader, can never stop evolving because nothing stands still.

I have organized the book into four parts - becoming a good leader of yourself (as all leadership starts with self-leadership), other people, and managing them effectively, leading business and change, and finally ending up with some more big-picture philosophical ideas that I find compelling.

I am sharing my own stories, examples, metaphors, models, and ideas that I have noticed resonate best with my clients and are most useful for me. It may seem like an eclectic (and maybe a bit haphazard) collection of thoughts and ideas but I make no apology for that. Each has proved useful and relevant at some point for me or someone else.

I also make only a vague distinction between a personal change and a corporate transformation. The essential challenges are the same, and the steps to follow are consistent. The reasons for failure are similar.

You may be a powerful leader, but you are still a person. I hope there will be something in here that brings you value or helps you think.

Some ideas are all my own, and some are other people's concepts that I believe are worth sharing. I aim to provide a reference whenever I talk about other people's work or ideas.

I have highlighted 30 key ideas throughout the text, which I have called the "Top 30" - so if you feel you can't manage to read the whole thing, you can try those and see if they tempt you in for more.

"Secrets to success" are so often just applied common sense, which is arguably our most useful tool for everything in life. This is absolutely true for being an effective and respected leader.

I find that a lot of success in life and work boils down to a fairly short list including:

- The relationships that we build and nurture.
- How well we know ourselves and our self-awareness.
- How well we communicate.
- How well we use the opportunities we are given to be good leaders, and make a real impact.
- What we do to feel more confident in ourselves, and create confidence in others.
- How we orchestrate our personal process of growth and evolution.
- How we define our own happiness and fulfillment.

Most important of all is to appreciate and accept that we only truly control ourselves. As much as we might like to feel we control the actions or ideas of others, it will be at best short-lived, and most likely an illusion or a delusion. Leadership is not about control.

And there is nothing easy about it either. Great leaders are truly dedicated and invest a lot of themselves to be just that. Whatever it is you are striving for, if you really want something, you will have to work hard for it, and nothing truly worthwhile comes to us easily.

Some people may seem lucky compared to others – but the harder you work at something, the more luck you are going to generate. In my experience, there really is no such thing as a free lunch in this world.

The ideas you will find here are all about working hard on being more comfortable in your own skin, whoever you are, being better at whatever it is you do, and getting more good things from people around you. And helping you to get to the place you want to go next.

I am a coach, and coaches like to ask questions. At the end of each chapter, I have included a short list of questions for you to reflect on. In some cases, you could try to give yourself a 'mark out of 10'. And if you feel you are a '5' - then what could you do to become a '7'?

Ask yourself: Based on what you read in the chapter, what might you like to be different? What actions could you take?

What questions do you have for yourself that you would add to the list?

Part 1

You (Leading Yourself)

Chapter 1: Self-leadership and me-pathy

Let's start off by thinking about what "leadership" really means, at least in this book.

Top 30 #1: Leadership Starts with You

What makes you a good leader? What do you think is a useful definition of leadership?

The dictionary defines it as "the office or position of a leader."

This is probably the idea that most typically comes to mind when thinking of leadership.

You are in charge of a group of people - and required to get them to do or achieve something together under your recommendation, guidance, or authority. And indeed, it certainly is true that a tremendous amount of thinking and effort goes into making people effective or better leaders of others in a hierarchical situation.

However, this is a very narrow way of thinking about leadership. Leadership capabilities begin within each one of us - and your capacity for self-leadership.

In a personal transformation process, or just in your everyday life, you have only yourself to lead. To achieve a goal or make a change, you will need to set realistic objectives and find a way to achieve them without delegating any responsibility to anyone else.

Later, we will discuss how to try to optimize leadership of teams and projects - but right here at the start, I want to make the point that leadership is something that you can be focusing on all the time, in everything you do.

Self-leadership starts with self-awareness. The best leaders, in every personal and professional relationship, are really good at understanding their own strengths and weaknesses - and the impact they make on others.

Every one of us has the opportunity to demonstrate great leadership behaviors in all the interactions we have every day. How you manage yourself, how you treat your bosses, how you interact with your colleagues, clients, or partners and yes… how you lead teams of people that report up to you

There is so much you can do to make those interactions and relationships more successful. You can constantly optimize every interaction you have and everything you do to drive toward a better outcome for yourself and for others.

If you are self-aware, good at managing yourself and your time, emotionally intelligent, and conscious of your impact, you are on an excellent path to being a good leader of other people.

Equally, if you are kidding yourself about your own capabilities or resisting changes that you know you need to make in your life, it is highly unlikely that others will be effectively or willingly led by you.

Essential Leadership Traits

What are the qualities of a good leader - to most effectively lead ourselves and others?

There are three elements, or traits, that I have observed all good leaders demonstrate. If you are an effective leader, you are likely to be:

- Conscious
- Responsible
- Intentional

Conscious - you are self-aware, present, thoughtful, understanding your own needs and the needs of others, aware of the situation, the environment, and 'what is happening.'

Responsible - feel that you have a role to play, can contribute to success, not just passive or observing, but engaging in relationships and activities at every level, you are always part of the solution.

Intentional - you have a plan, or you are working on one. You are driving toward something that you believe in and are committed to. You seek resolution, improvement, and outcomes.

When I talk about leadership in these pages, I want you to understand that I think of it always in this wider sense as a constantly recurring opportunity to do things better, in just about any situation, and in just about any relationship. Including our relationship with ourselves.

Leadership starts with you. We have lots to discuss more about leadership later, but let's first think about what makes you 'you.'

LEADERSHIP

Your Personal Brand and Impact on Others

Let's zoom in on your favorite subject. You.

How well do you know yourself? How conscious are you of your impact?

Nurturing your personal brand and intentionally 'marketing' yourself helps define who you are and what you offer the world and those around you. It will help you not only differentiate yourself and be memorable to others but also behave with confidence.

This is true for every one of us, regardless of whether you are the CEO of a giant corporation, a manager of a team, or simply responsible for yourself.

What Makes You Stand Out?

There are a lot of people in the world with an endless variety of personalities, likes, dislikes, and goals in life. The other day, I randomly decided to search for "Edward Ross" on LinkedIn. Up came nearly four thousand people sharing my name. So, before I even start to make my personal mark in the world, I am up against all those people with the exact same starting point as me – a name. We like to think of ourselves as unique and special. A lot of self-help books and popular thinking about being more successful revolves around the idea that each one of us is indeed a one-off, and that we are all capable of anything. And potentially, I am sure this is true.

To make a positive impact on others, which will certainly help you be more successful, you need to consciously work on your marketing plan for your personal brand – just as if you are a product that you are wanting to sell. As in any crowded and competitive marketplace, differentiation is a vital element of success.

Why are you different? What makes you stand out?

Are you memorable?

Are you appealing?

Are you conscious of your strengths, weaknesses, talents, or blind spots?

If we truly know ourselves, we are on a good path to understanding others and how they see us.

You are up against a big field of competition, and it's not easy to stand out. People who are regularly asked to speak at conferences usually have a particular personal story to tell that attracts or interests an audience.

However, not all of us can survive a plane crash, reflect on our time in jail, or explain how we had to learn to play the drums with our teeth. We need simply to focus on what it is we do well and emphasize that. Our story may not be dramatic or shocking, but it is still our story, and it is up to us to make it interesting and engaging.

Careful Who You Measure Yourself Against

Some of us can be tempted to compare ourselves unfavorably to others. We line up our weaknesses against what we see as other people's strengths. We haven't a hope if we do that to ourselves. We can always find people who seem more gifted, more successful, more popular, and apparently happier than us.

Even though we are aiming to stand out in some way, it is a mistake to start off with comparisons. We need to look carefully and honestly at ourselves and be clear about what we do well and can offer. In the world of work, that will often be mainly about our professional career experience and skills. Although our most powerful talents may be innate and highly personal to us.

Do you have certain unique qualifications? What do you have great confidence in doing? Have you lived in unusual places and maybe speak another language or learned from another culture that will engage people? Do you put others at ease? Are you especially direct and honest? Or maybe unusually charming and thoughtful? Or a good listener? What are your interests or passions? What can you bring, teach, or inspire others with?

Whatever it may be, those are your assets, they differentiate you, make you '*you*'. Being comfortable and clear about who, what, and why you are who you are helps to make you stand out and be memorable.

The more you actively work on whatever it is that defines and shapes you, the more confident you will be when interacting with people.

Good at Everything

Just as we need to be actively conscious of our strengths, it is equally important to be honest with ourselves about the things we are not good at.

It is unlikely and unrealistic to expect that we will all be good at everything. It would be an exhausting world to live in in that case. Admitting to ourselves and others that we have weaknesses and failings is, in fact, a great demonstration of confidence and strength.

Of course, we may wish to improve in the areas that we perceive as weaknesses and absolutely should do that. Deciding to work on something is, in itself, an admission that we can be better at it.

It is equally exhausting to spend time with people who cannot see their own failings as it is to deal with someone who sees no good in themselves. We need to strive for a healthy, honest balance. Knowing our strengths and how best to use them - and recognizing our weaknesses and having a plan to work on them.

I once had a colleague who was very bright, hardworking, demanding, and genuinely trying to be a good leader. Despite that, he wasn't that popular with people, as he lacked some hard-to-define personal skills that somehow made people feel uncomfortable around him.

One day, I was talking to another colleague, and we were casually discussing him. I said, *"What is it about him? What is 'off'?"*

She said, "*I know what it is - he never needs anything from anyone. He never asks for anything, never needs anyone's help. Never admits he has no idea what to do - even though I am sure sometimes he doesn't.*"

She was right. Even if he didn't feel that he needed advice and input from others, he would have benefited from involving others in his ideas and asking for their support. His desire not to admit weaknesses or to need help from others actually turned out to be a fundamental weakness.

There is a very big difference between being an 'incomplete leader' and being an 'incompetent leader'[2] - recognizing that you have areas where you are less powerful or experienced, and that you need help and input from others to make good choices and decisions is, in itself, a strength.

Making Your Elevator Pitch

How good are you at explaining who you are, what you do, and what you do well or less well... and why? When people are asked to introduce themselves at the start of a

---

[2] In Praise of the Incomplete Leader - Harvard Business Review by Deborah Ancona, Thomas W. Malone, Wanda J. Orlikowski, and Peter M. Senge From the HBR Magazine (February 2007)

meeting, have you ever noticed that they are often terrible at it?

Your colleague climbs uncomfortably to his feet at the start of a meeting and seems to mumble...

"Hi, yeah, um yes...I'm Frnk Smth, head of cnsm'r insights and...er... mkting. Yeah, good to be here.... Thanks"

But if we ask someone else to introduce Frank Smith, they will typically do a magnificent job, talking slowly and in a clear voice that everyone can understand.

"This is Frank Smith, our head of Marketing and Consumer Insights. He leads a team of 23 and spent 6 years at Google before he joined us last summer."

We need to work on getting good at talking about ourselves in a comfortable and confident way. Getting the right balance between overbearing or self-promoting and underselling ourselves and leaving a lukewarm impression.

We can start by setting out to be just as good at introducing ourselves as we are at introducing others. Speak clearly, develop your script. When you show confidence in yourself and what you do, and how you talk about yourself, you will put others at ease.

When I run strategy or team meetings, I always ask people to introduce each other - rather than themselves. If they don't know each other, this is also a good way to kick off a meeting and warm up a group. If they do know each other already, you can ask them to find out 'something interesting or surprising' about each other and tell the group about it.

Part of the reason I do this is that I have noticed how bad people are at talking about themselves.

What can you do to differentiate yourself, or at least make a positive impact right from the outset on the people you meet or work with?

Smile and Actually Mean It

How about starting off by just deciding to be a bit nicer? The internet is filled with research that shows that people who are positive and smile more often are onto a winning strategy. They enjoy better relationships, are healthier, live longer lives with lower blood pressure and less stress. They have increased success as being more 'likable' has been shown to be a significant advantage in business and the workplace.

It may feel that being 'likable' comes from people's naturally innate characteristics that belong only to some people — like being good-looking, extroverted, or gifted at something. The truth is that, like most things, being more likable is under our own control to a great extent.

In a study conducted at UCLA, subjects rated over 500 adjectives based on their significance to likability. The highest-rated adjectives had nothing to do with innate traits like being gregarious, intelligent, or attractive. Rather, the top adjectives were sincerity, transparency, and the capacity for understanding other people. So those are things you definitely can work on.

Friendly people are curious about others; they ask questions and actually listen to the replies. They look for the funny side, are forgiving, and patient. They don't take themselves too seriously. They laugh at problems and seek solutions without pointing fingers or blaming others. They are typically self-deprecating, good company, and generous.

You don't have to be nice or liked to be successful in life, and I am sure we all know someone who appears to be highly 'successful' but is also scary, mean, or not fun to be around. Do you want to be one of those people?

Or would you rather be one of those professional, strong bosses or colleagues who are also approachable, encouraging, thoughtful, consistent, and with a ready smile?

Consider the impact you make. How do you make others feel?

Are you concentrating on them and what they are saying, or just waiting for a chance to say something? Does meeting you make their day better? Do they want to stay and talk more to you, or are they edging away looking for someone more engaging, interesting, or maybe just nicer to be with?

There's a lot of emphasis on empathy and how important it is for leaders to be empathetic – and have *"the ability to understand how it feels to be someone else."*

But another important part of emotional intelligence is to understand the impression you make on others.

I call this **"me-pathy"** – the ability to truly understand the impact you have on others when they meet you, and deal with you.

Top 30 #2: Me-pathy

We've all heard of empathy, the ability to imagine what it's like to be someone else - to understand and share the feelings of another person.

It involves being able to put oneself in someone else's shoes and experience their emotions and perspectives without necessarily agreeing with their views or opinions.

Empathy is seen as a key component of emotional intelligence and can help you build stronger relationships, improve communication, and resolve conflicts. It's a great talent to be able to understand and connect with others.

But what about really connecting with and understanding yourself?

I call this "me-pathy" – the ability to truly understand the impact we have on others when they meet us and have to work with us. David Wheldon has additionally suggested that we call it our MQ, to go with our IQ, or EQ[3].

When you walk into a room, what do others see and feel? Do you know what your impact is on them?

If you have high levels of me-pathy, combined with good empathy, it is likely that you will be very conscious and in control of how you talk, act, and interact with others. That's a very good starting point for effective leadership.

We need to be honest with ourselves about the impact we make. If you are brave enough, you can ask people whom

---

[3] See Foreword

you trust for some feedback. You may be surprised by what you learn about yourself.

Having highly developed me-pathy helps you better manage situations and be more comfortable meeting new people or tackling new situations. You know yourself, you know what others are probably thinking about you, and you feel more confident and capable as a result.

It seems to be generally agreed collective wisdom that high levels of empathy make you a better leader - which I generally agree with up to a point. Nevertheless, my observation is that the people who actually make it into powerful leadership positions often do not achieve them due to their great empathy skills.

In fact, quite the opposite. Driven, single-minded, and clear-thinking people who are sure of themselves, their ideas, and their strengths very often are the ones chosen for the top job.

Leaders need to be decisive and strong - as well as thoughtful and caring. They need to make the right decision - not the popular one or the one that will create the least negative impact on others.

Me-pathy is just as important as empathy when it comes to being a strong and effective leader. Perhaps more important.

You need to listen well, understand how others feel in your presence, make sure they get your time and real attention to explain their ideas or proposals to you. You need to appreciate the impact you make on them, and how you make them feel.

Is there a significant gap between how you see yourself, and how others see you?

If so, it will certainly create issues for you in your relationships with bosses, peers, and teams. It is vital to be honest with yourself and have a good measure of your own me-pathy.

---

me-pathy
/ˈmiː - pəθiː/

noun
noun: **me-pathy**
1. the ability to understand your own impact on others

Practicing Tough Love

Your team is looking to you to lead them, and they need your steer, your guidance. Not everyone is going to like what you think. If you push your response to the next meeting to save someone's feelings, you may get high marks for empathy but low for me-pathy. You don't understand your impact, or lack of it.

Your team (even the ones who knew you weren't going to back them either) is disappointed to see you back down.

If we really care about something, we may say that we love it. Love is, by definition, an emotional and sometimes irrational state. Kind and thoughtful leaders get themselves into a position where they 'love' their people. They want to nurture them, teach them, and see them flourish.

But they also need them to perform, to respond, and to do better - learning from their mistakes. An effective leader practices 'tough love' with their team. A combination of empathy, me-pathy, and consistent focus on honest, constructive feedback allows people to question without fear of ridicule or failure, and be their true selves.

Doing What You Say

One measure of me-pathy is how honest you are with yourself about the extent to which you genuinely follow through when you say you will do something or help someone out.

When I first came to live in Texas some years ago, I didn't know a soul, but I wanted to establish a coaching practice. With that in mind, I set out to meet and network with absolutely everybody and anybody who would give me the time of day. During that process, I realized something.

90% of people that you talk to say that they will do something for you: connect you with somebody else, send you some information, invite you to an event...

But only 5% of people who promise you something (and that, I'm afraid, is being generous) actually do anything at all.

When you do come across a person who genuinely goes out of their way to help you, the impression they leave on you is enormous.

I had lunch in Dallas with an executive I had never met before. We had been connected by a person back in Spain that we both had worked with in the past. At our first meeting over lunch, he suggested two other people he felt I should meet.

By the time I got home after lunch, he had already sent emails introducing me to them. Both turned out to be critical to my future. After so many positive, friendly but ultimately fruitless chats, it was a shockingly different experience and made a deep impression.

Over time, we have now both helped each other out on a number of occasions.

Do you do what you say you are going to do?

If you don't, then you are not alone. But if you are one of those rare people who promise and then deliver on your promise, for no reward other than it being a good thing to do, you are a rare species.

Start with You

There are traditional sayings like *'lead from the front'* or *'don't expect others to do things you don't want to do'* which are useful ideas in terms of how you may be perceived as a leader.

Certainly, no one likes to work for a lazy boss or a person who espouses the "don't do as I do, do as I say" attitude.

I remember a manager on my team who had 3 or 4 direct reports, including two people with young children. She herself had children and would often disappear early from the office to take them to activities or collect them from school.

However, she was incredibly inflexible with her team - not allowing them to leave their desks until 5:30 pm. I think you can imagine the resentment and frustration this caused. Yet when I talked to her about it, she was surprisingly unaware and certainly unrepentant. She was the boss, so the rules were different for her.

She was demonstrating low empathy for her team's challenges (even though they were the same as her own) and nonexistent me-pathy for the impact she was making.

My suggestion is, before all else, to have a deep and genuine think about yourself. If you are serious about wanting to be a good leader of other people, then first of all, you need to be a confident and honest leader of yourself.

Self-awareness is the absolute starting point for becoming a person that others will follow. You know in your heart if you are confident, prepared, and fit to be in charge. If you feel that maybe you aren't, there are many ways to work on that, if you are prepared to do so.

Get to really know yourself: your strong points, shortcomings, preferences, capabilities, and how you are seen by others. Work on developing your me-pathy.

Let's continue to dig into the elements that make up your own personal brand.

Reflections

Here are a few key questions arising from the themes raised in this chapter

- In what ways could you be a better leader of yourself?
- How might you further develop your self-leadership skills?
- Can you be more conscious, responsible and intentional?
- Do you feel you have well-developed me-pathy?
- How might you better understand the impact you have on others?
- How comfortable are you when talking about yourself?
- How good are you at recognizing your own strengths and weaknesses?
- Do you do what you say you are going to do?

Chapter 2: Your personal brand perception

Your value proposition

Let's talk more about what makes you memorable or appealing. Why do people want to work with you? Why are you successful? Can you distill it down to any one thing?

You may have studied for years to improve yourself, to be a qualified professional at something like being a lawyer or doctor – or have years of experience in marketing, finance, senior leadership, or software development. But is it those qualifications or experiences that set you apart from others?

All the way back in 1908, the Carnegie Foundation published the results of research by a certain Charles Riborg Mann carried out with fifteen hundred engineers across the USA: *A Study of Engineering Education*[4].

He was interested to know what engineers felt was the key to a successful career. He found that "personal qualities" were cited seven times more often than technical skill or knowledge.

"...qualities such as common sense, integrity, resourcefulness, initiative, tact, thoroughness, accuracy, efficiency, and understanding of men..."

---

[4]

https://archive.org/details/studyofengineeri00mannuoft/page/n3/mode/2up

To further test his (what I suspect he found to be rather surprising) findings, he asked another seven thousand engineers across the USA to rank the following list "Technique, Knowledge, Understanding of Men, Efficiency, Judgement, and Character."

Over 85% placed "Character" at the top, and "Technique" was sent right to the bottom of the list.

Interpreted over the years, and updated with more modern language, this piece of work and its conclusions are known today as the "Carnegie Triangle." It's just as relevant as it ever was.

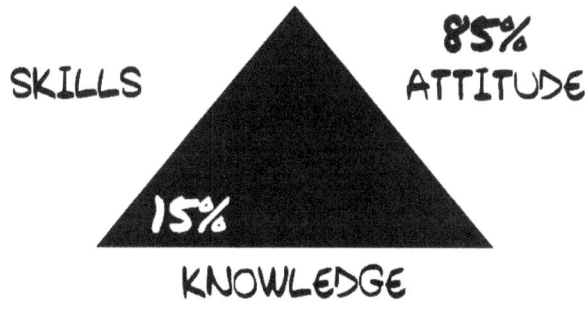

It reminds us that "Attitude" is many times more important for success than Skills and Knowledge put together. That was true over 100 years ago in the highly rigid masculine world of early 20th-century engineering—and it still is today.

You may have deeply impressive skills and voluminous knowledge, but the way you approach your work and how you interact with people is what really differentiates the impact you make. Your empathy and me-pathy are as, or maybe even more, important than all your degree certificates when it comes to your personal brand.

People are like Airlines

Imagine yourself in an overly narrow airplane seat, not very near the front, wedged between a person noisily eating a pretzel and a family of screeching infants. There are over three and a half hours still to go. It is slightly too hot. The drinks trolley is at least seven rows away and will be overpriced when it finally gets here. You are not enjoying this.

Have you ever stopped to consider how little we acknowledge or value the extraordinary human achievement required to fly us around in an airplane? Cabins equalized for air pressure, incredibly robust aero engines that never (well, hardly ever) fail, wings and fuselage filled with miles of electronics, and highly trained pilots who navigate us effortlessly to our destination.

Computers that land the plane on their own in thick fog. Yet, do we honestly care about any of that?

No, we expect it.

We judge our airline experience by ridiculously trivial factors when compared with the overall task of flying us around safely at 35 thousand feet: legroom, the food and the smile (or lack thereof) of the cabin staff are what we remember.

Airlines understand this slightly absurd state of affairs, which is why they don't talk about their core aeronautical competencies in their advertising (despite their pride in them) when they try to sell us and differentiate their airline. They know that the air journey is about the passenger experience, not the airplane or the flight plan.

Airlines talk about on-time performance, convenience, comfort, flat beds in business class, new exciting places for us to visit, and value for money.

In the same way, our own impact and proposition can often be driven much more by our emotional and soft skills than by our technical abilities.

How you behave and how you make other people feel can often be far more important in terms of creating a positive impact than what you know or your technical skills.

Most of us have at some point had the experience of interacting with a professional or technical expert (doctor, dentist, lawyer, plumber, etc.) and thinking, "I have confidence in this person's capabilities, but why are they so unfriendly?"

Our likelihood to recommend someone is often driven far more by our emotional experience than it is by their expertise, which we take for granted.

This "soft" impact we have on others is a massive part of our own personal brand perception. I think my dentist is a very good one. He seems to know his stuff, and his team seems happy and motivated. I trust him, and them. I've trusted him to do plenty of not very pleasant things to my teeth.

He is also very friendly and talks a lot—and is happy to chat with me about all sorts of things while he stuffs my mouth with wadding and fires up his drill.

Apparently, his team has code words to get him to shut up and move him onto the next patient as he gradually falls behind his daily schedule. They also obviously adore him, and that is also true of his patients. His personal brand as a trustworthy, professional dentist is underpinned by strong elements that have nothing to do with dentistry—and everything to do with his personal impact.

Your Personal Brand Needs Investment

Big, valuable, and famous commercial brands are supported by expensive advertising campaigns or offer a product or promise that people wish to be a part of and associate with themselves. The messages that companies deliver about their brand and products or services must be consistent with the experience that we all have when using or interacting with them.

Just as companies or products work hard and spend millions to develop their brands, you need to invest constantly in your own personal brand. How you look, how you talk, how you act, how you think, the clothes that you wear, how you treat people, how you react under stress.... All contribute to your personal brand impact.

The more you invest, the more impact you will make. It drives how you are perceived by others. Your personal brand is everything you say and everything you do. It underpins your me-pathy.

Building up your personal brand and reputation into something that has genuine meaning for people you interact with will have a profound impact on your success. However, creating and caring for a positive and powerful brand reputation is hard work and requires commitment, consistency, and clarity of purpose. You need to believe in its importance and understand how to care for it.

Your personal brand is like an iceberg. The small part that is visible to the world depends entirely on what is happening below the waterline. Your strength, sustainability, and stability come from inside you.

WHAT THE WORLD SEES

STRENGTH
STABILITY
SUSTAINABILITY

Your positive personal brand reputation will be built up by your behavior, capabilities, actions, and the impact you have on others. It all rests on your basic values and sense of purpose.

The more aware you are, and the extent to which you are honest with yourself about your own personal brand's strengths and weaknesses, are critical to your ability to optimize the way you are perceived.

Top 30 #3: Who Do You Need to Outrun?

A keen amateur photographer is out deep in the African bush, accompanied by a local guide. He is hoping to capture amazing pictures of wild African animals. As the two of them tread cautiously through the undergrowth, there is a loud rustle and a snort from a thicket some 50 feet away.

To their horror, an enormous rhinoceros emerges puffing and grunting, turning its head to look angrily at the hapless photographer and his companion. The beast lets out a bellow of fury and starts to charge towards them.

Panic-stricken, the photographer drops his camera in fright and makes to run away. As the rhinoceros bears down on him, he glances to his side, to see that his guide is calmly changing out of his boots into a pair of running shoes.

"What are you doing, you fool! You can never outrun this monster!" he shrieks.

"I don't need to outrun him," comes the calm reply. *"I just need to outrun you."*

Being good at understanding the context of a situation is a highly valuable skill. What is really needed? What is good enough? Will you need to beat everyone in sight to win or to get what you want? Or do you just need to be good enough or outperform certain people to win?

By constantly striving to achieve everything, you may end up achieving less than you hope - or even worse, not getting the things that really matter to you.

When you go into a situation where you want to achieve an objective (a sales pitch, an important presentation, a job interview...), how carefully do you ask yourself exactly what is needed to make that a successful interaction? How carefully do you define success? The more you do that, the more likely you are to achieve it. By trying to do too much, you may completely miss your target.

Perfect Is the Enemy of Good

Several famous thinkers over the years have gone on record as saying something similar about how, in trying to achieve perfection, you create the real risk that you will miss out on doing something that is "good enough."

Voltaire, the 18th-century French writer, is credited with saying *"le mieux est l'ennemi du bien"* (The best is the enemy of the good). It seems there may be an even more ancient Italian proverb that says, *"il meglio è nemico del bene."*

Even further back (500 BC), Confucius recommended that it is *"better a diamond with a flaw than a pebble without."* And let's not forget William Shakespeare in King Lear: *"Striving to better, oft we mar what's well."*

It seems like a consistent message through the ages. We need to do enough to be successful or achieve our target, and going beyond that can potentially ruin everything.

PERFECT
V.
GOOD ENOUGH?

Define Your Success Criteria

I once found myself presenting to a room of very senior technology leaders and investors. My task was to update them on our in-progress company-wide rebranding project. I thought it was very important and interesting, but I also knew that not all of them agreed with me.

They invited me to talk for an hour and update them on a lot of details about the project. I wanted to show off all the great work that my team and I had been doing, but I was very aware ahead of the meeting that they were going to be a tough crowd, short on patience with my fluffy branding stuff - especially the big boss.

I knew I needed three important things to be approved in that meeting, so I front-loaded those into my presentation. I even wrote them down on a paper in front of me and ticked them off as they got approved. After 15 minutes, I had only just gotten going with my presentation, but in terms of decisions, I already had what I came for.

After 20 minutes, the boss (as I had predicted) lost patience. *"OK, we've got a lot of important things to discuss today, how long is this going to take?"* he interrupted rudely. He wasn't at all a bad boss, very good, in fact, overall, just not very interested in the things I was responsible for. *"How much longer are you going to go on?"*

Despite this interjection, internally I felt supremely confident and comfortable. I wasn't upset about this treatment (I had anticipated it) and was able to reply, *"I can stop now if you like - you've already given me everything I came here for."* It was a good feeling.

There's another part to the story. The other senior executives in the room were woken up by this exchange between me and the boss. *"Well, do you want him to finish his presentation?"* he asked grumpily - they all said they all said "yes."

Knowing who exactly you need to be one step ahead of is critical to success. Trying to be one step ahead of everyone and everything is a sure route to disappointment and failure.

It is an important part of developing your me-pathy to know what is "good enough" to get what you need or want.

Looks and Body Language Do Matter

The world of work has changed significantly in recent years in terms of what is an acceptable way to dress. I find it hard to believe that for all those years I would put on my suit or jacket, fasten my tie, and shine my shoes before I headed to the office. It was just what everyone did.

Obviously, all that has changed. Flip-flops and shorts are quite acceptable in many companies.

Nevertheless, if you are setting out to convince someone or make a good impression, it is still worth it to spend some time thinking about the impact you make in terms of what you are wearing or your general appearance.

The old saying goes "you can never be overdressed," but I am not sure that is true anymore. When offices were typically "smart dress" places, it was probably true that a tie or skirt was a safe bet for an interview.

If you turn up now at a tech start-up in a suit, you may give off an impression that doesn't fit well with the values of the company. At the technology company where one of my sons works, suits and ties are actively frowned upon.

As with most things, the key here is to find the balance between what you feel is comfortable and appropriate to wear and how others will see you.

How you dress and present yourself definitely is an element of me-pathy. It makes sense to try to "mirror" the way that you think the person interviewing you might dress and so expect you to dress, but not to such an extent that you feel uncomfortable or fake.

The decision about whether or not to wear makeup or get a shave is truly yours to make - but avoid anything that is likely to make you feel self-conscious either way. Be you. But equally, if you don't get the job or the contract because you couldn't be bothered to smarten up or dress down to suit your audience - then it is your choice.

You can't control how someone will "see you" but you can decide to make your appearance a plus factor or minus factor in your chances of success.

You want to influence their perception of you as a good candidate or working partner that will not just do good work but also fit in with the work environment. Are you looking for an investor or to increase your budget? How you turn up to a meeting may well be a factor in helping someone else to build their perception of you and will influence the outcome for you.

Most importantly, how you dress is a key factor in how YOU feel about yourself. To an extent, it is similar to body language, albeit much more consciously controlled.

Body Language

Body language has been shown to have an important impact on how we are perceived by others. If we are open, positive, and look others in the eye, we are more likely to be listened to and get what we want.

If we are closed up and reserved and seem uncomfortable, we can make others uneasy and unwittingly stifle enthusiasm for us. It's difficult to control our natural body language tendencies, but recent research[5] seems to indicate that perhaps we can even change our own feelings about ourselves by using more positive body language. We release different hormones when we pose like a superhero than when we curl up in a ball.

When it comes to what we wear and how we show up, we should aim to give ourselves the best possible chance of feeling good about ourselves and giving off the right impression to others whom we want to impress.

What is definitely true is that whatever someone chooses to believe about you, or anything else, is the "truth" from their point of view.

---

[5] https://www.forbes.com/sites/kimelsesser/2020/10/02/the-debate-on-power-posing-continues-heres-where-we-stand/?sh=7b5eef50202e

Top 30 #4: Perception is Reality

We believe what we perceive to be accurate, and we create our own reality based on those perceptions. Our perceptions feel completely real to us; that doesn't mean they're necessarily factually correct - and certainly, it does not even slightly guarantee that others will have the same perception.

Our perceptions are built on our culture and previous experiences, education, emotions, ideas, self-interest, biases, and who we have been influenced by or choose to believe. Our perceptions are intensely personal, and we are comfortable when we spend time with people who have similar perceptions of the world as our own.

If your next-door neighbor has wildly different views from you, then you will always be at odds with him, and the annual neighborhood barbecue night will always be uncomfortable. It doesn't matter how long you talk to him; he's just never going to agree with you - or you with him.

Even though there may be actual facts available to support his, or your, argument, perceptions are much more powerful than facts, as they are rooted in beliefs.

So for each individual, their perception IS their reality. And this is very important to remember when you are trying to navigate a personal situation or a leadership challenge. If we set out to directly challenge someone's perceptions, we will immediately come up against their closely held personal belief systems, and those are well-defended and hard to change.

When we want to achieve something, we should start by remembering that what others see, feel, and believe is their reality - even if you see something totally different and also believe you have the facts to prove it. They are not "wrong" - just see things differently from you.

To be successful, we should aim to understand very well why they have a certain perception of a situation and work with that, helping them gradually see it in a different way but remaining respectful of their starting point.

Often, I hear clients say to me, *"but they have totally the wrong idea, they are seeing this all wrong"* - so I remind them that "perception is reality" and that we need to start from there to build a plan to make things different.

We need to carefully work out what and why others perceive if we have any hope of making them see things in a new way.

When I was living and working in Madrid, as a long-term "expat," I was sometimes asked to talk to people who were thinking of moving to Spain or who had already moved there and were struggling to adapt to Spanish life.

One night, I went for drinks after work with a person who wasn't enjoying the experience. He proceeded to go on an energetic rant about all the things he found annoying about life in Madrid in the late 1990s. His list included things like: the summer heat, the local food, the way people drive and park, how late everyone eats and goes to bed, how people are often late to appointments, a perceived lack of discipline, and a general quite relaxed attitude to the "rules"…

I listened carefully, and I imagine he was expecting me to offer a sympathetic ear as another Englishman abroad in Spain. Once he'd finished, I had to admit to him that just about everything he hated about life in Spain… was what I loved about it.

We were living the exact same experiences but perceived them entirely differently. Neither of us was *wrong.*

What Others Think of Me, How Little Others Think About Me

Another well-used saying (originally from the playwright and author Oscar Wilde, this time) is that *"the only thing worse than being talked about... is NOT being talked about."* Many of us do have a tendency to be sensitive about what we believe others think about us.

We can be so worried about "appearances" or what others will think of us or are saying about us that we can become paralyzed and unable to think for ourselves.

It is generally true that in any group of people, there will be a tendency to "gossip." It is human nature, and if we are ready to admit it, everyone does it to a certain extent. In his book "Sapiens," [6] the author Yuval Noah Harari argues that gossip has been an essential element for human evolution.

Gossip means that we keep in touch with what is "really going on" in an organization and find out things that are not being officially communicated.

In the case of early mankind, this was a matter of survival as you discovered there was a tiger loose nearby or which people you could trust or not.

In the modern workplace, it helps to build trust inside teams and to strengthen bonds between groups. People build trust by talking about others. Of course, gossip can also be malicious and purposefully false, which can be very damaging to an individual or an organization's culture.

I have always been fascinated by how terrible organizations are at keeping important things secret. If you tell someone something in "strict confidence," they will tell one other person almost immediately.

If you pass on your secret at 9 am to your one trusted confidante, within an hour, they have told one other person, and according to my math, by the end of that day, over 100 people are in on it.

If you really want something to be a secret, then don't tell anyone.

---

[6] *Sapiens - A Brief History of Humankind* by Yuval Noah Harari - Harper (2015)

How you handle gossip about you and are seen by others as generally managing confidential information is also an element of your me-pathy. As always, it's all about finding the right balance for you and the people you interact with.

You don't want to be seen as someone unreliable with sensitive information - that's a bad look for a leader. But also, it's good to show people that you are in touch and know what's going on in your team or group.

In reality, when it comes down to it, most of the time, people are far too focused on themselves to worry too much about what you are thinking or doing.

Stay true to your own values and beliefs, focus on what you can control, and don't worry unduly about what anyone may think. As another famous saying goes, versions of which have been attributed to various different writers and commentators over the years[7]:

"You'll worry less about what people think about you when you realize how seldom they do."

Less To This Than Meets The Eye

Along similar lines, it is sometimes also easy to feel that everyone else knows what is going on, and yet somehow you are in the dark and out of the loop. Worse still, you can feel you are being deliberately left out.

---

[7] David Foster Wallace? Olin Miller? Lee Traveler? Ethel Barrett? Mark Twain? John Steinbeck? Anonymous?

This is particularly true at the time of corporate reorganizations or changes. Everybody knows that something is being worked on and will be "announced soon," but nobody seems to know yet what the details may be.

In these situations, rumors and gossip will appear and flourish with incredible speed. You can quickly begin to get a feeling that *"there is more to this than meets the eye."*

Everyone but you is in the know. Whatever is being planned will be terrible for you, and that is why so far your boss (or your boss's boss) hasn't said anything about it to you.

Quickly, you and whole organizations can develop a powerful narrative of gloom, negativity, and suspicion fueled by a lack of information and collective paranoia.

Realistically, in some cases things might indeed turn out to be as bad as your worst pessimistic predictions - and then you will be justified to have believed, *"Just because I'm paranoid doesn't mean they aren't out to get me."*

However, I have noticed that in most cases, there is, in reality, often much less to this than meets the eye.

The reason your boss hasn't told you anything is because he or she also doesn't know anything either, or maybe knows you are not affected, so hasn't even thought about talking to you.

How often does the "big announcement" turn out to be not so big after all, and the rumors about individual or team changes just plain wrong?

As a leader, it is so important to understand how vital it is to communicate well and often, so that rumors and gossip are starved of the oxygen of individual or collective imagination that they need to thrive.

When faced with uncertainty or worry about what may be about to happen to you or your team, keep your imagination under control and don't allow yourself to be a part of the "rumor mill." And if you are really worried, look your boss in the eye and share your concerns. You may be surprised to discover how little they know, or how little is really going on.

Imposter Syndrome

Have you ever been in a meeting and found yourself thinking something like "how on earth did I get here? I am not up to this. Everyone is going to see that I am hopelessly out of my depth and I will be exposed as a fake and a fraud?"

If so, you are most definitely not alone. Different studies suggest that between 65-85% of people suffer from some version of self-doubt or feeling that they don't deserve to be where they are at some stage in their careers.

I will admit to being highly suspicious of anyone who claims NOT to suffer from some level of imposter syndrome. Overconfidence and arrogance are much more likely to lead to wrong decisions and mistakes than feeling nervous or uncertain about your place.

An actor about to go on stage can find a certain amount of nerves and self-doubt is healthy and completely normal. A manageable amount of imposter syndrome helps us to ensure that we prepare well and perform at our very best.

As is so often the case, the secret here is to get the balance right and not allow feelings of inadequacy to hinder your growth or performance. Rather, let them fuel a process of building up your experience and overcoming your self-doubts, gradually replacing them with a healthy confidence in your own abilities.

"The right amount of imposter thoughts may provide just enough motivation to bring out our best work" [8]

Learning to manage yourself well, and know and recognize your own strengths and weaknesses and how to get the best from yourself regardless of the challenges you face, is key to success and happiness.

Let's dig in more to how you can better manage and understand yourself as your life or work constantly throws you (at best) exciting new challenges to tackle or (at worst) what can seem like an endless series of terrifying curveballs.

---

[8] Quoted from interview with Basima A Rewfik, MIT Sloan professor in HBR 2023 Summer Special, Page 114 - "Imposter Syndrome has its advantages"

Reflections

Here are a few key questions arising from the themes raised in this chapter

- What differentiates you from other people?
- Could you consciously work harder on your soft skills?
- How would that help you?
- Are you good company?
- Could you maybe smile more?
- Can you define what is "good enough" for you?
- Can you improve your body language, and how you are perceived?
- In what ways do you care about what others think of you?
- Can you keep a secret?

Chapter 3: Managing Yourself

Where do you live your life?

How do you feel about your life and the things that happen in it? Do you feel like you are constantly being swept downstream in life's river, with little or no control over what happens, whether it's good or bad?

Have you noticed a pattern developing in your life or work where it seems like everyone and everything is working against you, leaving you feeling frustrated, angry, and resentful?

When things go wrong (again), do you immediately create an inner narrative that says, 'Here I go again, trying my hardest, but as always, there are people or events getting in my way'? Maybe you even share this personal narrative with your colleagues, friends, and family.

You talk about how unlucky you are – or rather, not so much unlucky but constantly blocked. It feels like a conspiracy against you. No, it truly is a conspiracy against you.

You deserved that promotion. You worked harder than anyone else, but of course, they didn't give you the job. No one sees the work you do or your true value.

When things happen, like someone pulling out in front of you while driving, how do you react? Or perhaps a waiter in a restaurant isn't giving you the attention you think you deserve. Do you verbally attack them? Do you feel like these negative events are just more proof that the world is against you?

If any of this sounds familiar, then you are living your life 'below the line.' It's a place where you constantly feel like a victim, where things are happening 'to you.'

You don't feel in control, so your actions or explanations become attempts to protect or defend yourself from blame or accountability. You may do this passively by throwing up your hands and saying, 'There's just nothing I can do.' Or you may become more aggressive by directly attacking or blaming others, highlighting how they have wronged you or worked against you.

The unfortunate thing is that your constant negativity creates a self-fulfilling prophecy. It creates a negative feedback loop, a vicious cycle that will continue to provide more evidence in your mind of how poorly you are treated and how powerless you are to change it.

Even worse, when you constantly live below the line, you actually push people away. They can sense your simmering sense of injustice and victim mentality and consciously or subconsciously choose to avoid you. Resentful, self-centered victims are simply not enjoyable to be around or work with.

They know that you will always point the finger of blame at someone else, never at yourself, and maybe that finger will eventually be pointed at them. It's incredibly frustrating for you when you feel that if only you could get others to behave differently, to see things your way, everything in life could be different. Why won't they see that you are right and that what they see, think, do, or feel is wrong? Especially when it comes to you?

Top 30 #5: You Only Control Yourself

A lot of very annoying and frustrating things go on in our lives as a leader, and many times we can feel, with some justification, that everything, or everyone, or maybe just one particular person, is stopping us from achieving our own plans and desires.

WHO DO YOU CONTROL?

Others are getting in the way of what we need or want. And this may well be true. But is the answer to try to get them to move, or for us to choose a different path?

Our tendency is to feel that they need to change. They need to realize that their behavior is unreasonable, or their performance is not good enough.

So we set out to try to change them - to give them feedback, advice, and opinions. We tell them how they make us feel or make others feel. We give examples to show them what we are talking about. Quite possibly, we eventually lose our cool when none of that seems to change anything much, and they carry on exactly the same.

The situation can be different if we have leverage or power over someone or a situation. As a boss, we can impose changes; we feel we have some control over others. But do we really?

The reality is that the only person you honestly control in this whole world is you. Once we come to accept this reality, it is very liberating.

You stop thinking about what we want others to do or how we want them to be different and focus on what YOU can do. And it is often the case that by keeping that focus on your own actions, you will bring about change in others.

Perhaps you feel that you are in partnership with someone who is not pulling their weight. You work every hour of the day to make the project work - but they are often late for meetings, miss deadlines, and take days off. You still appreciate their contribution, and you don't want to constantly fight with them. It is very frustrating.

Naturally, you will give them your feedback and express your unhappiness. They may or may not react.

The answers to creating a situation that truly works for you lie with you.

Can you accept them for what they are, create a way to live with their different approach from yours, and focus on what you want to achieve?

You can also decide that enough is enough and walk away. The point is that you stay in control of the one and only thing you genuinely can control. You.

When I was younger, I desperately wanted others to see things my way and to get on board with my ideas and enthusiasms. Sometimes they did, and often they did not. I gradually came to realize that people do not change and adapt to your way of thinking if they are happy and embedded in theirs.

The challenge is to find a way to make it work for you without expecting big changes from others.

As a leader or a boss, you have a responsibility to ensure that others are doing whatever it is that they need to do, and ideally for their well-being as well as performance. Nevertheless, often people just don't seem to react in the way you expect.

You can encourage, coerce, bribe, reward, threaten, shout, and scream as much as you like - people may respond, they may change - but you will never be in control of another person - and they just may not change at all.

The 'control freak' has a miserable life - as they will constantly come up against a world full of uncontrollable people.

"When the control freak loses control, you just get a freak"

ABOVE THE LINE:

1) OWNERSHIP
2) ACCOUNTABILITY
3) RESPONSIBILITY

BELOW THE LINE:

1) BLAME
2) EXCUSES
3) DENIAL

Above the Line Magnetism

In contrast to the victim who languishes below the line in a constant state of frustration, self-pity, and negativity, people who live above the line are positively magnetic.

Your most fundamental trait if you live above the line is that you are ready to take ownership, accountability, and responsibility for everything that happens to you.

You may not be able to control events, but you can certainly control how you choose to react to them. You know this – and when things go wrong, you remain philosophical, solution-oriented, and empathetic.

You tend to look at events, both good and bad, as experiences to be learned from. You also have a very clear idea that if you do well, it is because you have worked hard, done some things right, and probably had a bit of good luck.

People who live firmly above the line are enjoyable to be around and work with as, by taking ownership of everything that happens to them, they are always working to be a part of the solution, rather than just another part of the problem.

To be realistic, we know that no one really lives entirely above or below the line – like everything else involving people, there is a typical bell chart distribution with extreme cases, and most of us are somewhere in the middle.

And we will vary from day to day or year to year, depending on what we are doing, our mood dictated by our triumphs and disasters. Even if we are typically positive-minded above-the-liners, when we hit a series of setbacks, it is easy to become negative and a little paranoid, and cast around for reasons why these things are 'happening to us'. Or others to blame for our woes.

The key is to remain conscious of the model and ask yourself if you have slipped below the line and have become negative and defensive. What is important to remember is that if you do go there, it tends to be a lonely and pretty miserable place. Nobody really enjoys the company of a 'victim' who feels hard done by and sorry for themselves, as deep down we know that to a great extent our own destiny is in our control.

What is also true is that our tendency to be above or below the line is often deeply rooted in our personality and our previous life experiences, people around us, or sense of self-worth. Sometimes we can pull ourselves out of the negative spiral, but it can be very hard at times when you have faced many setbacks.

Aim for objectivity and don't let yourself be drawn into subjective 'what if' mental self-torture. Mental resilience is a great asset, and recognizing that you only control yourself is a key to building up that resilience.

If things really aren't going well, get help. A therapist or a coach, depending on what you feel will work for you, can make a big difference.

Aim to keep the high-level view and focus on the positive and your achievements. You are consistently successful and appreciated in so many areas of work and life. It's a journey you are on and will lead you somewhere positive without a doubt. You do lots of things well and are doing things to grow and evolve. You hope others will see that - but if they don't for some reason, it's about them, not you.

That Little Voice in Your Ear

The 2021 Disney-Pixar film *'Luca'* is about a little Italian boy who is actually a sea creature (better that you go and watch it than I try to explain…) who tackles a series of enormous challenges and gradually overcomes his significant and often crippling self-doubt.

His friend Alberto (who is much more self-confident and a risk-taker) advises him to say to himself, *'Silenzio*

Bruno!' every time he hears that voice of 'you can't do this' in his head.

By giving that voice a name, Luca was able to dominate it and overcome his fears and achieve some incredible things.

We all hear those voices, and it is up to each one of us to learn to control them and remember that they really are just our own inner creations.

THAT VOICE IN YOUR EAR

During one coach training program I took part in, they were described as 'passengers' (as they constantly travel with us), and we were encouraged to give them names and develop strategies to silence them or at least manage them.

Those passengers can also be positive, and we can develop them into encouraging voices that tell you 'yes, you can do this'. Working out who or what your passengers are and when and how to either bring them forward or send them back is a skill well worth developing.

By giving them names (*the captain, the superhero, the witch, the nay-sayer, the optimist, the pessimist, John, Bruno, Jane...*) you will also be able to imagine yourself overcoming, managing, or summoning them.

You might find that it is helpful to use objects or a personal talisman to support your process of controlling your voices or supporting your inner process of positivism.

Perhaps it is just a post-it note stuck to your bathroom mirror that just says 'Yes, you can!' and that you see every morning before you start your day.

I have been wearing a red wristband for over six years that reminds me every day to be 'funny' and to see the funny side of things. I have noticed that with increased age, we gradually get more serious - and as seeing the funny side of things has always been a key to my own happiness, I wanted to reinforce that for myself. It works for me.

Optimism, Pessimism, and Realism

My father was a terrific, self-confessed pessimist, and was often happily surprised when things turned out better than he expected. We used to enjoy playing golf together, and I would say, 'see you on Tuesday for golf', and he would gloomily reply that it would almost certainly be raining, and we would have to cancel.

In general, I am an optimist, and I would confidently retort that it would be perfect weather for our golf game. Looking back, I'd say we were both right about half of the time.

Who knows why some of us usually take a positive slant on life and expect the best, while others regularly predict a negative outcome? Once again, it is a combination of our personality and our experience.

Optimism in excess can be just as wearing as overt pessimism. The leader who is constantly determined to expect better results or more positive outcomes, despite a lack of real reason for that hope other than optimism, soon loses the respect of their team.

There is a fine line between optimism and hubris – the unrealistic belief in a positive outcome. Realism is far more useful than either overt optimism or pessimism.

Look objectively at why you think something will turn out well or badly and base your prediction on facts, observations, and evidence.

The realistic leader provides an environment of honesty and safety where people can speak up and contribute. If your team feels that any kind of doubt or misgiving will be seen by you as negative in the face of your determined optimism, then they will be afraid to voice their opinions or tell you the truth as they see it.

As always, it is important to have a good sense of your impact – do you transmit pessimism, optimism, or realism? You may not be able to change that inherent personality trait, but it certainly helps if you know how you are seen by others.

We are not necessarily even directly in control of how we may see, feel, perceive, or even remember things. Did you know, for example, that you have two brains?

Your Communicating Brain And Your Experimenting Brain

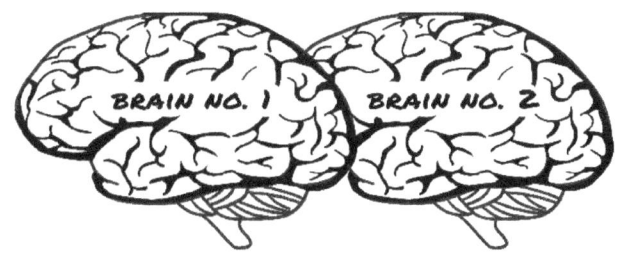

Some years ago, I took part in a fairly extreme mountain bike event. It takes place every year at the highest mountain in Spain – the 12-thousand-foot ex-volcano called El Teide on the Canary Island of Tenerife.

It is a grueling all-day activity, starting before dawn from a village halfway up the mountain and concluding some 11 hours later (at least that's how long it took me) at the same village. Almost 80 miles of tough off-road cycling and around 9,000 feet of up and down.

The last 10 miles were the worst – the organizers clearly had a sadistic streak as we struggled through cloying mud to reach the village and the final, unnecessarily uphill ride along the village's main street, to agonizingly wobble across the finish line.

They call it a 'race' - but like most of life, it is much more of a personal challenge of survival rather than a question of beating anyone else. Only half of the original 400 riders who start it even get to the end. I am very proud of my 'finisher' medal.

It was so obviously a terrible ordeal. My backside was rubbed raw, at times I even closed my eyes hammering down near-vertical, rock-strewn descents, or my brain was numbed in despair as I ground up never-ending hills. At one point, it started to snow. It seemed like an endless, drawn-out torture.

So, why then was it that at dinner that evening, did I feel like I wanted to go back and do it all again as soon as possible? Why are all my memories of that day made up of my family cheering me across the finish line? Or of the incredible views from the top of the mountain? Or of how good the sandwiches tasted at the halfway point? All my memories of the agony and suffering have magically gone away.

This is because we have two brains. [9] The 'experimenting brain' registers and records everything that

---

9

https://www.ted.com/talks/daniel_kahneman_the_riddle_of_experien ce_vs_memory?language=en happens to us. It locks those memories away somewhere for future use – to help you learn, manage future situations, and avoid danger.

It's the 'communicating brain' that decides what you are actually going to actively remember and recall about what happened – and the communicating brain likes to paint an optimistic and positive picture of the past for you to enjoy and to give you reasons to keep moving forward.

It's what keeps you going and keeps you coming back for more, even though everything would indicate you'd be better off not repeating the experience. Your past reality is presented to you through a lens of positivism that inspires you to keep advancing.

It is thanks to the communicating brain that most of us exist at all. The pain of childbirth is notorious for being excruciatingly terrible, and even more so during all the centuries before epidurals were invented. What woman would willingly go through all that torture more than once if she could accurately recall the pain?

The communicating brain remembers the incredible feeling of cradling the newborn baby and the joy of a new life created.

It's useful to know about these two elements of our brain and how they affect how we remember things. There are many situations in life, leadership, and business that we may look back on with greater nostalgia than we felt at the time.

We have to be careful not to let our communicating brain trick us into making the same mistakes twice or underestimating a new challenge.

As a leader, you should aim to be conscious of these unconscious forces at play and take them into consideration.

Light v. Heat

Many brilliant scientists of the 19th century worked on the challenge of trying to create a light bulb, an invention that unquestionably changed the world. Thomas Edison finally patented the first commercially viable version in 1879.

A lot of good things have happened to light bulbs since then. Even the early versions were effective at providing light, but unfortunately also gave off a lot of wasted, and sometimes dangerous, heat.

A typical incandescent light bulb from only a few years ago wasted 90% of its energy in heat. A modern powerful LED bulb gives off a strong light, using up to 85% less energy than a traditional incandescent bulb, and generates very little heat at all.

When dealing with people, or better managing ourselves, you should aim to be more like that modern light bulb - providing plenty of light without generating unnecessary, useless heat.

Just as scientists have worked on optimizing the light bulb, much work has been done over the years to help us all to be better leaders and managers.

We benefit from all the experience, mistakes, and successes of those that have gone before us.

Despite all that knowledge and best practice, when things get complicated and challenging, do you, your teams, or even whole organizations start to generate unnecessary heat that reduces effectiveness? And even worse, can that heat lead to a danger of burnout and permanent damage?

Be aware of when your light/heat ratio starts to tip from providing useful illumination to generating unhelpful and uncomfortable heat.

There is no excuse for being a scalding incandescent light when you can be a cool, calm but still brilliant LED.

Thinking v. Acting

There is a time to act, and there is a time to think carefully before you do anything. Sometimes we act when we should think, and think too long when we should act.

On many occasions, leaders are criticized by their teams for overthinking decisions and taking too long to act.

History recalls the generals who won a great victory on the battlefield, and even those that lost. History does not bother with the generals who couldn't make up their minds whether or not to engage in battle.

It is also true that sometimes, perhaps through emotion or because we feel under pressure to act, we act when we should think some more first.

A friend of mine was married for 25 years to a man who was consistently unfaithful to her. It was a terrible thing to witness, and he just seemed unable to manage himself. She stuck by him, and many times I wondered why she didn't leave him.

He was successful and well-off, and as time went on, their children left home, and it seemed as though at least they had a very comfortable life. Then suddenly, way past her sixtieth birthday, she announced that she was leaving him, and she marched out without demanding any of his money and set herself up alone and had to find a job to support herself. It was a very hard time for her.

You are thinking that she has gained her independence, and that is certainly true. I find myself wondering whether, at that stage in her life after all she had been through, if she had thought more and acted less, could she have still obtained her independence but also suffered less?

There is definitely a moment when we need to act – but it is important to make sure that we have really done just the right amount of thinking beforehand to ensure the outcome we want.

Escalate or Placate?

It's late on a Tuesday afternoon, you are tired and you want to go home. Suddenly, you receive an email from a colleague that greatly irritates you. You're itching to fire back your own message and show your displeasure. How do you respond?

You look down at your keyboard and suddenly see only two possible keys to press - 'E' for escalate or 'P' for placate.

We are regularly faced with these testing moments in our lives, especially in the world of work. My experience is that it is almost always better to choose to press, at least initially, the 'placate' key. That is not to say that we should allow ourselves to be bullied or let genuine issues that need addressing pass.

If there is something significant that has to be handled, then it almost certainly needs some clear thinking and calm analysis to ensure the best way to handle it and create the optimum outcome.

Maybe write your angry reply and then put it in your 'drafts' and read it again in the morning. How does it sound in the cold light of day?

Firing off an angry email riposte may be satisfying at that moment, but 'escalating' and raising everybody's blood pressure is very unlikely to contribute anything to solving the issue.

Think carefully before you act. If you decide to escalate, make it a conscious decision that you have thought through with a calm mind. Placating in the short term does not mean you are giving in or showing weakness. It buys you time to think more.

'Thanks for your email. I will call you tomorrow so we can discuss together what is the best thing to do.'

Top 30 #6: You Make Reality

Earlier, we talked about how perception is reality and that you only control yourself. We can go further - how you choose to act in a given situation and the extent to which you control yourself can radically change the consequences or reality of that situation - despite the actual 'facts' being just the same. Let me explain with an example.

You are driving along in your car and you stop at a red traffic light. The driver of the car behind you is fiddling with their phone and applying their brakes too late, smacks straight into the rear of your car. There is a nasty tinkling of glass, and both cars are damaged. You leap out of your car and rush towards the other driver, who is just emerging from their car, looking shaken. You say...

"Are you blind, or stupid or both? Look what you've done to my car?"

Your voice is getting louder, and you are getting angrier. *'I hope you know that this is exactly what happens if you text and drive! It's people like you that make our roads unsafe - you should have your license revoked!'*

The other driver responds angrily to your outburst - *'Hey! You stopped suddenly, you could have made that light! Who do you think you are to shout at me!?'*

The whole situation gets worse quickly. The police are called, and you spend a fractious hour at the traffic light. The other driver is angry and claiming you stopped suddenly, which means that, although the other driver's insurance will eventually pay up to repair your damage (it was his fault), he chooses to contest your version of events, so it all takes months to sort out.

You eventually drive on, furious and very late for your meeting.

Or how about...?

You are driving along in your car, and you stop at a red traffic light. The driver of the car behind you is fiddling with their phone and applying their brakes too late, smacks straight into the rear of your car. There is a nasty tinkling of glass, and both cars are damaged. You leap out of your car and rush towards the other driver, who is just emerging from their car, looking shaken. You say...

'Hey are you OK? No worries! Thankfully not too much damage and insurance will pay for that! Let's swap numbers and insurance details and be on our way.'

You help the other driver out of their car. They are obviously relieved, as they know the accident was all their fault. You swap insurance details, and you are quickly and calmly on your way to your next meeting, still arriving on time. The other driver's insurance pays for your damage without any issues.

The interesting thing about these two stories is that the facts of what actually happened are exactly the same: there was a collision, both cars were damaged, and it was the car behind's fault.

Yet the way you handled it completely changes the nature of the incident. In the first example, the other driver only gets annoyed as they are challenged and feel abused. It has nothing to do with the actual accident. An additional problem is created on top of the basic incident.

How we react to things that happen, keeping ourselves in control and focused on a satisfactory outcome for everyone involved, can radically change consequences for the better.

You only control yourself - so losing your cool and admonishing the other driver for their shortcomings brings no material benefit other than allowing you to let off steam. It does, however, create more problems for you.

You don't control what happens to you. You do control how you react.

How You See Yourself

What we choose to believe, or 'see' about ourselves can have a radical impact on how we feel, how we behave, and how others see us. The extent to which we can overcome our own self-doubts or negative self-imagery can have a profound effect.

Many years ago, I had two very good friends that formed part of a larger group of people that spent a lot of time together. We'll call them Bill and Fred. There was one thing that everyone in our group of friends knew about Fred: he wasn't a tall person.

There's no other way to say it than to recognize that Fred had a complex about his height. This had a powerful effect on his life and his relationship with everyone around him. As everyone knew it was a 'sore point,' we were very careful never to make fun of him or in any way reference his height.

In some ways, that made things worse, as we all knew we were doing that - and so did he. Unfortunately, this just reinforced his own self-image and everyone else's discomfort.

Occasionally, there would be some incident when Fred felt challenged in some way, and he would even react quite aggressively - perhaps subconsciously compensating for his own perceived lack of height compared with others. Who knows...?

What I do know is that looking back on that time, being shorter than most other people was a troubling issue for Fred.

One day, I was walking down the street among our group of friends, heading somewhere together. Bill and Fred were a little way ahead of the group, walking along together.

Suddenly, I realized something, and something that I had never noticed before. Bill and Fred were exactly the same height.

In contrast to Fred, Bill had absolutely no self-consciousness or negative feelings about his stature. It just wasn't something he ever worried or even thought about. As a consequence of his total lack of concern about it, no one else worried about it either, or even noticed it.

Bill lived his life in happy ignorance of any idea that how tall he was had any kind of negative impact on him, or his success or happiness.

There are so many ways in which by recognizing that you only control yourself and accepting that you are the only owner of your own destiny, you can be happier and more successful.

You are not just 'part of the solution' - you are the solution to your own needs and desires.

Although you also need to accept that by truly accepting control of things and recognizing your power to bring about improvements or changes, you also must accept accountability for outcomes.

Top 30 #7: Get Hold of Your Own Steering Wheel

If you are traveling in a car, do you prefer to drive or be driven? I guess your answer may depend on how much you want to stay in control of where you think you are supposed to be going, the route chosen, and where you will finally end up.

If you want to drive but find that someone else has taken the wheel, it can be an uncomfortable feeling. Are you at least sitting in the front seat where the driver can hear you clearly and you have a good view? Or do you feel like you are in the back seat? Or worse still, are you right back in the third row with the noisy kids and are being totally ignored by those in the front seats? Or even worse, are you tied up in the trunk?

Sometimes my clients tell me that they feel things are out of their control and they feel helpless or limited in their ability to make changes or be heard. They are not holding on to their own steering wheel; they are letting someone else drive, and often they say that they *'have no choice'*.

If you aren't holding the wheel, then you can't expect to control where you are going. It can make a tremendous difference to how you feel when you do decide to take back that control - but it also comes with pressure and responsibility. You are driving now.

WHO'S GOT HOLD OF YOURS?

When you take real control of things in your life or work, you will also have to stop asking for permission. You may have to stop asking others to sign off on the decisions you make or give you their reassurance or approval. You may have to accept new levels of exposure and accountability that may make you uncomfortable.

When you first learn to drive, it feels unnatural - you have to think about everything - mirrors, brakes, clutch, other drivers, road signs, speed limits, etc.

As you gain experience, all that becomes second nature and easy. After a while of being truly in charge of the journey, you'll find that driving and steering, and being more responsible for your own destination, becomes natural and you can't believe how difficult it seemed.

When you get comfortable, you will be able to focus on other things apart from just the driving. And you are recognized by others as a competent and reliable driver that others are happy to let you do the driving.

If you never learn to drive and truly grab hold of your own steering wheel, it means that you are accepting that you'll constantly be driven around by someone else. That is your choice.

Reflections

Here are a few key questions arising from the themes raised in this chapter.

- Have you ever felt like the world is against you?
- Have you had experience with another person behaving like a victim?
- How did that seem to you?
- To what extent do you feel you take accountability for everything that happens to you?
- How can you spend more time 'above the line?'
- Do you believe you can control others? Why or why not?
- Are you an optimist, pessimist, or realist?
- How does that affect you and your impact on others?
- How comfortable are you in your own skin?
- Do you like to drive, or do you let yourself be driven?

Chapter 4: Choices You Make

Why We Want Things

René Girard (1923-2015) was recognized worldwide for his work on human behavior and culture. In 2005, he was inducted into the Académie Française. He was a Professor Emeritus at Stanford University.

When he was still quite young, he got a job teaching French literature despite not knowing much about it. He hadn't even read most of the books he was supposed to teach.

To stay one step ahead of his class, he read many classic literary works and began to notice similarities from novel to novel. He unearthed a simple but important pattern across all those novels that no one before him had apparently noticed. He identified a consistent thread of "imitation."

A lot of traditional stories have a similar narrative and are based on conflict between characters. Girard realized that the people in these classic stories are not fighting each other due to their differences of philosophy or fundamental beliefs. They are, in fact, in conflict because they are incredibly similar and are in pursuit of the *same* things.

This is not just because they want and need the same things, such as food, material goods, riches, and power, but because most of all they want whatever will make other people (their enemy in particular) envious.

Humans have been blessed with great intelligence and a unique capacity for planning ahead. We can make choices and decisions in a way that animals simply cannot. Along with that capacity to plan and choose also comes risk, uncertainty, and anxiety.

We don't know what the best choice to make is, so we look to others for ideas and reinforcement of our choices. We are capable of desiring just about anything, as long as other people seem to reassuringly desire it as well.

This sums up Girard's concept of "mimetic desire." People tend toward the same objects of desire, jealousy, and rivalry, which inevitably creates social tension between individuals or groups.

"Man is the creature who does not know what to desire, and he turns to others in order to make up his mind. We desire what others desire because we imitate their desires."

- René Girard

We all subconsciously tend to assume that there's a simple relationship between us and what we want.

We convince ourselves that our desires are independent and autonomous. We want to pursue something because it makes sense or is the right thing to do for us, or it's just what we want, deserve, or need to be happy and fulfilled.

All that is happening outside of our conscious awareness. Few of us question why we want the things we want; we just want them.

However, it turns out that maybe the value we place on objects is ironically not objective at all—it's subjective. The subjective value we assign to possessing or obtaining something is "mimetic." It is based on our relationships with and observations of other people.

According to mimetic theory, we assign value to things (and therefore desire them) not according to what we want, but according to what we see other people want.

The people whom we subconsciously look to for guidance about what to want directly influence our choices.

You are shopping with a friend, and they see some shoes that they like. You aren't especially interested in them. However, the moment your friend decides to buy them, they are no longer just a pair of shoes - they are the ones your friend chose to buy.

When your friend starts to show interest in the shoes, they become different from the few moments before they started wanting them. They've now become your friend's choice - and so changed your own relationship with them. From now on, you'll never be able to make a genuinely independent choice about what you truly feel when considering those shoes for yourself.

The never-ending process of new clothing fashions, hairstyles, or popular music is underpinned by mimetic desire. Suddenly everybody wants to wear skinny jeans... and will never be seen dead in last year's baggy ones. Is it possible that suddenly all those individual people independently changed their taste all at once?

These forces on our decision processes are especially difficult (perhaps impossible) to control as they are mostly subconscious. But once again, it is useful to understand more about what is happening and why we may feel that we want something.

Understanding more about this can be important when aiming to make wise choices about when to alter your destination or stick with what you have.

Top 30 #8: Going Towards Something New, Not Away from Something Old

You'd be amazed at the number of times my phone rings and I hear, "I'd like to get your advice on something..." and it turns out to be about a headhunter call, a potential new opportunity, or maybe even a job offer already on the table. Sometimes, it's just someone expressing a great desire to get out of what they are doing and into something else.

When people tell me they have a great new opportunity and are seriously considering a move, I am almost always initially (and intentionally) quite unenthusiastic and cautious.

Not because I am against changing jobs for something better, quite the opposite. In fact, most successful careers include several significant, and sometimes risky, job moves.

My concern is that I want the assessment of the opportunity and the decision process of making a move to be careful and objective.

It is so easy to run away from one situation that you don't like just to end up in another that is just as bad, or worse. The key before you make any move is to be sure you are heading towards something you judge to be genuinely better - not away from something you have gradually grown fed up with. Familiarity breeds contempt.

It is human nature to feel that the grass is greener on the other side of the river. In reality, we don't know much about that grass over there, we only know about our own grass. And we know a lot about it, usually too much.

The trick is to make a genuine, unemotional comparison between what we already have and what we might have if we make the move.

In the story of "The Golden Windows," written by Laura E. Richards and published in 1908[10], two small boys set out to find the house on the other side of their valley whose incredible golden windows shine every morning as the sun comes up. Why can't they have golden windows too?

They are determined to find out the secret of this magical home. They travel all day and finally reach the house, only to find that it has disappointingly ordinary

---

[10] From the book *"The Pig Brother and other fables"* (1908) by Laura E Richards (1850-1943)

windows just like their own. The sun is now setting, and as they look back across the valley, they are amazed to see that their own house magically now suddenly also has impressive golden windows.

Their perspective - and their feelings about the good things they already had going for them - change in that moment.

We know a lot about our family, friends, colleagues, workplace, or job, and we have a tendency to believe that it all compares unfavorably with what others have or is available elsewhere.

Your new opportunity needs to be significantly and objectively better than whatever it is you are leaving behind - not just a change of scenery or a higher salary.

There will be difficult colleagues, unreasonable bosses, and daily frustrations at your new job too. Don't let your confirmation bias convince you that the grass is greener over there. It is just different grass, and as yet unknown and untested.

Confirmation Bias

The more you find out about an exciting new opportunity, the more attractive it seems. You actively look for positive signs, ignoring warning signals, and see the people who interview you or the new organization you are hoping to join in a good light.

You WANT the opportunity to be everything you are hoping for and will, to a certain extent, be ready to convince yourself that it is. You are at risk of making yourself a victim of your own confirmation bias.

Confirmation bias is the tendency to subconsciously search for, identify, and recall information that confirms or supports your existing beliefs, values, or desires.

You select information that supports your view, ignoring contrary information. You interpret ambiguous evidence as supporting your case. The effect is known to be strongest for desired outcomes, for emotionally charged issues – like moving to a new job, for instance.

The more objectively you assess any situation, the more likely it is that you will make good choices asnd decisions. We are generally good at advising others to be objective and rigorous in their thinking but less good when it is about ourselves.

I recommend creating some process and structure around your decision-making when considering a new job or any other big decision. Write down the pros and cons, make a table, and attach weightings to different elements of the decision, and highlight what you know and don't know.

Ask yourself very honestly if you are convincing yourself that the new job will be great in part because you are fed up with the old one.

Be Aware of What Drives Your Choices

The concept of "going towards, not away" and watching for confirmation bias applies to so many key decisions that you will make as a leader, both for yourself in terms of career moves, but also regarding people or business decisions.

The more objective you can be, using evidence and facts to support your thinking, and getting other people's views to compare with your own, the more likely you are to make good choices.

When hiring new people to work with or for you, watch out for other innate biases that might cause you to make a poor decision. People will turn out to be what they are, not what you want or hope them to be.

It is easy to be over-optimistic and over-enthusiastic about a new team member, which can also be annoying for your existing team who may feel you are overly positive about someone just because they are new - albeit as yet unproven.

We all also have a tendency to hire people who are "like us," as naturally, we find it easy to work with people with a similar "style" to ourselves. We will talk about personality assessments in Chapter10, and how they can help you to build a strong team of people with diverse skills and personalities.

Planning for a career change

If you are feeling that it is time for a change of job, then the more specific you can be in terms of your future ambitions, the more likely you are to successfully land a great next move.

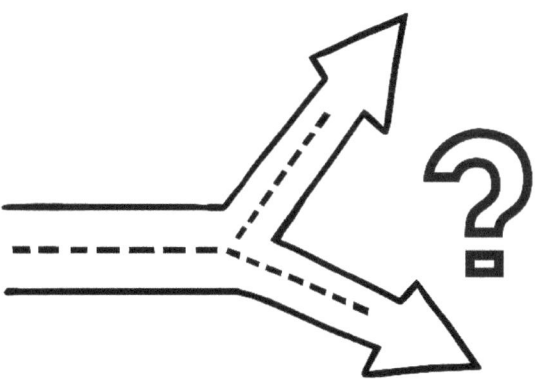

Do you have a clear idea of the sector you want to work in, or the type of job you want? Can you specifically name 10 companies that you would like to work for (even if no job is available as far as you know)? Who do you know that might know someone at one of those companies?

Once you begin to drill down to create a more genuine picture of that future role, you start to create that "target" to move towards. Your current job and its shortcomings will become less important as a decision factor - you've already started to get some detail on that "greener grass" on the other side of the river.

Ticking Career Boxes

Consider your career as a series of achievements or experiences that gradually build up to form your professional and personal proposition in the world.

When you think about your current role or the company where you work, have you ticked all the boxes you can? If you have, then it could indeed be a good idea to move on. Also, ask yourself how this new role is going to open up new boxes to tick.

Similarly, if you have an opportunity to move into a new area and tick new boxes but are feeling insecure or risk-averse about taking yourself out of a comfortable job into something new, ask yourself the same questions. How many more boxes will I tick if I stay put? Have I already ticked every box available to me in this role or in this company?

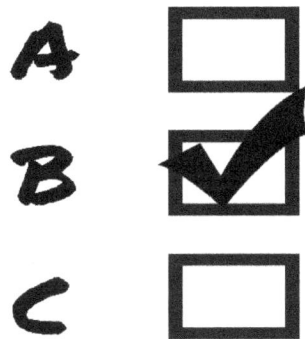

If you have reached a certain level of seniority, are earning a good amount of money, and enjoying what you do, then that in itself is another box to tick. It is a real achievement to be satisfied with what you are doing. Will moving up or out bring you something new that staying put will not?

If you have genuinely ticked all the boxes in your current role, then your reasons for staying in it need to be consciously about enjoying stability, security, or certainty. It's no good going to your boss asking for more money to do the same thing.

If you desire more money or more responsibility, then objectively recognize that all your current boxes are ticked and it's time to make a move up or out to seek new things.

You Own Your Career, and It Is Your Responsibility

If you work for a large company, it is tempting to feel that the organization should be looking after you and actively helping you to tick more of your boxes with internal moves or promotions. You may see others apparently getting that treatment and become resentful of the organization, your boss, or HR.

At one point, my office on the 11th floor overlooked the eight-lane circular highway that surrounds Madrid. Every evening after dark, there would be a mass of red taillights trying to go north and a mass of white headlights trying to go south. Hundreds of Madrileños on the move, going home for the evening.

It seemed to me that at this time of the day, people would often come into my office and start to grumble to me. They talked about how the company *'should do this or that'* for them, or how something wasn't fair, or in some way, they were missing out or being hard done by.

I would point out of the window at all the cars below on the hectic highway and remind them that not one of those people worked for our company, and that there was always a choice to leave and go elsewhere and seek 'better treatment'. It's up to us.

They were all dreaming about some non-existent future role in terms of their dissatisfaction with their current situation and their perception that somehow, someone, somewhere in our company should be looking out for them for promotion or advancement.

Your career belongs to you only, and it is your sole responsibility to manage and develop it as you want and as best as you can. Don't outsource that responsibility to your boss, HR, or anyone else. If you really want something new or different, then you must make that happen yourself. Remember, you only control yourself and grab onto your own steering wheel.

Your Career Arc

Often, we feel stuck or frustrated at any one point in our career. Our job has become boring, or maybe it has changed and is not as enjoyable or interesting as it was. It is then easy to feel that we urgently need to move on and do something different. But don't be too hasty.

Take a step back and look at what you are doing from a wider perspective. How will what you are doing right now at this time impact the overall trajectory or arc of your career?

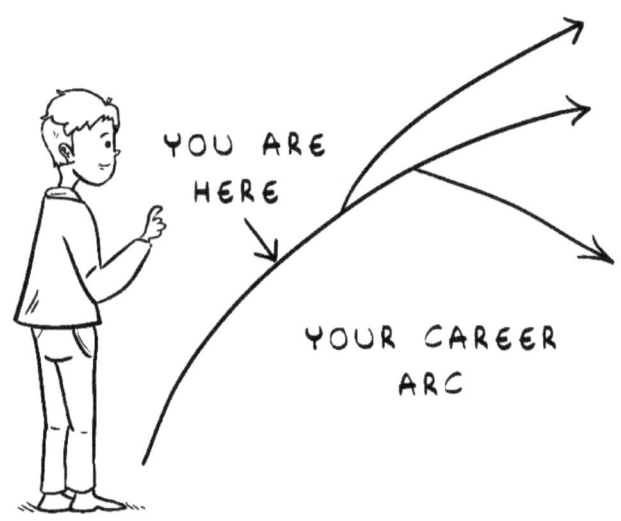

Perhaps another six months or a year in this role can truly consolidate your experience? Typically, I feel that one should aim to stick with any given job for at least two years - even if you are getting itchy feet after less time.

Managers who look at many resumes may view a candidate with suspicion if they have moved very quickly from one job to another. Bosses look for ambitious and active people, but they also want commitment and stability in their team.

If you are objective and clear about your plan for your long-term career and professional goals, it will help you judge when is the right time to stay put and further consolidate your position - or to move on to something new.

It is almost always the case that stepping back and looking at the bigger picture of where you are in your personal or professional trajectory will give you good insight into what is needed or when your next move may become the right thing to do.

Reflections

Here are a few key questions arising from the themes raised in this chapter

- Have you ever thought about why you want certain things?
- Do you agree that we tend to feel the grass is always greener elsewhere?
- Have you experienced confirmation bias?
- Do you want to change your job? If yes, do you know why?
- How clear are you about what you want in the future?
- Who do you think is responsible for your career?
- In what ways do you support your choices with facts and evidence?

Chapter 5: Managing Your Time and Your Ambitions

Knowing your limits, setting goals, allocating time realistically.

Top 30 #9: Focus, delegate, park

Do you feel overwhelmed by your "to-do list?" Like you are half-buried or drowning under the daily pressure of meeting deadlines and keeping up with the demands of your life and work? Maybe you have other personal, family, relationship, health, or money worries that impact your ability to manage things?

If so, you most definitely aren't alone. The UK Mental Health Foundation[11] carried out a major study of stress. It found that 74% of people reported that at some point in the previous year, they had "felt so stressed that they were overwhelmed or unable to cope".

We only have a finite amount of time each day to invest, and it is arguably our most precious commodity. "Time waits for no one."

Faced with a to-do list that is bigger than your can-do capacity, you need to step back and get some perspective.

I recommend sorting your ideas, opportunities, goals, ambitions, obligations, deadlines, children's sporting commitments, family time, friends, video calls, business priorities, bosses' demands, etc., into three action groups: Focus, Delegate, or Park.

Focus is for the stuff that just has to happen. Yes, or yes. You will know what these things are. You will also know that your critical focus on them is eroded by other less

---

[11] UK Mental Health Foundation 2018 Study of Stress - 4,619 respondents

important things. Recognize that you must do these things, and probably do them yourself.

Delegate is for things that have to happen, but where someone else realistically can support you. At home, kids can be asked to make their own bed; at work, you just have to let go and ask people to do more for you. You can pay someone to mow your lawn or to sort out your LinkedIn page. Your team can do more. Recognize that you can do these important things, but only with help.

Park is what you need to do with all those things that you would like to do but just cannot get to. They hang over you, making you feel guilty and frustrated because you never seem to get to them. Take positive action and consciously "park" them. You can come back to them later. Recognize that you cannot do these things now.

FOCUS, DELEGATE, PARK

You may find that over time some of your goals, activities, or ideas that you have consciously parked become less important, appealing, or necessary. If so, consider going one step further, and press "Delete."

Whether a business, a project, a team, or a person - faced with an overwhelming list of stuff to do, and a finite amount of time to do it - get organized and focus, delegate or park…and delete.

Managing Your Capacity (Circles on a page)

There are some things that are just not flexible. For example, there are only 24 hours in a day, and at some point, you need to eat, sleep, and do other things apart from work. However much we might like the idea, the 25-hour day is not going to happen.

The flexibility has to come from you, as you attempt to squeeze all of your commitments, meetings, and deadlines into the space available. Many of us live with a constant feeling of being overwhelmed.

One simple idea that I recommend is to take a single piece of paper - the paper represents the natural limits that we live in, and I ask people to draw circles that represent the different elements that fill up that finite space - the more time needed, the bigger the circle.

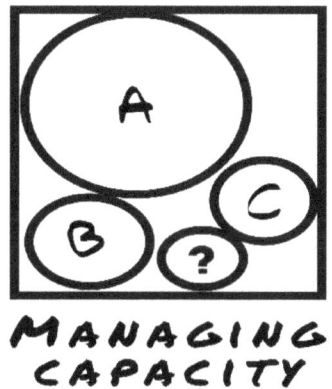

MANAGING
CAPACITY

It might be that the paper represents your overall life at this moment - so the circles represent your mental and time commitment to: work, family, friends, relaxation, keeping fit, etc. You will know what needs to be on your list.

If the 'work' circle is enormous, the 'family' circle is very small, and the 'time for me' circle is a tiny dot... then it is a great way to represent the challenge you face.

You can play around with the size of the circles to see the proportion of your time that you really want to spend doing what. If you want to add in a new activity (like going to the gym, for example), then you can immediately think about what has to give up some space to make that happen.

This simple exercise helps to visualize your commitments and how you spend your time. Despite its simplicity, I've found it can be very useful for people. It brings home the truth.

This also works as a tool for thinking about the projects or challenges you are working on professionally. Do the circles of everything you have on your plate fit into your single page? Or is it patently obvious that you just have too much to do? So what is going to give?

It will help you to more clearly see your situation and the challenge ahead of you, and to make a structured plan to improve things.

Opportunity Cost

When thinking about how you use your time, I find that it helps people to think in terms of the economic concept of "opportunity cost."

"When you choose one option, you lose the potential benefits of the other options[12]"

Whatever we are doing, however we choose to spend our time, there is always something else that we could be doing instead. If we lose track of how much we are investing in any one activity or project, it is likely that some other aspect of our work or life in general will suffer.

If we stay conscious of how one activity is taking more than its fair share of our time, then we can hopefully address it or manage it as a short-term problem. If we allow ourselves to become chronically out of balance and lose sight of that, it is almost certain that the opportunity cost of our over-focus on one thing will have a negative impact in other areas.

Maintaining our work-life balance, spending enough time with our families or loved ones, eating well despite a busy schedule, and getting enough sleep are all important to most of us - and yet they can be, and often are, pushed aside by the prioritization of work commitments.

Rather than thinking only about the cost of not keeping up with professional objectives and time commitments, think also about the cost of ignoring or

---

[12] Definition of Opportunity Cost from the *Oxford Learners Dictionary*

avoiding those other activities that you know are important but that you constantly deprioritize.

In the work environment, it is easy to become over-focused on aspects of your job that you enjoy or feel you are good at, or a team that you like working with. Your excellent work in those areas can be outweighed by the opportunity costs of what you are not doing elsewhere.

Keep a careful eye on the opportunity cost of your decisions and how you choose to spend your time.

Helicopter Pilot Training

When I was about 15 years old, my father took me to visit an old friend of his who had become an admiral in the British Royal Navy and was in charge of a naval air station in the UK. I was given a memorable tour of the base and got to look closely at fighter jets, as well as sit in the pilot's seat of a big helicopter.

The pilot was explaining the controls to us, and my father asked him, *"How long would it take you to teach my son to fly this helicopter?"*

The pilot replied, *"Oh, I could teach him to fly it in a couple of days, but it would take me two years to teach him what to do when it goes wrong."*

Similarly, when we look at how we use our time and organize ourselves, we need to build in capacity and be prepared to deal with the unexpected.

Things will go wrong, tasks will take much longer than expected, technology will fail, people will let you down, and it will rain on your parade.

If we haven't factored in these negative surprises and made plans to mitigate issues, misunderstandings, or delays when they do happen, their impact will be so much worse.

It is vital to consciously consider what can go wrong and be ready for that. There is great satisfaction in flying your metaphorical helicopter on a perfect day with blue sky all around and not a care in the world. That positive feeling is greatly enhanced if you feel fully confident that we also know what to do when the weather turns nasty or the engine cuts out...

Washing Up Theory

Imagine you are back in college and you have a lot of homework or studying to do. You really do not feel like doing it. You get home and the last thing you want to do is settle down with your books.

Then you notice that there is a nasty pile of washing up in the kitchen sink. Under normal circumstances, you would avoid it at all costs. But now it has started to look strangely attractive as an alternative to doing what you actually really need to do but don't feel like doing.

You embark on the washing up with enthusiasm, turning on some music to keep you company and drying each dish with great care before replacing it in its place. Given your sudden focus on attention to detail, the whole washing up process takes almost an hour...and now it is really too late to study...

Have you noticed how minor, and perhaps mindless, tasks can become a much more appealing option compared to the difficult thing that is really hanging over you?

We are all human, and we can forgive ourselves for putting things off and procrastinating in the face of difficult or maybe tedious obligations.

In the end, we do have to get the important stuff done. We don't get paid or pass exams because we do a great job of washing our dishes. One way to tackle that challenge can be to do the hard things first and get them out of the way.

'Eat that Frog'

Brian Tracy, the self-help and business guru, has written no fewer than 80 books to help people be more successful. He must be fairly well-organized and self-disciplined himself to have made that happen.

My favorite idea of his, and I suspect his best-selling book, is about eating frogs[13]. Essentially, he says that if the first thing you do every morning is eat a live frog, then everything else you do after that will seem easy.

He also suggests two additional rules: if you have to eat two frogs, eat the ugliest one first. And if you do have to eat a frog, do it now. It won't get any easier to eat by delaying or just looking at it.

I think there is a lot to be said for tackling your day's most difficult or unappealing task as soon as you can, and before all others. You get it out of the way, and everything does seem easier after that.

We always know which things are the ones we least feel like doing - and if you really can't delegate, park, or delete - then it's really best just to get on with it.

There is a tangible physical feeling of release, a weight lifted off your back, when you have completed a dreaded task.

---

[13] "Eat that Frog" by Brian Tracy, published by Berrett-Kohler Publishers, Inc. (2017)

You've no doubt got a lot of things to do and little time to do it. You can't afford to waste any of that time procrastinating. But how do you even find the time you need to get everything done? Let alone the time you need for yourself, to think and plan.

Own Your Own Schedule

Time is your most precious asset, and most of us are very busy with multiple demands on our time, all coming at us constantly.

Finding the time in your schedule to answer emails, read reports, or even just think a bit, is hard – so you end up doing emails in bed, not reading any reports, and doing precious little thinking. But a good question is: Who really owns your schedule?

When you are asked to attend an internal meeting at 10 am, but you already have a client meeting at that time, you just say, *"Sorry. No, I can't do it."* You don't feel guilty or unprofessional.

Nobody questions you about it. Everybody has commitments, right? But if we have set time aside just for ourselves, we somehow feel guilty if someone else wants us to use that time differently. However, that time is just as important, maybe vitally so, for you to perform at your best.

So, block yourself 90 minutes in your schedule, label it "ER & T Committee" (E-mailing, Reading, and Thinking), and then stick to it. Don't let anyone bump you off that spot. No one will ever question what you are doing, and the other meetings will get rescheduled.

You get 90 minutes to do what you really need to do, and as a result, you will feel better, more in control, and be a happier and more effective employee. Try it this week.

Recognize that YOU own your schedule and don't allow yourself to be bullied out of time you allocate to yourself.

Your Goals Are Yours

If you want to achieve something, it is generally accepted that it makes sense to set yourself some goals. Having a clear idea of what you want to do, by when, is obviously an important step in turning an ambition into a reality.

As they say, "what gets measured gets done," and it is indeed highly satisfying to set a target and then achieve it. Most people know about SMART goals, and that framework certainly makes a lot of sense.

If your goals aren't specific, measurable, achievable, relevant, and time-bound, then it seems likely that they may not be that useful as a plan for you.

On the other hand, perhaps you have other types of more intangible ambitions that are not so easy to put into the SMART frame. What if you want to be happier at your work, get better at relaxing, or learn to keep your temper when things get really annoying? Those things might be very important to you, and yet they may be very hard to measure, and even harder to achieve.

```
┌─────────────────────────────────┐
│                                 │
│   SMART GOALS                   │
│                                 │
│   S-SPECIFIC                    │
│   M-MEASURABLE                  │
│   A-ATTAINABLE                  │
│   R-RELEVANT                    │
│   T-TIME-BASED                  │
│                                 │
└─────────────────────────────────┘
```

Goals are sometimes imposed on us by our work, bosses, etc. Ideally, you will be, at the very least, a major part of setting that 'contract' between you and your boss about what is expected of you and how your progress will be measured. Nevertheless, there is a big difference between ambitions we set for ourselves and ones that we must achieve to keep our jobs or get promoted. It's important to make that distinction and make sure there is a healthy relationship between the two.

There is a risk of 'goal tyranny' when the goals we set ourselves, or are set on us by others, actually are a source of anxiety for us. Rather than helping us to move forward with energy, they can actually contribute to our worries and stress.

That is why we need to have a healthy relationship with our goals and remember that they are OURS. Even if they have been suggested or even imposed by someone else, we have decided to accept them - and as such, need to live up to them and aim to achieve them.

Realistically, we will not achieve anything if we outsource our responsibility to someone else or blame others for our own lack of conviction or belief. Remember, we only control ourselves.

I am a fan of short-term goals. Trying to set goals for what will happen months ahead in time does not create any real incentive for immediate action - there's plenty of time, no need to stress too much about it now….

A goal that you set out to achieve today, by tomorrow, or next week is far more tangible and has a much greater chance of being met. When setting goals for other people or for yourself, think short term to get things done.

Most importantly, be conscious of your relationship with the goals you have in your life. If you don't really believe in them or are shifting responsibility for them to someone else - then you have an unhealthy relationship with them. You will not achieve them.

Top 30 #10: Scoring goals v. playing well

When it comes to achieving goals and making progress, I find the analogy of a soccer game to be useful. You are playing very well. You've done some brilliant runs down the wing, sent over some amazing crosses, and shot four times at goal. However, your efforts have either bounced off the crossbar or just missed the goal by inches. You are playing the game of your life!

Even if you are not into soccer, I hope you will get the picture. Lots of effort and work, but no actual goals scored.

The final whistle blows. You feel very satisfied with your performance. But then you notice that the crowd is booing. You and your team did play well, and you tried very hard. But you didn't score any goals, and you lost the match.

Unfortunately, that is what will be remembered, and that is how you are judged on your performance. Organizations are the same. They say they appreciate hard work and engagement, but they only really reward results.

I was a newly appointed CEO of a franchise organization in the UK, owned by private equity. There were a lot of issues to tackle, and I was fired up with enthusiasm to fix the business, with a long list of urgent projects underway in many areas of the company.

One of our board directors was a highly experienced ex-CEO of a large legal publishing group in the USA. He took me out for lunch, and we talked about my new job and priorities.

He said to me that while everyone on the board was very impressed with what I was trying to do with the team, the customer satisfaction and the NPS score, the marketing plan, the new website, etc., there was only one thing the owners actually cared about. That was to generate new sales and grow the revenue of the business.

He said that in the end, all my other good work would become irrelevant and ultimately forgotten if I could not deliver that.

All the other stuff was evidence that I was playing well, but I needed to score goals to win the game. And if I couldn't win the game, all my efforts were eventually wasted, and in vain.

He pointed out to me that my bosses were only interested in the results that mattered to them. It made me think hard about how I was spending my time and where I was putting focus for my team.

Work out what counts as 'Scoring a Goal'

This one is so important. I find with my clients that often they are frustrated because they are working so hard, yet they do not seem to be successful in the eyes of their superiors.

HOW DO YOU SCORE A GOAL?

It is critical to figure out what really matters to your bosses. What is it that they expect from you? If it is different from what you are doing, you have an issue at review time.

Often, you have to step back from your big list of tasks and challenges and ask yourself, *"What will really move the needle for my bosses, and therefore for me?"* And how much time are you really spending on that? How much time do you spend on the really key stuff?

From your boss's point of view, what counts as "scoring a goal?"

Active Waiting

Notwithstanding all of our efforts to be in control of what we do and to be well organized when we are doing it, sometimes we just have to wait for someone to decide something or for something to happen that will allow us to move forward with whatever it is.

I find that people often say to me, *"There is nothing I can do - I am just waiting."* But is that really true? Is there truly nothing you can do?

Sometimes, how well you use your waiting time can have a dramatic effect on the successful outcome of whatever it is you are waiting for.

Practice "active waiting" - ask yourself what you can do to be more ready and more prepared. Stay in control by using your time wisely and not shifting responsibility for your inaction onto someone else.

What can you read? Who can you talk to? How can you better prepare for when whatever it is finally happens?

Action!

When faced with difficult decisions or choices, it can be tempting to decide to do nothing at all. *"Sometimes it is wisest to do nothing"* - but is it really?

When does kicking the can down the road really solve anything? The only real effect of delay is to lose some of the most precious and rare commodity of all - time.

As Tony Stark (Iron Man) says to his father Howard Stark in Avengers Endgame[14], *"No amount of money ever bought a second of time."*

The best time to do something that needs doing, really almost always is - now.

---

[14] Marvel Studios *Avengers Endgame* (2019)

Reflections

Here are a few key questions arising from the themes raised in this chapter:

- Do you feel you have enough time for everything you want, or need, to do?
- Do you measure or track how you spend your time?
- If you don't, how would that be useful?
- How do you plan for the unexpected, or things going wrong?
- Do you feel in control of your own schedule?
- Do you know what your bosses consider to be a 'win' in terms of your work?
- How could you spend more time on the things that really make a difference to your success?
- To what extent do you feel you are action-oriented?
- How do you organize yourself to get things done?

Chapter 6: Become a Master Communicator

Presenting Yourself and Your Ideas

In life in general, and most definitely in the work environment, being able to present your ideas or work with confidence is a core skill.

It's amazing how a mediocre idea can gain traction if powerfully communicated - and equally, a great idea can be wasted by poor presentation that fails to grab the attention of an audience.

There is no job in the world, however technical or buried in the back office, that occasionally doesn't require you to come out into the light to sell, explain, or share in some way.

Whatever your natural personal style may be, you absolutely can become a competent and memorable speaker or presenter. Becoming good at it, and even learning to enjoy it, is time very wisely invested.

Big Objective

When faced with the need to give a presentation, I find that many of us quickly dive into the details of what we want to say: which facts to include, which graphs to show, which numbers to use. We concentrate on what we think the audience needs to see or hear from us in order to be impressed or convinced.

Before you even start developing the content of a talk, the first step is to step back, consider the big picture, and ask yourself, "What am I trying to achieve?"

What do you want people to think, feel, or do after listening to you? Having this clarity may radically change what you decide to include or leave out. Perhaps your mission is just to tempt people to find out more or to participate in another, more detailed presentation? In that case, including too much information now would be a mistake.

Being absolutely clear about the overall objective of your speech or presentation will make it much easier to put together the elements that will achieve that goal. I want them to find out more, visit my website, buy my book, give me money, be convinced, be impressed, be shocked, be happy, be angry... The list of possibilities is endless.

Top 30 #11: Not What You Say, But How You Say It

When it comes to creating personal impact, such as with a presentation, a speech, an interview - or even just a conversation - we tend to focus a lot on what we are going to say.

And what we say is obviously very important - although not as important as one might think. Your personal impact in these situations is driven by three factors: your:

-Content

-Competence

-Charisma

As you rise to your feet to speak, it is expected that you will have strong content. Certainly, if your stories are boring, your facts are wrong, or your numbers are out of date, then your audience will not be impressed. And, of course, they will be happy to hear an interesting speech with compelling or original content.

However, when it comes to grabbing attention and being memorable, research has shown that your content is only responsible for about 10% of the impact mix.

Technically-minded presenters often make the mistake of thinking that excellent content will make up for poor presenting skills.

Working on your Competence (i.e., skills and techniques like clear and precise diction, breathing, eye contact, body movements, avoiding notes, use of media, structure of ideas, rehearsing, etc.) is time very well spent.

Charisma is more of a personal thing, but often it is about relaxing and being 'you'. I have seen some excellent speeches and presentations given by people who initially do not seem likely to enjoy speaking or be good at it. Just because you are shy, quiet, and a bit introverted does NOT mean you can't captivate an audience. Quite the opposite, in fact.

NOT WHAT YOU SAY...

By practicing, gaining confidence, and getting experience of talking - in presentations, conferences, or even just in meetings - you will develop your charisma. How you say it turns out to be more important than what you are saying.

We instinctively feel that some people just naturally are charismatic. Really, it is nothing more than a set of behaviors applied with confidence. Work on developing your empathy, me-pathy, self-confidence, and assertiveness. Be authentic and think about what your body language is saying to people. Be you, and like it.

If you look like you are enjoying yourself, then others will enjoy watching you and listening to you.

Practice Makes Perfect

When it comes to becoming a great presenter or speaker, there are many ways to go about perfecting or improving your skills. Sign up for a course, join Toastmasters[15], video yourself, or ask friends or colleagues to give you honest feedback. Most importantly, get out there and do it - practice and learn from your mistakes.

Ask some friends over for the evening and ask everyone (including you!) to make a speech after dinner.

Many people have a genuine fear of public speaking, but it can be overcome - and overcoming it will unquestionably help you be more successful at whatever you do.

If you are lucky enough to be a naturally confident speaker, you can still put in some time to be really good at it and become not just a natural communicator, but also a highly professional one.

Here are some ideas that I have found to be useful for being a better speaker or presenter.

It's a Show

Whilst it may be a professional work presentation, it's still a show. People like to be entertained and absorbed by what you are doing for them and will remember and appreciate you more for entertaining them.

---

[15] https://www.toastmasters.org/

That doesn't mean you have to be hilarious or tell jokes. Rather, aim to be supremely professional and on top of your story and personal presentation technique.

Put yourself in the shoes of your audience. Would you enjoy listening to you? During a play at the theater, the "magic" can be broken by a mobile phone going off in the audience or an actor who forgets their lines. Think of your presentation as a show and aim to fully capture and captivate your audience in the time they are listening to you.

Don't Apologize

How many times have you heard a speaker start off with some kind of apology or excuse?

"Oh, I'm sorry I'm late - the traffic was awful." (Well, we all made it on time). "I am a terrible presenter - but I'll do my best... haha."

"Oh dear, I've got the wrong slides..."

"Oh, I don't know how to work this clicker..."

As an audience, we want to be put at ease, informed, and ideally entertained. We don't want to listen to an incompetent person. Can you imagine an actor starting a play by apologizing that they haven't really had time to learn their lines?

However late you are, or however nervous you feel, you won't get sympathy from the audience with apologies and excuses.

Tell a Story (Beginning, Middle, End)

Every good story has a beginning, a middle, and an end. Your presentation is no exception, and the more you work to give it that structure, the better it will be. In general, people can more easily absorb ideas when presented in groups of three (once again, a beginning, middle, and end), so bear that in mind when you organize your points. It's easy to overwhelm an audience with too much data or a long list. Think of your presentation as a story that you are telling.

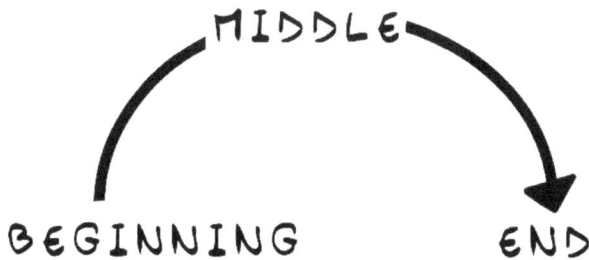

Consciously organize your material into these three parts. Don't be afraid to explain your structure, your agenda, or to repeat your main points at the end.

"Tell them what you plan to tell them, then tell them, then tell them what you just told them."

It is an anticlimax when a presentation has gone on for 30 minutes and suddenly just abruptly ends, *"Er - that's my last slide."* Work on your ending to make it memorable and a satisfactory conclusion to your message. It may be the moment to ask for a next action - or just to say thank you for people's time.

The Power of Stories

We all enjoy a good story. If you can find ways to include stories in your speech, you will transmit a more personal impression. The story comes from you and your experience. By illustrating a point you want to make with a personal anecdote, the audience will be much more likely to remember it.

People will warm to you.

If you stand up to make a presentation of the quarterly sales results and you start off by saying, *"The other day I was on the bus, and I noticed it had started to rain. I looked out of the window and I saw a man who had obviously forgotten his umbrella start to..."*

Everybody will now be listening to you, suddenly keen to find out what happens next in your story.

Don't feel embarrassed to include stories just because it is a work meeting. Your audience is still just people. You might want to start out with the first part of a story and then conclude your talk with its resolution - nicely giving structure to your talk.

Use Your Time Wisely

If you have a 30-minute slot for a presentation and have carefully prepared 45 slides, then you are heading for a bad situation. Audiences do not appreciate speakers who cannot stick to their allotted time. It is a sign of disrespect, suggesting that the speaker's time is more important than the audience's.

If you are using slides to support your talk, then work out exactly how long each one will take to discuss. Even the most basic slide can occupy a couple of minutes of your speech. Practice the timing of your talk in front of a mirror and then add extra time – it always takes longer in front of a live audience.

One great slide is better than 10 that you rush through.

Give yourself space to complete your talk easily in the time you have and be sure to have adequate time to deliver your ending or request your call to action. Do you need to leave time for questions?

Using Slides to Support Your Message

Your audience will read slides with lots of words on them and stop listening to you as a result. If you do use words, choose short statements or single words as anchors to what you are saying.

Slides with strong, engaging visuals that support but do not distract from your story can be good for everyone. They keep the audience's attention and are also a way for you to keep track of your script and remind you of your key points. Less is more with slides. They are a visual stimulus, not a source of information. You are the source of information.

If you want people to read something, then ideally provide it to them in a written format that they can hold in their hand and give them enough time to read it.

If you are presenting to a meeting with less than ten people, avoid projecting slides onto the wall. Instead, provide each person with a printed copy of whatever will help them to follow or remember your message. That might be a single page designed to have all your important messages and information on it.

Projecting a slide with a written list or paragraphs is lazy and ineffective. By the time you have gotten to point 2, your audience has already read everything and is getting restless as they know or think they know what you plan to say. It's critical to keep your audience engaged and keep them guessing.

If you want people to take something away with them, make sure it has been properly designed for its purpose. Giving people a copy of your slides with pictures or numbers that made sense while you are speaking will become meaningless in a very little time. Provide a document that will be readable and useful for them and is consistent with your speech but not just a repetition of it.

Only Extrovert People are Good Speakers

That is completely wrong! In fact, I have found that some of the very best public speakers I have worked with are those who are naturally shy and do not enjoy the spotlight.

They know that strong speaking skills are a core asset for their success, so they have made up their mind to overcome their fears and get good at it.

Sometimes, very extroverted people can fail to prepare properly or not engage well with an audience because they are overconfident. They think they are great at public speaking because it doesn't scare them. They may fail to listen to feedback or be ready to learn.

An audience enjoys authenticity and appreciates you when you make an effort to prepare well - and have put thought into what and how you most effectively communicate your messages and ideas.

Build Your Communication Competencies

However natural you think you are (or are not) as a speaker, the more skilled you become, the more impact you will have. Getting good at developing eye contact, mastering your body language, and being comfortable with different types of media or tools can all help you to be a first-class communicator.

Learning to present without notes, keeping your head still, knowing what to do with your hands, how to vary your voice in terms of pace or volume, and how to naturally engage audience members are all key elements that you can learn about and work on. The list is long, and the rewards are real, as people who present and speak effectively are always appreciated.

Enjoy Yourself

Aim to relax and enjoy giving your presentation. This feeling will be transmitted to the audience, and they will, in turn, relax and enjoy the experience of listening and watching you.

Your impact really is all about 'you' and much less about what you are talking about. If you are talking about something engaging and you are a confident speaker, you are in a great position.

Have you ever been to a show by a stand-up comedian and found yourself laughing constantly throughout but then afterwards had difficulty remembering the actual jokes? The comedian uses timing, storytelling, and audience connection to engage you. In many cases, the comic narrative uses no 'jokes' at all - but you are pulled in by the confidence of the speaker and the competence of their delivery.

Aiming to become good at speaking in public is one area in which we are absolutely in control of our own destiny. Practice, a bit of bravery, and getting some help and advice can make a massive difference in how well you communicate and, thus, typically get what you want or need.

Being a poor and nervous speaker is a serious shortcoming that can hold you back in many ways.

Being a confident and effective speaker is a great personal and professional asset that you will use time and time again and constantly get better at doing.

Reflections

Here are a few key questions arising from the themes raised in this chapter

- Do you present your ideas with confidence?
- When you make a presentation what do you mainly focus on?
- How might you further develop your competence as a speaker?
- Do your presentations have a clear beginning, middle and end?
- What kind of stories could you include in your presentations?
- Do you always keep to the time you have been allotted?
- When you give a speech or presentation, do you consciously aim to enjoy yourself?
- How could you enjoy yourself more when speaking in public?

Part 2

Leading Other People

In Part 1, we focused on how to be more aware of yourself, more conscious of your own brand, your own personal qualities, and the impact you make on others.

We discussed how to manage yourself and your emotions, how to use your time wisely, and how to make good decisions and choices.

We also explored how to most powerfully present your ideas.

Now, let's shift our focus to the challenges of leading other people.

Chapter 7: Our Most Important Asset

How many times have you heard the leaders of a company or business (perhaps your own leaders) say that their people are special, unique, and amazing?

"Our people are our greatest asset! We must always remember that we owe all our success to them. They are so talented, amazing, and special."

What they don't say out loud is the second part of the sentence that they are all thinking.

"Our people are our greatest asset. We must always remember that we owe all our success to them. They are so talented, amazing, and special. And if we could think of a way of running our business without any people at all, we would do it in a heartbeat, as they are an absolute pain most of the time."

Even in the newly dawning age of AI, it is very likely that you will need to employ or manage others to achieve your business goals.

Being an effective manager of people is challenging and a never-ending task, mainly because people are endlessly complicated and demanding.

People Are a Pain, and Need a Lot of Attention

Every individual is their own mini-universe of experiences, ideas, feelings, opinions, cultural influences, insecurities, ambitions, and aspirations. Never make the mistake of thinking that because people are lower down in a hierarchy, paid less than others, or part of a big team, they will somehow be individually easier to please or less focused on what they want. Why would they be?

PEOPLE = PAIN

Humans are complicated and surprising and don't always behave in the way that you expect, and hardly ever in the way you ideally want them to.

You can never underestimate the effort that you need to put in to effectively manage your professional relationships and get the most from the people you work with every day.

At least 80% of my work as a coach is helping people to tackle 'people-issues' in their job. Sometimes this is a situation involving a boss, colleague or peer, a team member, or maybe managing a group of people, a client, or a provider.

Whoever and whatever they may be, they are all issues that are created by the unexpected behavior, expectations, demands, reactions, or performance of people.

I am constantly amazed by the range of problems and crises that us humans can come up with. When it comes to people, things are rarely simple.

There is no easy way around working out how to get the best from your people, create a happy and engaged team, and a good working culture. You just have to work extremely hard at it. Being a good leader and manager of people is both highly challenging and also extremely rewarding when it goes well.

Top 30 #12: Never Stop Communicating

It cannot be overstressed how important it is for leaders and managers to maintain constant communication with their teams, peers, bosses, clients, and any other important stakeholders.

That sounds obvious, but in so many cases, I have seen how what seemed like "enough" just wasn't.

This is especially true now with so many people working remotely. You may spend a lot of time on video calls with your team, but do you take the time to talk to them not just about projects and work matters, but also as people?

You may feel that there is "nothing to communicate," but people aren't necessarily expecting "news." They yearn for a constant flow of natural communication that helps them feel well-informed and respected as part of a team.

If, for example, a senior person has left the company and perhaps you are tempted not to make a big fuss about it or say anything. After all, it's not really relevant to most people or their job that this person has left.

But a vacuum will always be filled by something, and people left with a scarcity of information will start to generate their own version of what happened and why, and in the absence of an "official" explanation, total nonsense can somehow become the "truth."

Suddenly the office will be rife with whispered rumors about why that executive suddenly departed. Time will be wasted. People will wonder why you didn't want to say anything or explain what happened.

This situation is so easily remedied by just providing people with a version of the truth (ideally the complete truth, but this isn't always possible) that satisfies their curiosity and allows them to refocus on their work.

People are self-centered, so if someone is let go without any explanation, they may think "that could be me next."

Never underestimate how important it is to keep communicating—and the constant need people have to be informed.

Relationships Need Constant Nurturing

All of us have personal relationships. Even if we don't have a wife, boyfriend, or significant other, we typically do have a neighbor, a mum, or a grandad. Every human relationship has one thing in common—it needs to be constantly worked on.

There are best practices, guidelines, and expectations. There are ups and downs, critical moments, and sometimes there are breakdowns.

Our work relationships are no different and must be actively worked on constantly to create the optimally enjoyable, effective, and productive partnership - and the best outcomes for everyone involved. It's good to think of your work relationships in the same way that you think of your personal ones.

They need constant nurturing. They need honesty and trust. They require effort.

For relationships to function optimally, the most important investment you can make is time spent on working out how to communicate well…and time spent on actually communicating.

We may be IT developers or marketing executives, but underneath that, we are still humans and we will be happier and more productive if we have healthy relationships with our colleagues.

Never underestimate the importance of working on your relationships at work and how good communication will make those relationships work better.

Relationships are like a log fire. If you don't pay attention to it and put on more logs now and again, it will definitely go out. Keep investing in it and caring for it, and it can burn forever.

1-1 Meetings

Most managers have regular 1-1 meetings with their team members, or direct reports. If you don't, you really need to think about why not. Perhaps you feel that you are always talking to your team, so why the need for a 1-1?

It is the time that your team member gets your undivided attention, and when you can really find out how things are going both in terms of work projects, but also the state of engagement of the individual, and sometimes even get insights into what is happening in the wider organization.

As the boss, you need to make it clear that these meetings are "owned" by your team member. They should always prepare an agenda, which ideally should be sent in advance. Of course, you can always have an agenda of your own, but your direct report should come prepared to talk and to update you on progress, or to ask questions, etc.

If you allow it to happen, people will just "turn up" expecting you to do all the talking - after all, you are the boss, right?

If your own boss is not disciplined about 1-1 meetings and their structure, it is in your interest to propose improvements. Offer to bring an agenda each time. Think about what you want to achieve from these meetings, create some objectives for yourself. You have the boss all to yourself, how can you benefit from that?

Healthy and effective 1-1 meetings are absolutely critical to run an effective and engaged team and to make sure that projects stay on target.

You can avoid micromanaging and interfering with your team members' work by establishing this regular reporting process. Your people know that you will give them autonomy and space - but that 1-1s with you need to be well-prepared.

After 1-1s follow up in writing with a brief email on anything that was agreed. Try to have clear, mutually agreed action points or deadlines for things. I recommend a work/project-based 1-1 update meeting every two weeks at least - keep them short and to the point.

Then, once a month, have a 1-1 which is specifically identified as a more personal conversation - a check-in on how your direct report is doing - not just as a worker but also as a person. I call these meetings "sacred spaces."

Top 30 #13: Sacred Spaces

If you are running a team, you will be constantly talking to your colleagues and team members. Most people have more tasks on their plate than time to manage them comfortably, so conversations are focused on information, projects, data, results, feedback from clients, and reports.

It is very easy to get into the habit of communicating a lot with your team but never actually talking to them about anything other than work and never about them as people.

They can start to feel like they are only elements of a working process that has certain tasks to complete and deadlines to meet.

It is absolutely vital to build meetings with people into your schedule that are specifically and intentionally used for talking about anything and everything other than the job in hand that week. Whatever THEY want to talk about.

Your team members should "own" these meetings, just as they own all 1-1 meetings with you. It is up to them to plan and bring the items they want to discuss to you each time. You can always bring up your own points, but the responsibility of preparing for that time lies with them.

Usually, these are 1-1 meetings, probably once a month, and for no more than 20 minutes or half an hour. I call them 'sacred spaces'.

They are sacred because they should not be shifted for other priorities and not canceled as they 'aren't really important'. They are incredibly important.

They are used for talking to each other as people, not just as workers. To dig into what is going on in people's lives, how they are feeling about their job, their career, and anything else that is important to them. Do they need a grumble, to be listened to?

Sacred spaces also provide the moment for you, or whoever you are talking to, to bring up important matters that are hard to introduce into the normal hurly-burly of everyday work communication. Feedback, requests for a promotion or more money, concerns about a colleague, advice on an opportunity, or an explanation of an incident.

Just because sacred spaces are intentionally not all about work or projects doesn't mean they shouldn't be planned in advance and have structure. An agenda sent to you by e-mail beforehand and some agreed action points afterwards will make these meetings even more useful and effective.

Retreating Into Caves

When times are tough (which, in most corporate organizations I work with, they seem to be most of the time), communication becomes even more vital than ever.

The danger is that when under pressure and feeling stressed, members of your team can gradually "retreat into their caves" – taking refuge from everything going on, and also gradually withdrawing from you and the rest of the team.

In the remote environment, especially, it is easy not to recognize that this is happening. People still turn up for their meetings, but without you realizing it, they are gradually becoming less engaged. The withdrawal process that has recently been called "quiet quitting."

Communication needs to be more than just you talking to your people. Organize group meetings and discussions where you put challenges and topics out for joint consideration. Make sure everyone is participating.

Ask different people to lead those meetings and ask the group for ideas about what matters to them and what they would like to talk about. This may sound like a lot of time out of your already packed schedule, but it really is worth it.

Team Building

The most effective way to organize a "team building" is actually the simplest and least expensive option. Allow people the opportunity to talk together about what they do every day and jointly agree on ideas and proposals on how things can work better.

Create a forum where team members or guests from other teams can present what they do to their colleagues. Everybody likes talking about what they do and why it is valuable. Learning more about other people's contributions builds trust and appreciation between teams.

It is tempting to take your team to the bowling alley or try out archery, but while this may be a good outing, it will not be as useful for your team as getting together to discuss their work and actively share experiences.

Traditional team building exercises, while enjoyable for some, can sometimes accidentally expose potential divisions or differences in the team beyond the work scope.

I attended one event that was organized by a very enthusiastic and sports-minded senior leader who had his team spread across several countries. It was well known that there was constant tension between him and one of his direct reports in another country. He and she just did not connect well.

The people flew in from all the different countries to take part in the highly planned team-building day. It involved a kind of treasure hunt in the countryside with clues and objects to discover. As we all gathered in a woody clearing in our tracksuits and running shoes, we suddenly realized that this particular lady had chosen to turn up in a very bright pair of red high heels.

It was the clearest statement possible that she did not appreciate the boss's team-building plan and did not intend to be a part of it.

The Right Relationship to Have with Your Team

Getting the balance right in terms of what kind of relationship you aim to build with your team members is not easy. It is certainly a big mistake to try to become everybody's best friend.

You are the boss, and that means that a time may come when you have to make tough decisions and choices about people. That might be a performance issue that needs to be resolved or just a case of cost-cutting or a reorganization that is imposed on you from above.

If you have populated your team with your friends, this already stressful situation will become highly unpleasant for you. Your team members may turn on you personally as they feel you have let them down as people, not just as employees.

Perhaps for that reason, I have seen some leaders take a distant and rather cold stance with their teams. Aiming to avoid the pitfalls of being too close to people, they end up seeming remote and not greatly appreciated as leaders. Neither of these approaches is ideal. But how do you go about achieving the right balance?

I-it and I-you

Martin Buber (1875-1965) was a prolific writer, teacher, and philosopher born in Vienna, who later lived in Israel. Perhaps his most famous work is a short book first published in German in 1923, and later in English in 1937, entitled "I and Thou". It is all about relationships between humans (and his personal relationship with God to an extent) and is not a light read.

It does have some essential ideas that are useful when thinking about leadership and our relationships at work. He describes two types of relationship: "I-it" and "I-you."

I-it relationships are transactional and ignore our humanity; the human interaction that takes place might as well be between a person and a machine or a computer. An example might be buying a train ticket for your morning commute to the office.

"One return ticket to London, please."

This interaction is all about the desired output, and the traveler might be just as happy (or even happier) getting the ticket from a ticket machine.

The "I-you' relationship" version of this interaction might be:

"Good morning, Fred. How are you today? And the kids? Great! My normal return, please. Thanks, see you tomorrow, and say hello to your wife from me."

Clearly, an effort has been made by the traveler to know something about the ticket seller, and as such, the interaction recognizes him as a human who has a life and family beyond the act of providing the ticket.

This extra relationship effort has no practical impact on the transaction - the ticket gets bought just the same. The difference is that the two people have an exchange of human interest, as well as just the practical process.

Importantly, the traveler is not "friends" with the ticket seller. They will almost certainly never spend any time together beyond the bounds of the ticket transaction. The traveler doesn't actually know the man's wife and has never met his kids. He probably doesn't even know where he lives.

Nevertheless, their morning exchanges create a sense of something intangible beyond the transaction. The two of them are creating a "culture" by an awareness of their wider lives. However, their relationship only exists because together they buy and sell the train ticket.

There is something very useful in these ideas of Buber's when considering the ideal relationship to build with your team members. Make an effort to know an appropriate amount of background information about your people.

If they have children, find out their names and ages; if they are getting married, congratulate them. If they are learning a new language, be encouraging and ask them how it is going.

Set out to consciously build a relationship with your team that goes beyond just the work that has brought you together. Recognize them as humans with wider lives, but don't try to venture too far into those lives.

It is a respectful but genuine approach that will help to build a culture that goes beyond, but not too far beyond, your work relationship.

Seek your deeper, more personal relationships beyond the workplace to satisfy your desire to really know people intimately. It is very easy to get close to team members, as you have a lot in common and plenty to talk about. But the power dynamics will create potential problems for both you and the people that work for you.

Strive for powerful, healthy I-you relationships with your team members, and you can potentially build a working culture that is as pleasant to be a part of as it is hopefully effective at delivering good work.

The Double Agent

Sometimes you can find that someone is struggling in your team, or in a more junior role in someone else's team with a different leader. You may have a lot of sympathy for their situation, especially if you like them and appreciate them as people.

They are suffering with their issues with their manager and come to you to share, and possibly complain. You can and should listen and offer suggestions and ideas to improve the situation.

But beware. However well you get on with this person, you must take great care to keep your involvement at arm's length and not allow yourself to 'take their side' behind closed doors, or worse still, join in with them in criticizing your own peers or bosses.

You must remain loyal to your position as a manager in the hierarchy - offer to share their grievances or to support them in sharing directly. Don't encourage their position by supporting it behind 'closed doors.'

If you are tempted to join in their narrative of criticism of others, you risk becoming a "double agent." You are trying to play both sides of a situation and saying different things to different people. The risk is that *everyone* will eventually not trust you. Your "confidential" words of support can easily be shared, putting you in an embarrassing and uncomfortable position with everybody.

In spy films, double agents always end up dead. And sometimes it isn't even clear who finished them off, as no one fully trusts them.

Starting in a New Role

Beginning in a new leadership role will mean that there will be increased expectations placed on you, and you will be focused on delivering those and showing your bosses that they made a good decision to trust you with this new responsibility.

If you are also taking over a team of people, it is very important to invest adequate time in getting to know your team in the early stages of the new job. With a big group, remember that they will be delivering much of what will make you successful.

I strongly recommend setting out to meet every member of your new team personally at least once within 3 months of taking the role. If the team is very big, then this will have to be arranged with town halls or group meetings, and if geographically dispersed, then via video calls.

However, if you can physically do it, try to meet everyone one-on-one, even if just for a small amount of time. This is the vital first step in building your I-You relationships with your people. You are showing that you actually care about them as individuals, and not just as workers.

You will make an important impact on your team who will be pleasantly surprised that you have shown this level of interest in them. This will bring you future benefits as well.

Everyone who works for you will recognize you - you are the boss. It can be an uncomfortable feeling to meet someone in a corridor after six months in your new job who greets you warmly (you are the boss, they know who you are) - but whom you don't recognize.

When I took over a department of around 100 people, I made the effort to meet every person. It was quite a commitment and hard work to arrange and fit it all in - but I never regretted it. If your team is 30 or 40 people, then it is a must.

If you are the CEO of a massive organization, then obviously the challenge is different, although the benefits of meeting as many people as possible will still be significant. Perhaps you aim to meet the top 100 and brief your communication team to create a plan for you to speak and interact with everyone.

Never underestimate the impact of your extra effort with people.

Never Underestimate People

Whatever business you are in, it is almost certain that to grow it or your own responsibilities within it, you will need to hire or manage increasing numbers of individuals.

However good you are at developing software, selling ideas, knowing the law, selling insurance, designing new things, etc., you will absolutely also have to be good at managing and leading people to be truly successful.

Decide to be good at this. Be an expert at understanding and getting the best from the people that work for you, and with you.

There are many ways to do this, and an endless range of types of people that you must deal with and be flexible enough to handle appropriately for a good outcome. With people, there are rarely easy answers. Every person is their own mini-universe of ambitions, perspectives, and beliefs.

Never underestimate the power of people to build up or destroy whatever it is you are trying to do. Excellent communication is the number one rule for successful and happy teams - and you will have to work on that every day and put in much more effort than you ever imagined was necessary.

And it can, and almost certainly will, still all go wrong at some point. Leading people is far more an art than a science. It is a challenging, surprising, and at times exhausting assault course that never ends.

Reflections

Here are a few key questions arising from the themes raised in this chapter

- How would you rate your communication efforts with your team?
- Do you constantly work on nurturing your key relationships?
- Do you have 1-1 meetings with your team members?
- Do your team members prepare an agenda for those meetings?
- Do you also make sure there is an opportunity to talk about more than just work and projects?
- What is the type of relationship you aim for with your team members?
- How might you make your work relationships stronger?

Chapter 8: Getting What You Want (or Need) From Others

You live and work in a complex community made up of individuals who all have needs and ambitions. You want certain things to happen, but then again, so do they.

How do you make sure you get what you need from other people to be successful? And how can you be better at helping people to get what they need from you?

I wonder how many meetings you have attended this week? In how many of those meetings did you really get what you wanted or needed? Did you come out feeling that somehow the time got away from you, and you left a little frustrated?

Who Controls the Agenda?

So many people have talked to me about their frustration that somehow they don't achieve the decisions or outcomes they need when they get together with their bosses, teams, colleagues, or other departments.

I have found that one very small idea, which seems almost absurdly simple, can make a big difference. I have practiced it with incredibly good results.

You write down your agenda for the meeting and take it with you. You might send it around beforehand, put it up on the screen as the meeting starts, or if it is a traditional face-to-face meeting, print it out and distribute it physically to each person.

Just because you are not the chair of the meeting or perhaps the most senior person in the room does not mean that if handled with a bit of tact, you cannot make your agenda extremely clear to everyone involved.

If you are looking for a clear decision on a particular topic, you can make that very obvious by writing "decision on project x" in your agenda.

You can always end your agenda list with *"Any Other Business"* so that no one can be offended if their pet project is not on your list. You can actively request other agenda items from all participants and enlarge the agenda there and then.

By actively bringing a written and pre-prepared agenda list to the meeting, you have begun in a small but powerful way to control the meeting.

Over the years, I have been amazed by the effectiveness of this simple practice. You arrive at a large meeting of various groups from within the company, and there are a lot of things to discuss. Perhaps someone is going to stand up and suggest brainstorming the topics for the day.

To everyone's surprise, you stand up and announce that to save time and be helpful, you have brought an agenda. You produce a copy for everyone.

Is anyone going to say, *"No, I don't like that agenda!?"*– even if they may be thinking it. You have successfully taken the initiative, and they will now have to add their extra ideas to your list.

It shows everyone that you didn't just turn up for the meeting, but that you prepared for it in advance and thought about what would happen.

Pre-Identify Outcomes

In the same way, thinking carefully beforehand about the decisions or outcomes that you want from any particular meeting can have a tremendous impact on the likelihood that you end up getting what you want.

So often, you can turn up to a meeting with only a vague idea of how it is going to go and suddenly realize that it is not going in the direction you want. Someone else is controlling the agenda, and someone else is getting what they want from it.

Before going into any meeting, spend some time thinking about what is going to happen there, the personalities involved, and the outcomes that work for you.

If it is really important, get a group of trusted people together and brainstorm it out. By predicting the way it will go and defining the outcome you want, you may get a much better result. [16]

Reconnaissance

My father always used to say *"time spent in reconnaissance is rarely wasted"* and I think there is a lot of truth to that. Whenever you interact with another person or another group of people, finding out a bit about them beforehand creates a double advantage for you.

First of all, you can show them that you have bothered to go out of your way to do some research, which will probably make it easier for you to create a good impression.

In a video call meeting with someone for the first time, it is much more powerful to say, *"You are based in Boston, right?"* than *"Where are you based?"*

It sends a message that you have done your homework and looked the person up beforehand. Thanks to LinkedIn, this is really extremely easy. There is no excuse for not doing a basic search on people that you are about to meet for the first time.

---

[16] See page 42 - Define Your Success Criteria

You may discover that you have something, or someone, in common. Once again, LinkedIn is a wonderful tool for that. You can see instantly if there are some people you both know, and that can be an excellent icebreaker.

When you have spotted that you both worked in the same city ten years ago, you are leading the conversation.

The second benefit of doing some reconnaissance before whatever it is you are doing is that you may find out information that may put you at an advantage in some way. Knowing something about the history of a person or an organization before you meet with them can be extremely useful.

I am often amazed by how lazy people are about doing some basic research before they start an interaction with someone else, especially if your aim is to get something from them or sell something to them.

In essence, you are appealing to their individual or collective ego by showing them that you care enough to find out about them before you meet them. I find that you don't need to know very much to be a step ahead when it quickly becomes obvious that they haven't done any reconnaissance and don't know anything about you.

Certainly, everyone has an ego, and with a bit of care and tact, you can use that to your own advantage.

Top 30 #14: Playing the 'Ego Card' (1) – Asking for Advice or a Favor

Everybody has an ego. In some people, it is more highly developed, and it can certainly be exhausting dealing with individuals with extremely big egos.

Overall, the idea of 'ego' seems to have developed a negative connotation, as it is associated with selfishness, not listening, or being narcissistic.

In reality, our ego is just what lies behind our sense of self-esteem and confidence. But even if you are extremely shy, avoid the limelight, and always put others before yourself, you are kidding yourself if you think you have no ego.

And understanding that everyone has an ego can be powerful when you want to achieve something or obtain something from someone - particularly somebody's support or advocacy. The trick is not to flatter but rather to let someone know that you appreciate them - that you 'see' them.

It can be terrifying to go to a more senior or experienced person and ask them for something - but sometimes it is the very best way to achieve what you want. And first recognizing why you came to them can set the scene for success.

When you "play the ego card," it is important to recognize to yourself that you are doing it. So that you choose your words carefully. You are not trying to blow the other person away with admiring words that may sound hollow when you say them. No one likes a flatterer. Rather, aim for an honest description of how you feel that puts the other person in a good light.

"I respect your opinions and feel you have good judgment, and will tell me the truth. That is why I have come to ask for your advice..."

"I know you are good at this..."

"I have watched you handle similar situations, and I believe I can learn from you..."

"I am lost, and I believe you can give me some wise counsel..."

You are appealing to their ego, to their own sense of self-worth, by recognizing their power, experience, or status - and explaining why you feel they can be of help to you.

It is an unusual person who does not respond positively to a genuine and honest stroke of their ego.

Before you say what you have come for and make your request about yourself - you have first made it about them. You have made it easy for them to be generous with their time, advice, contacts, or whatever they can give, as you have already given them something.

People forget to think about how the other person feels when they ask for something. It is just another form of empathy and respect. It is a measure of your own me-pathy.

However much you may feel that you "can't ask" - you can - but do not be ashamed to play the ego card, as you may be far less successful if you don't.

All you are doing is embracing human nature and being appreciative of what someone else can do for you by recognizing them as an individual.

WHEN TO PLAY THE EGO CARD?

Revisit Themes After a Meeting

Sometimes you can come out of a meeting feeling like you wanted to say more or didn't achieve what you needed. This can especially be the case when there were a lot of people in the room and your voice was just one among many.

If your objective is something important, or at least important to you, think about how you can re-engage on the subject directly with your boss or whoever you need to influence.

Often, I would hold back my comments or opinions in a meeting chaired by my boss and think of an excuse to go back later that day (when the subject was still "hot" but everyone else was no longer there) and talk about it again.

Sometimes, keeping quiet in the moment can be a wise choice.

Selfish v. Sensibly Self-Centered

Rarely are very selfish people well appreciated by others. We all know who is really only interested in themselves. However, it is also true that you need to be careful not to be over-generous with your time.

I had a personal experience with this as a leader of a department, as I would always want my team to feel that my 'door was open' for them.

I learned gradually that I had to protect myself and my time. People would turn up at my office and engage me in conversation. *"Oh, just wanted to let you know what happened with x,"* or *"do you have 1 minute to discuss y?"*

The trouble is that it is never 1 minute. I would find myself falling behind with my own priorities as I allowed people to bring theirs to me in an unstructured way.

Eventually, I communicated a small but rather obvious process. If my door is shut, I am working on something, so please *"do not disturb."* If it is open, then please say hello but don't be offended if I ask you to wait for our next 1-1 or to send me an email. Everyone was fine with that.

Trying to be unselfish with my time, in fact, made me rather stressed and inefficient.

Equally, you must get the balance right in terms of the hours you are working overall and be a little self-centered to preserve your capability and do your job well. You cannot be 'on the run' from your job, boss, or team.

There's a big difference between being selfish versus taking sensible measures to protect your time and the ability to do your job well.

Blaming Others

When things go wrong, or are evolving in a way you do not like, it is tempting to find someone to blame. It may be that there is justification in that, and you can legitimately blame someone else for a situation. In which case, you should be thinking about how to express your feelings and give some honest feedback.

Pointing fingers is rarely helpful, and you have to be very sure that you are not just inviting others' fingers to be pointed back at you.

BLAMING OTHERS

Another interesting dynamic is when it is inconvenient or challenging to blame the person who is actually responsible for a bad situation (usually the boss, or perhaps yourself), and so fingers are pointed unfairly at an easier target.

This is called "projecting" or blame-shifting and is not constructive or likely to lead anywhere good.

I had a boss at one point who was rather weak and made some poor decisions about people. He appointed some people he liked to positions of responsibility before they were ready. What I noticed was that my colleagues preferred to blame the individuals themselves and constantly find fault in them and be irritated with them, etc.

They chose to blame them rather than our boss, who was actually responsible because it was easier for them. It didn't help the situation in any way.

Before you rush to blame anyone, think carefully about what has really happened and who (if anyone) is truly responsible.

Satisfaction v. Loyalty

Have you thought about the difference between generating satisfaction compared to creating loyalty? This applies in so many leadership situations.

Driving satisfaction or loyalty from your clients or customers, regardless of your business, is the obvious example that comes to mind. But we also want to create those positive feelings with our bosses, teams, and colleagues.

We want people to be satisfied with what we do with them or for them - and ideally, we hope they will be loyal to us. The two ideas seem similar at first glance but they are totally different, albeit related.

Satisfaction is transactional and is essentially dictated by whether you actually do what you say you are going to do.

Do you pick up the phone in less than three rings? Do you deliver your projects on time and on budget? Do you keep your promises? Do you offer people a consistent result that is aligned with what they are expecting from you?

Take Amazon, for example. It offers its customers a well-defined service that typically delivers exactly what it promises. You find what you want, you press 'buy,' and in a well-communicated timeframe, it gets delivered to your door. What's not to like? People have high levels of satisfaction with Amazon.

Domino's Pizza would be another example - you get exactly what you expect, in a consistent way, for a decent price.

How loyal are you to these services?

If you find a similar or perhaps arguably better product online but not via either of these brands, and they also offer a great delivery service, etc., will you reject them due to your brand loyalty?

Another question: If you use Amazon or Domino's, does it impress your neighbors? Does this service make you look good? This is a key distinction between satisfaction and loyalty.

Loyalty is created when you feel that a person or a service provides you with something that you perceive enhances your own standing in the world.

In the case of consumer brands, you are prepared to pay over the odds for an iPhone, a BMW, or a smart hotel not just because of what it does, but for how it makes you feel about yourself.

Equally, in your relationships with people, you will be fiercely loyal to people that you feel provide you with something that makes you look better in the eyes of others.

If that makes it sound like quite a selfish concept - that is because it is. We are loyal to things or people that make us feel or look good.

When you set out to create loyalty in a person or a team, it is important to keep in mind that they will become loyal to you only if you can help them to seem somehow better.

This works both ways in terms of your relationship with your boss and with the people that report to you. What are you doing for them that helps them to grow, learn, or triumph?

What can you do behind the scenes for your client, boss, or partner that will enhance their reputation?

A colleague of mine had a client that had poor English skills. Unbeknownst to everyone in the client's organization, all of his memos, important emails, and presentations were checked, edited, and sometimes completely written by my colleague. This generated an exceptional level of loyalty. The client almost could not do their job without this support.

As a leader or manager, you can create loyalty in your team by letting them shine, speak up, and be recognized for the work they do. To create personal loyalty, you need to be giving something of yourself away and creating something for someone else.

Managing Up and Down

We know that leadership is not just about managing people who are "below you" in a hierarchy. On many occasions, you may obtain great benefit from actively managing your boss.

That may seem somewhat unfair or unreasonable. Isn't your boss meant to manage you?

That may be true, but if it helps to get what you want and need from your boss, then it is worthwhile to invest time in how best to manage them and to work out what will make them happy or annoyed.

If the boss seems stuck on an important decision, how can you facilitate a way for that to happen without making it look like you are undermining their authority?

I noticed over the years that a lot of my colleagues would give surprisingly little thought to what they could do to make their boss more loyal to them by working out what they could do for them...rather than just the other way around.

Bosses are just people and will have their failings and shortcomings. If we think we can help them be better bosses, we should absolutely make that effort.

The Priorities of the Boss

An example of this is trying to work out what your boss really cares about, what they consider priorities or of key importance.

I worked for a demanding but fair boss who had a reputation for constantly assigning work and making requests to her team. There was a joke about her that if you ran into her in the corridor, you should try to avoid eye contact, as if she looked you in the eye, she would probably give you an "action point."

She would often call me to her office and ask me to do certain things for her, perhaps a list of three tasks: some numbers she needed, making a phone call, or finding something out. She would say *"no rush."*

I would then try to determine which of these tasks she really cared about and wanted done quickly. I would go back to my desk and immediately carry out the task that I felt she was most likely to want done quickly.

Sometimes it only took me 10 minutes and I could send her a quick email with the answer or solution. I know that over time, we developed a higher level of mutual trust as I worked hard to help her quickly get what she most wanted or needed.

Make it about them

Often, I am asked about the best way to go about requesting something from a boss. One thing to consider is whether there are alternative approaches to simply presenting your request as something you want or need. While that approach is fair enough, it may not always be effective.

Simply asking straight out risks making it "all about you."

Can you find a way to make your proposal or request more interesting and appealing to your boss by also making it, at least to some extent, about them?

For example, if you want to take a day off on Friday, you could start by talking about the tasks you will complete by Thursday night. Or if you want to book your holiday dates for the summer, let your boss know that you have already checked their planned dates to be away, and so seem to have taken them into account.

Before requesting anything, stop and think about how it can impact others or how it may be perceived. There may just be a slight adaptation in how you go about it that can make all the difference, so you can get what you want and everyone is happy.

We can become too focused on what we want or feel we need and forget to consider the bigger picture. Figuring out how to make things appealing and beneficial to others can ultimately help you get what you want.

You want, and even expect, your boss to be empathetic toward you and understand how you feel about things. Practice that in reverse and think about how your boss is feeling or how they may react. Work out "what's in it for them" as well as for you. It's another dimension of me-pathy.

Top 30 #15: Playing the 'Ego Card' (ii) – Getting Something You Want by Understanding Them Better

"If you don't ask, you don't get." True enough. But understanding the motivators of those you are asking and how you go about asking them may be a massive factor in getting what you want or influencing an outcome in your favor.

I worked for a while for a very senior leader who had a fierce reputation for being hard to please. She was highly intelligent, knowledgeable in her field, and did not suffer fools gladly. She was well-respected but also known to be very 'difficult' to deal with, and occasionally people would emerge from her office demoralized and literally shaking after a severe dressing down.

I worked with this person a lot and also had a lot of respect for her, and I had my fair share of difficult moments when she was displeased with me.

However, after a while, I gradually cracked the code of how to work much more successfully with her. So much so that I began to have a reputation as someone who knew how to 'handle' her, and people would even seek my advice before important meetings.

There were some basic things to know about working with her, like being well-prepared and knowing what you were talking about. It was very unwise to admit you had no idea about something she felt was important, and she hated it if you blamed others.

I watched a couple of times as she roasted people for offering replies like "Well, it's not really my responsibility..." She detested that as she thought everyone should be able (and brave enough) to offer an opinion.

Those are all pretty standard demands from a good, exacting boss. The secret wasn't any of these things.

What I realized was that if you wanted to get something from her (more budget, an approval, a signature, a recommendation, a decent amount of her time, etc.), you had to find a way to make it about HER, not you.

The secret to getting what you needed or wanted from her was all about managing her ego. Often, this was simply about how you framed a request or a conversation.

"I think you will really like this idea" rather than *"I want to tell you about my idea."*

"I believe it will be greatly appreciated by the local team if you speak at their annual conference" – rather than *"I recommend you should speak at that conference."*

"Agreeing to this project will allow you to…" – rather than *"This is why you should approve this project."*

"I know you are frantically busy today, but if you can spare me 10 minutes, I believe you can really help me solve this."

She would reluctantly agree to the ten minutes but, in the end, give you an hour or more as she would gradually engage with whatever your problem was on that day. Asking for her help was about needing *her*, not about what you needed.

Sometimes she would go very quiet and think deeply about something. The key was to wait quietly. If you interrupted her thoughts, it showed that your time was more important than hers.

Perhaps she sounds like an unappealing boss? Well, in truth, she was an excellent executive and leader who went out of her way to do the right thing – but she saw things through her own personal lens, and once you got that clear, it was so much easier to work well with her.

The reason for including this story here is not because I feel that every person you work with will respond as described or may even have this kind of highly developed ego.

Rather, I want to stress that it is time very well spent to consider the personality, drivers, and motives of anyone that you need or want to help you or support you in some way. Just going 'straight at it' with your request may lead to disappointment when more careful observation and preparation of your approach can yield a much better outcome.

You may be letting *your* ego take control and get in the way of getting what you want from someone else.

Making It Someone Else's Idea

If you really want something to happen, and you are dealing with someone with a big ego, it can even be worth it to gradually convince them that your good idea was actually theirs all along.

This is a low-ego route for you, as you may not get the credit you deserve, and that can be frustrating. On the other hand, once the boss is happily reassured that you are doing what they always wanted you to do, things can be easier for you as well.

This can be quite a gradual process, and as a project develops, no one remembers very clearly how it all began. Rather than reminding everyone that it was your brilliant idea, it may be worth your while to see who *really* wants to lay claim to it.

I have found that in the end, most people have a pretty good idea of who was behind a successful piece of work, and you may not need to reclaim your authorship to generate a positive outcome for yourself and everyone else involved.

In one team I worked for, we used to joke that if we really wanted our ideas to be taken seriously, the first step was to convince our boss that, in fact, it had been his idea in the first place.

Fire with Care

Sometimes, you will find yourself in a situation where you have no other choice but to fire someone. We won't talk about why you may have reached that point, but if you have, then it is worthwhile to think and act wisely as you go about that.

First of all, it is a mistake to make the act of firing someone all about you. Explaining why you have no choice, have tried everything possible, been extremely patient, etc. is really quite selfish, as you will seem to be justifying a decision that you have already made. And why? To make yourself feel better?

Equally, once the words "you are fired" or something similar have been said, the person in question is no longer listening to you. You may start explaining the reasons for the decision, or the cost-cutting pressure, or that it isn't your idea... but none of that is of any consequence to the person who is being fired.

Equally, do not dish out rebukes or let the person know what a terrible job they have done, or in any way criticize them or insult them. You will need to tell them the straightforward facts about why they are being fired, but do not embellish or seek to justify the decision. You gain nothing. They are being fired, that is enough.

What they do want is practical information. What happens next? Can they make an appeal? Are there other options? How much money will they get? Will they get a reference?

Others who are not being fired that day will be watching with great attention to see how you, and the organization, treat this person who is losing their job. How you go about this unpleasant task can have a big impact on how you are perceived as a leader.

Also, remember that this person may reappear again in your life at some point. Although they may be upset or angry at the time, if you behaved in an honest, authentic, and fair way towards them when you fired them, it will make a big difference when one day they buy the house next to yours.

Never Burn Bridges

Further to this, as you move on with your career, aim to leave your past relationships in as good a state as you possibly can. You never know when your toxic ex-boss or that irritating colleague will turn up again.

At one point, I was moving from one job to another at a new company. I was quite angry with a couple of people for how they had behaved, and I was sorely tempted to give them some strong feedback as my 'parting shot'. In the end, I talked myself out of it and departed on outwardly excellent terms with both people.

As it happened, a lot of unforeseeable events over the next couple of years completely changed my expected plans. I found myself in a situation where both those people suddenly became important to my new revised career options. I was extremely grateful that I kept my counsel.

When you are moving on to a new job, what is there to gain by upsetting or angering your old colleagues by criticizing them as you head for the door? Nothing at all. You are moving on.

If they pop up again later, you will be glad you stayed friendly and quiet.

Reflections

Here are a few key questions arising from the themes raised in this chapter:

- When you attend meetings, do you control the agenda?
- Do you plan ahead or the outcomes you want?
- How do you go about that?
- Are you good at 'playing the ego card'?
- Do you ask others for advice?
- If things go wrong, should you look for someone to blame?
- How do you generate loyalty for yourself from others?
- How well do you know what your boss wants and needs?
- If you move on to something new, what do you do to leave with a positive reputation?

Chapter 9: Setting Goals and Giving Feedback

Short-Term Objectives

There is no doubt that we all function better if we are working towards clear goals. If you are leading a team and people do not have a clear picture of what you expect from them, or how they will be measured, it is likely that their work will disappoint you.

This may sound incredibly obvious, but I have been amazed by how many people go to work every day without clear objectives.

To be useful, objectives should not be overcomplicated. Established companies often create complex systems for setting people's objectives and measuring performance.

Usually, this is an annual process that takes up a lot of management time that could be better spent actually doing the job. How effective are annual goals? A year can be a very long time.

I recommend setting short-term goals (2 to 3 months) and revisiting them regularly with your team members to review progress, and update as needed.

At one point, I took over a team of about 40 people and was surprised and concerned to discover that no one had any established objectives, even though everyone was undoubtedly very busy.

I requested that everyone on the team must have at least three (but only three) objectives for the next three months, written down on a single side of paper and mutually agreed upon with their manager. I made it the responsibility of each individual to take their proposals to their manager, and then for the two of them to agree.

The key to this is the mutual agreement part. Objectives or goals are a contract set between a manager and the team member. Agreeing on them should be a negotiation. That is why it is so much more effective for each person to initially tell their boss what they want, or believe they can achieve. The boss can (and almost always will) add in their own opinions and desires.

The effect of this for my new team was profound. Suddenly everyone felt responsible for knowing what would be achieved in a certain timeframe. In reality, the end result of this process was often a more complicated or longer-term set of agreed-upon goals. The point was, we started with a simple idea that everyone could understand. We didn't let the process get in the way of the outcome we wanted to achieve.

Top 30 #16: Outcome Focus

Keeping an "outcome focus" implies maintaining your concentration on the desired results or outcomes that you truly want or need, as opposed to being distracted by all the accompanying noise generated by the processes or activities that are happening to try to achieve those outcomes.

Your primary focus is on what you will achieve, rather than how you or others think it should be achieved. You value results over process and encourage creativity and innovation in achieving the desired outcome.

We create unnecessary complexity and complication with endless meetings and presentations to justify actions and supposedly provide supporting information for decisions. It's all too easy for these decision support processes to take on a life of their own, with hours spent debating options, numbers, and scenarios - and in the end, we are avoiding the one thing we really need: a decision or a clear action.

It is useful to define the shape of a satisfactory outcome from a meeting or a project at its start. Have everyone clear from the very beginning what success will look like - even if yet to be exactly defined.

In more personal situations, we can easily get caught up in our frustrations, opinions, and emotions that actually get in the way of what we want to happen.

You may feel that somebody is behaving unreasonably and have a great desire to let them know how you feel, but in doing so, you may delay or derail the process of getting what you want.

If you need to cut costs in a business project, focus solely on the number you need to hit - don't be sucked into details about why it's going to be hard to hit that number.

In every situation, keep asking yourself: are we keeping the outcome focus we need to achieve the task or solve the problem?

Projects

One way to get people focused on a specific outcome is to create temporary short-term teams of people, taken from apparently random departments or work areas, and ask them to complete a one-off project task. These are mini-transformations.

You start by clearly defining the outcome you want, explaining why it is important, and why you have chosen this group of people to tackle it. You appoint one person to lead the group and set very clear deadlines for progress reports and for the job to be completed. Projects should always have an end-date.

Usually, these kinds of projects do not fit neatly into a departmental area, so it makes sense to gather people with different skills. It can also be refreshing for your team to interact with people they rarely work with under normal circumstances.

It can also help to avoid departmental silos as your direct reports get used to having to provide resources to tackle these one-off projects from time to time.

Delegating

As a manager of people and someone responsible for aligning the goals of your team, your skill at delegation will be a critical factor for success. If you have previously been used to managing your own time and being responsible only for yourself, then learning to delegate can be very challenging.

Delegation is the path to growth. Only by becoming good at getting others to achieve tasks for you can you create more time for yourself and deepen your own opportunities to do more.

Once again, the process of delegation should be a negotiation, not a set of orders. If your team member just agrees to your demands to please you, the job may not get done, and you will not achieve the outcome you want.

The delegation process is all about the person who is going to do the work, not about you telling them what to do. They need to own it. Your task is to explain clearly the outcome that you would like to see and then to ask your team member what they need to get it done and by when you can expect it.

It is not necessary on many occasions for you to ask how it will get done. Does that matter? What matters is that your desired outcome is achieved.

Always ensure that a time frame is mutually agreed upon. *"We'll meet again next Friday."* Once your team member goes off to do the work, leave them alone to do it. There is nothing more frustrating than a boss who delegates a task and then calls up every 5 minutes to ask what you are doing and how it is going.

You may discover that your team member is not reliable and does not deliver a good outcome on time. If so, you will need to adjust and investigate and discuss with them what has gone wrong.

You must stick to the rules of the delegation process, as if you do not, it can be you who is the blocker to success.

Your team member may blame you (openly or not) as it has not been possible to achieve the desired outcome since you have not let them work on it in their own way, without interference.

Stating Needs

Setting useful goals and effective delegating are key elements in building a healthy and productive working relationship between team members. They may be work colleagues, but you are certainly 'in a relationship' with each one, and like all successful relationships, you will have to work hard for it to work well.

Whether it is from the boss to the team member or the other way around, learning to 'state your needs' can be extremely powerful for everyone to get to their optimal outcome.

Explain exactly what you want or need to be able to work at your best. If you need more time or more resources, then ask for that. If you need someone to talk to you differently, slow down, or explain again what they want from you, ask them.

In work relationships (and this is also very true of our personal relationships), problems so often arise because we do not know how to explain that our essential needs are simply not being met for us to be able to progress effectively.

If we don't ask or explain (or sometimes demand), how will our boss realize that we are not getting what you need from them? That clarity will make for a better future outcome, even if it does require some short-term honesty that may be hard to communicate.

Equally, as a leader, it is your responsibility to clearly state your needs. Make it crystal clear what you expect and by when. Check that there is genuine understanding. Do not fall into the trap of thinking that by being extremely direct and demanding, that perhaps you are being unreasonable.

State your needs clearly and allow the other person to state theirs. You will together get to a much better outcome.

Effective Feedback

When things do not go well, and also when they do, you will need to provide feedback to your team members. Despite the fact that useful and honest feedback can be the greatest gift you ever give to anyone, many managers are very poor at it. They find it uncomfortable to talk about your performance and to have to tell you things that you may not like.

And also, there may sometimes be opportunities to give feedback "up" to your boss. This is hard, but if you do manage to communicate what you see and feel, your boss may get insights that can be game-changing for them.

You can be too "kind" and not say what you really think or feel, so no real learning is achieved. Or too harsh, and the opportunity to improve is lost in feelings of resentment and anger.

So often, managers feel that giving feedback is all about them – they need to explain what somebody on their team has done wrong, they need to give advice and suggestions. That is their job, isn't it?

But on many occasions, people are very aware that their work, or a particular situation, has not been good, or work not done to the standard expected. If you "tell them" about it, you are really just confirming what they already know.

They don't have to work very hard because you are doing all the work explaining your opinions on how they have gone wrong and what they should do about it. All they really have to do is to agree with you.

How much more effective is it to ask them questions, let them talk and explain, and ask or demand that they tell you what they are going to do differently in the future. Make them do the work.

Top 30 #17: Energy of the Conversation

One of the most common subjects that comes up time and time again with my clients is, *"how do I give this difficult or negative feedback?"* Certainly, telling someone that they need to improve, have performed badly, or are in trouble is not fun or easy.

You might logically begin by describing to the other person why, in your opinion, they have failed or performed below expectations. You may offer some evidence. You tell them very directly that their work, behavior, or performance is not acceptable.

What have you just done? If this were a game of poker, you have just laid out your cards directly on the table.

The person will now react to the feedback – they now know what they are dealing with. Maybe they will fight back, or disagree, or begin a strategy to overcome the situation you have presented to them with an apology, excuse, or a promise to be better.

What you have done is that by telling them what you see, feel, or want you have kept the energy of the conversation on your side of the table, allowing them to respond to that without too much effort.

It is so much more powerful to make them do the work and keep them guessing, thinking, and unsure about exactly what it is you know or think. You force them to keep the energy.

You do this by asking them powerful questions and requesting them to describe what happened, why it was not optimal, and what should happen next.

Instead of *"Last Tuesday's meeting was terrible – you were late, unprepared, and there were mistakes in your analysis that made us look unprofessional,"* try:

"I want to talk about last Tuesday's meeting, how do you think it went?"

As necessary, you follow up with questions like *"Did you feel prepared?" "How did the client feel?" "Was the work of the right quality?" "Do you really think that?" "How do you think I felt?" "What do you think the consequences may be?"*

Keep them guessing – they don't know exactly how you feel. You can use that energy to make sure they are really working hard, thinking about, and feeling the situation, as you force them to describe it – rather than you describing it for them.

You will get to the same place (you are indeed providing the feedback) – but they will eventually tell you what went wrong and why – as they surely know it. If not, you can ask them why there is a gulf of perception between how you and others see it, and they see it.

And you make them keep the energy as you decide what should happen next. *"What do you think we need to do here?" "How can we avoid this situation in the future?" "What are your ideas for putting this right?"*

As leaders, it is a constant temptation to take over and keep the energy, and do the work and the thinking for others. It often feels right and more comfortable. But by doing so, we let people off the hook.

It is so much more powerful for a person to admit to you, and to themselves, that they made a mistake or fell short of what is expected. Then they will be a real part of finding a solution and a path to improvement.

The Power of Questions

Never underestimate how effective it is to ask people really good questions and truly let them answer. Coaching is based on the principle that the coach asks good questions that force their clients to think for themselves and develop their own answers to their challenges.

Allowing someone to come up with their own ideas and solutions as a result of a series of powerful and appropriate questions is so much more effective than telling them what to do. Immeasurably so.

When something is genuinely "your idea," you take ownership of it and embrace it in a way that you never will when the boss tells you what to do.

Develop the art of asking questions that force people to think, and in doing so, make sure they "keep the energy."

Closed or leading questions are not effective and only serve to shut down the conversation. "*Do you think it was a bad thing that the project failed? Were you disappointed?*" (Yes. Obviously...)

Ask open questions that don't include the answer:

"*How did you feel when you heard that the project had failed?*

Why do you think that happened?

What could we have done differently?

What else?

What three things do you think we should change now?"

Quantitative questions can also be a good way to push people to give a more specific answer. Instead of "*Do you think she is a good manager?*" (Er..yes, not bad) ask:

"*What mark out of ten would you give her as a manager?*"

(6)

"*OK, so what would she need to do better for you to give her an 8?*"

Asking people quantitative questions also allows you to compare answers between people more easily and include simple graphs in feedback reviews that can help to clarify or underline an issue or a strength.

Asking great questions is without doubt a core strength of an effective leader. You also need to be good at listening.

Three Levels of Listening

Are you a good listener? It's easy to tell when someone is really listening to what you are saying. We can always tell when someone is nodding their head and smiling away as we speak – but we just know they aren't really listening properly. They are waiting for their turn to speak.

There are considered to be three "levels of listening," and it is useful to recognize when we are using or experiencing each one. Knowing whether you are a good listener is an important part of your self-awareness as a leader and a key contributor to your me-pathy.

Level 1 listening is when you appear reasonably engaged in what someone else is saying, but in truth, you are itching to say what you want to say. So, you are really just waiting for them to pause so that you can jump in with your opinion or interesting fact. You will probably get impatient and start to interrupt or talk over others as you want to get your point across. Your mind is not fully focused on what is being said to you.

This happens to most of us at times, and try to be conscious of when you are in Level 1 and how that feels for whomever you are talking with.

Level 2 listening is when you REALLY listen. You exclusively focus on whoever is talking and take in every word. You push all other distractions and thoughts from your mind.

When you are in Level 2, you know it, and whoever is talking knows it too. This is a powerful message, and knowing that your boss or colleague is truly listening intently to every word you are saying puts you under more pressure than if you think they aren't properly listening to you.

When you are giving feedback or talking one-on-one with a colleague or a team member, if you can develop your capacity to practice Level 2 listening, people will notice and appreciate that.

Level 3 listening is about listening to (and observing) what is going on in the room, or a group, or a meeting around a table, for example. As a leader, you can often notice very important signals by listening to what is being said (or maybe not said) in a room. When one person is talking, keep an eye and ear on what others are doing or saying to their neighbors.

The Headmaster's Study

When you were at school, were you ever sent to the principal, or the headteacher, because of your poor behavior or schoolwork?

At my school, this was a pretty terrifying prospect. Our headmaster lived in a house on the school grounds, and we had to use a big door-knocker on the heavy wooden door that led to his dark and scary "study". When you knocked, he shouted "come!"

Rarely would you ever be in that room because of something good. If you were unlucky enough to find yourself inside and standing in front of his big desk, you were in trouble and you only had one mission: to get out of there as soon as possible.

You would pretty much say or do anything that would shorten the interview. Therefore, the process of receiving feedback from the headmaster was flawed from the outset as it was all about saying as little as possible, avoiding punishment, and making your escape.

As a leader, you have to be careful not to become like that headmaster and create a situation where your people are just working out how to "survive and escape from your study".

You may be the big boss, but you need to know why things happened, as well as what happened – and how to make things better for the future. You need to listen as well as tell. You need to be ready to receive feedback as well as give it out.

Eliciting Feedback from Others, 360 Surveys

Giving honest feedback to the boss is not always easy – and if you want to find out how your team really feels about you as a leader, then it will be wise to create a process to enable that.

Just asking people one-on-one who work for you *"What do you think of me?"* or "How am I doing?" is very hard on everybody concerned, including you. Nevertheless, that information, if it is honestly given, is absolute gold dust for you as a leader. It is critical to understanding your empathy.

Subjecting yourself to a confidential 360 review process also sends a message of confidence to your team, peers, and bosses that you are ready to listen and learn from your colleagues.

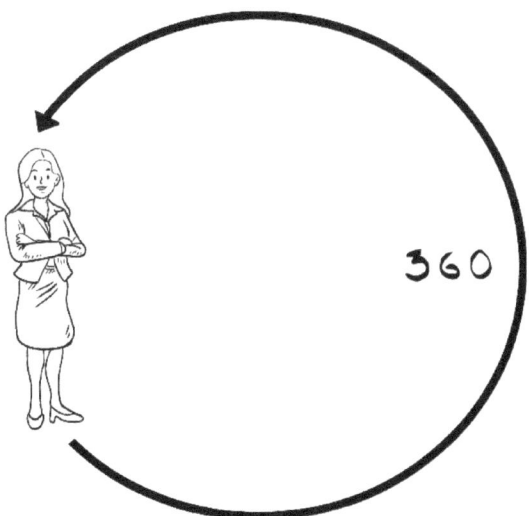

Sometimes it is an HR policy for leaders to be reviewed in this way, but if not and you instigate it, it shows that you are not afraid of feedback and will set the tone for everyone below you in the organization.

If the CEO is open to a 360 review, then everyone else in the company should be as well. Equally, if the CEO is definitely not going to participate in a 360, then it is highly likely that others in the organization will resist it.

There are plenty of 360 tools available that allow people to write their feedback confidentially online in response to questions about your qualities and shortcomings. These may be multiple choice or offer a scale or maybe free text, allowing people to write more personal comments.

The confidentiality element is important, and if your team or colleagues feel that you will not react well to feedback or will try to work out who said what about you, then the process may be pointless. You must embrace it as a genuine opportunity for you to learn and grow.

Another option is to ask somebody you trust (your coach, for example) to conduct structured interviews with people on your team or peers and put together a confidential feedback report.

You can help create the questions so you get the information that matters to you. Once again, your colleagues must trust the interviewer to respect their confidentiality if you are going to get genuine feedback from them.

Reading about yourself can be traumatic, especially if your self-awareness and me-pathy are low and you are confronted with unpleasant surprises about how you are perceived.

However, the benefits of learning that information are immense for you to evolve and improve as a leader.

Appreciative Inquiry

Sometimes, it is necessary or useful to obtain feedback from the broader organization, and many companies have established "engagement" surveys to measure how employees are feeling.

When a more one-off type of internal research is carried out, one potential drawback can be that employees can see an opportunity to grumble about the leadership or organization, and the results can be overly negative.

One research methodology that I have used on several occasions specifically aims to overcome that problem. "Appreciative Inquiry"[17] asks questions that have an intentionally positive slant. *"What has been your best moment since joining the company?" "What do you see as the strongest values shown by your colleagues?"*

Typically, if there are significant grumbles that need to be aired, they will still come through with this approach, but the positive framework pushes people to think about what they do like about their job, and not just focus on the negative.

---

[17] https://en.wikipedia.org/wiki/Appreciative_inquiry

Top 30 #18: Evidence-Based Feedback, and Specific Recommendations

How can you make the feedback you provide to others genuinely useful and as effective as possible?

Make your feedback "evidence-based" - that is, directly replay things that people said or describe a situation unfolding exactly as it happened, as if it were a video recording.

Imagine yourself in a meeting and a colleague has been overly harsh in your opinion. You tell them how you feel. They respond, *"Oh no, it was OK. I didn't say anything much, really."* Left there, it is just a case of perception and memory, and nothing will come of it.

But imagine if you are able to respond, *"Well, I can tell you exactly what you said because I wrote it down,"* and then you read out those harsh words, and there is no escaping the truth.

In a similar vein, imagine you have an employee in your team who is constantly late. Eventually, you lose patience and say, *"Fred, you are always late, and I won't put up with it anymore."*

Fred can easily respond, *"Always late? Now hold on. I've been on time a lot lately."* Fred will push back because it's just really his perception versus yours.

How much more powerful to tell Fred, *"I've been keeping a record of how often you are late to meetings, and here are the results - 6 minutes late on Tuesday, 8 minutes on Thursday, etc."*

This is a simplistic example, but the more you can offer indisputable evidence for something that you would like to see change, the more likely it is to actually change.

In the same way, how specific can you be about what "good looks like" in the future? So often, leaders will say, *"I want to see significant improvement,"* but this does not really help the person to know exactly what is expected of them or what will be enough for you.

The more specific you can be when providing feedback and when requesting change in the future, the greater chance you have of bringing about real changes in behavior.

The Power of Silence

When you get good at asking great questions and at really effective listening, you will also observe how powerful it is to remain silent after you have asked a question.

"What do you think you could have done differently?"

Silence…

As the silence becomes increasingly uncomfortable, it is so tempting to jump in and start to answer the question yourself or to ask another question.

But leave the silence there, and eventually the person will start to answer – and it will be *their* answer and not a build on your partial answer or what they think you want to hear.

When giving feedback or in an intense 1-1 conversation, leaving a silence to linger long beyond when it feels comfortable can be a great way to get to the truth or a more honest answer.

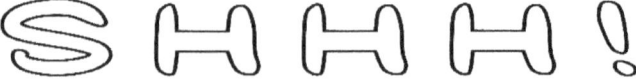

Everybody's Favorite Subject

Even though giving and receiving feedback can be embarrassing and uncomfortable, it is powerful because, at heart, everybody's favorite subject is... themselves.

You do want to know what people think about you, and then you will decide whether to take others' opinions and observations on board or not.

In the same way, your team members do want to know what you think about them, partly to ensure you are happy with them and their work and will keep their job, but also because they are deeply curious about your opinion of them.

This is a natural human tendency, and it is why it is important in the workplace to set good objectives and goals, create opportunities for honest feedback, and take a genuine professional interest in the people you work with.

You really cannot over-communicate. Many problems with individuals and teams are caused by leaders not communicating enough and not giving enough attention to each individual's favorite subject.

Reflections

Here are a few key questions arising from the themes raised in this chapter:

- What kind of goals do you set for your team?
- What are your own goals like?
- How can you stay focused on "outcomes?"
- When you provide feedback, who does all the talking?
- Could you say less and achieve more?
- Are you a good listener? Could you be better?
- Do you know what others think about you? How could you find out more?
- If you give feedback, how can you support it with evidence?

Chapter 10: What People Want and Need

Finding the Sweet Spot of Engagement

Which is the most effective way to motivate people? Carrot or stick? Do they respond best to a kind, thoughtful, caring approach where your teams know you are looking out for their every need?

Or, conversely, is it all about keeping people in line and warning them of the severe consequences if their work is not good enough?

There is no single correct answer to that conundrum - it depends. It depends on the situation, on the people involved, and the task to be undertaken. It also depends on you - your approach as the manager of the team.

Do you believe that people are essentially hardworking, trustworthy, and have good intentions? Or that they are, at heart, lazy and irresponsible and must be checked up on and pushed to work harder?

Theory X and Theory Y

During the 1960s, social psychologist Douglas McGregor created an approach to explain how a manager's beliefs about what motivates their team to do good work affect their style of management.

In his book *"The Human Side of Enterprise"* [18], he described two contrasting styles of management - Theory X and Theory Y. Theory X is an authoritarian style, and Theory Y is a participative approach.

If you believe that your team members dislike their work and have little motivation, then, according to McGregor, you'll likely use an authoritarian style of management. This approach is very "hands-on" and usually involves micromanaging people's work to ensure that it gets done properly. McGregor called this Theory X.

On the other hand, if you believe that your people are self-starters, take pride in their work, and see it as a challenge, then you'll more likely adopt a participative management style. Managers who use this approach trust their people to take ownership of their work and do it effectively by themselves. McGregor called this Theory Y.

Theory X managers tend to take a pessimistic view of their people and assume that they are naturally unmotivated and dislike work.

Theory Y managers have an optimistic opinion of their people, and they use a decentralized, participative management style. This encourages a more collaborative, trust-based relationship between managers and their team members.

Theory Y managers encourage people to develop their skills and suggest improvements. Appraisals may be

---

[18] *The Human Side of Enterprise* by Douglas McGregor published by McGraw-Hill (1960)

regular, but unlike in Theory X organizations, they are used to encourage open communication rather than to control.

As in most things, in practice, things are not so binary, and most managers will likely display a mixture of the two theories, with Theory Y being the more typical approach in modern organizations.

It is worth asking yourself where you put yourself on the X-Y axis about what really motivates people to work most effectively.

Top 30 #19: Aiming for the Productive Zone

Ronald Heifetz and colleagues, the architects of the adaptive approach to leadership, described the "productive zone of disequilibrium" in their books about leadership (We are going to talk more about this and these ideas in Chapter 13).

They were focused on situations of change and how to engage people to think differently and be part of a solution to do things better.

"[There is an] optimal range of distress within which the urgency in the system motivates people to engage… If the level is too low, people will be inclined to complacently maintain their current way of working, but if it is too high, people are likely to be overwhelmed and may start to panic or engage in severe forms of work avoidance…"[19]

The idea is applicable to just about everything we do.

Finding that productive zone is critical for teams, organizations, and individuals. If there is too much pressure over an extended time, we will all start to crack and fail. Initially, high-pressure environments will yield results, but neither the pressure nor the results are sustainable without consequences.

Equally, if people are not busy enough and not feeling any pressure, this will be just as ineffective for generating good results. Humans quickly adapt to an

---

[19] Quoted from *The Work Of Leadership* by Ronald Heifetz and Donald Laurie HBR Article 2002 (4150) page 4

undemanding environment and will arrive late, leave early, and take long lunches, knowing that they can still hit their targets. After a while, even those targets become onerous and start to be missed.

AIMING FOR THE PRODUCTIVE

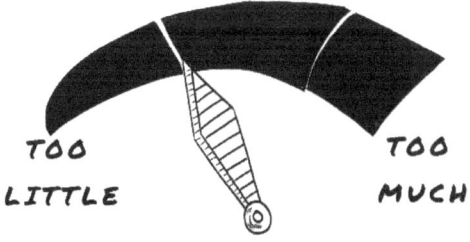

The trick is to create a situation with just the right amount of stress to keep focus and engagement high, but not so much as to create anxiety.

As primarily a leader of yourself and also of others, the ability to identify when you are working in this 'most productive zone' is a vital skill. Recognizing it will not only bring better results but also avoid crises of burnout that waste time and resources.

Living and working with a consistent level of healthy pressure to get things done is probably more effective than frantic bursts of high tension interspersed with more relaxed recovery periods. Sometimes, that is unavoidable, and something urgent has to be done at all costs. Then, unusual amounts of stress and focus will be needed for a predictable amount of time, to get the job done.

Identifying the situation, conditions, and environment in which you and your team are most productive will have dramatic implications for your effectiveness and the engagement of everyone.

Getting the Basics Right

It is important to try to understand what motivates individual people and where they may be in the evolution of their ambitions for themselves and their careers. Every individual is different, but there are also models that help to remind us what drives people's engagement and mindset.

Most probably, you know about Maslow and his 'hierarchy of needs'. Have you ever really thought about how important and relevant it is to understand our motives and desires?

Abraham Maslow (1908 - 1970) was an American psychologist who grew up in Brooklyn, New York, after his family fled persecution in what is now Kyiv.

He believed in focusing on the 'good things' about people. That made him a bit different from most psychologists of his era, who tended to see people as a big collection of problems and issues to be tackled. He published his hierarchy in his 1954 book *"Motivation and Personality"*.

Maslow presents his hierarchy in a pyramid shape, with basic needs at the bottom of the pyramid and higher-level, less tangible needs at the top. We can only fulfill the higher needs when our basic needs are adequately met.

At the very bottom are the basic human survival needs: food and water, enough rest, clothing, shelter, health, and the ability to reproduce. We do see this in our daily lives when, for example, an illness threatens us - it immediately becomes our only focus of attention. All our other plans and goals become secondary until we are healthy again.

Next up among the lower-level needs is safety. Safety needs include protection from violence or theft, emotional stability and well-being, health security, and financial security. Most of these are still quite basic.

If employees in your team don't feel safe for some reason, it will be very hard to expect good work from them. If they feel their medical insurance is poor, and so leaves them or their family exposed to risk, they will not be engaged.

This is the level where compensation for the work they are doing must be adequate to support their essential needs. If you are not paid enough to support yourself and your family adequately, you will not be happy in that work.

The next level up is relationship and belonging needs. We are social beings, and our social requirements for happiness are on the third level of Maslow's hierarchy.

This level is about friendship, family, and community. Our need for physical and emotional closeness to others to enjoy intimate emotional bonds. Being part of social groups contributes to meeting these needs - from belonging to a team at work or being part of a club or a group of parents at a school, or a group with a common interest.

Once we have achieved the requirements of the first three levels, we have a lot of what we need to live a satisfactory, albeit maybe simple, existence.

Realistically, over human history, many people did not progress much beyond this level. They felt safe, they were reasonably healthy, had enough to eat, received adequate compensation for whatever they did, and were part of a group or family where they belonged. They often did not expect much more from life.

In the modern setting, it is common that the first three levels of Maslow's hierarchy are not just well established but also often taken for granted. But still, we can see that when some kind of major crisis, like an illness or sudden loss of income after losing a job, or moving to a new city where you don't know anyone, these more basic needs can suddenly become very important.

Equally, the 'cultural' aspect of work (relationships with teammates, bosses, and a feeling of belonging, for example) is also in these critical foundational levels of the model.

Having a 'toxic boss' can have a catastrophic and fundamental impact on a person's engagement, happiness, and effectiveness at work.

Feeling that you are being appropriately and fairly compensated for what you do every day is a fundamental need. It may sound obvious, but sometimes organizations get this wrong, with profound negative consequences.

Similarly, at times of change in an organization, people's relationships or essential sense of security in their jobs can feel threatened - and it is easy to underestimate the impact of change on individuals or teams.

The top two levels of Maslow's model are when things really start to get interesting. These are the 'ego' needs.

The fourth level is about 'esteem'. The key elements are self-respect (the belief that you are valuable and deserving of dignified treatment) and self-esteem (confidence in your potential for personal growth and achievements).

Maslow says that self-esteem can be further divided into two types: esteem which is based on respect and acknowledgment from others, and esteem which is based on your own self-assessment. Self-confidence and independence arise from this last type of self-esteem.

It's at this level that me-pathy is key. How you see yourself and understand your own impact are directly linked to your own image of yourself, and your conscious belief in yourself.

The highest level of Maslow's pyramid is "self-actualization". This is about the achievement of your full potential as a person. Self-actualization includes your level of education and skills or the development of talents in areas such as music, sports, art, building a house, or writing a book...

Also, caring for others, giving away your wealth, and broader goals like learning a new language, seeing other parts of the world, or winning awards for your work or your contribution to society are all at this level.

Maslow referred to the top level of self-actualization as a "growth need," and so distinct from the lower four levels, which he named "deficiency needs."

According to Maslow, if you cannot meet your deficiency needs, you will experience harmful or unpleasant results. Essential impacts ranging from illness and starvation to loneliness and self-doubt are the outcome of not meeting your deficiency needs. Your self-esteem is a critical factor in your success and happiness. It is not a "nice to have."

On the other hand, fulfilling self-actualization needs will make you happier, but you are not essentially harmed if these needs go unfulfilled. You may be disappointed, but you can still operate successfully.

Your own perception of "what matters to you" is a major driver. So, if you do not want to learn another language and, realistically, you do not need to, it follows that you will not feel bad about not having done it. Self-actualization needs become a priority only when the other four foundational needs are met.

If you move to another country and must learn the local language to survive and flourish, then that becomes a deficiency need.

When you are thinking about yourself or the people in your team, it can be worthwhile to reflect on Maslow's hierarchy. You will not be able to bring about "self-actualization" in yourself or others if the more basic needs are not being met.

Equally, it is important to recognize that if the first four levels are truly being satisfied, then it is human nature to yearn for greater self-actualization and the achievement of "higher" goals that will "leave your mark on the world."

MASLOW'S HIERARCHY

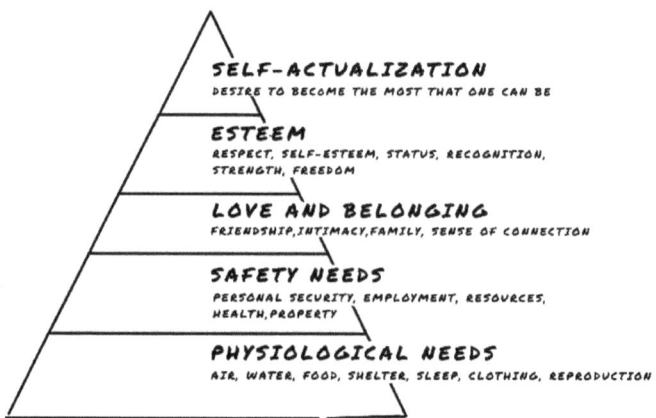

SELF-ACTUALIZATION
DESIRE TO BECOME THE MOST THAT ONE CAN BE

ESTEEM
RESPECT, SELF-ESTEEM, STATUS, RECOGNITION, STRENGTH, FREEDOM

LOVE AND BELONGING
FRIENDSHIP, INTIMACY, FAMILY, SENSE OF CONNECTION

SAFETY NEEDS
PERSONAL SECURITY, EMPLOYMENT, RESOURCES, HEALTH, PROPERTY

PHYSIOLOGICAL NEEDS
AIR, WATER, FOOD, SHELTER, SLEEP, CLOTHING, REPRODUCTION

SCARF

Another framework that I find useful when thinking about people and why they act in a certain way is the SCARF model, as developed by Dr. David Rock.[20]

Earlier in Chapter 3, I talked about how our brain controls subconsciously what we remember and dictates our choices and decisions. Rock's work is all about the neuroscience of our behavior and delves into the subconscious way we react or feel in different situations.

SCARF is a "brain-based" model that can help us collaborate and work more effectively with people by understanding how they will react to perceived threats and rewards.

Rock coined the term "Neuroleadership" and is the Director of the NeuroLeadership Institute, a global initiative bringing neuroscientists and leadership experts together to build a new science for leadership development.

Rock felt that brain research was a missing piece in our understanding of how to be more effective leaders, managers, or coaches. He has written three books on the subject: *"Quiet Leadership,"* the textbook *"Coaching with the Brain in Mind,"* and *"Your Brain at Work."*

He coined the term "Neuroleadership" in 2007 and now contributes to running a global Institute involved in research and education to improve organizations through

---

[20] https://davidrock.net/

the use of neuroscience. I met him in 2012 when he came to talk to our MSc class at Oxford University.

An essential function of our brain is to decide when to approach or avoid something - "fight or flight". This mechanism has developed over many years of evolution and has helped humans stay alive and thrive.

We are innately motivated to move away from threats and go towards rewards. A positive emotion creates action, whereas a negative emotion or punishment creates a threat stimulus in our brain, leading to avoidance.

The idea of the SCARF model is that, in the office environment, the brain causes us to behave in certain ways aiming to minimize threats and maximize rewards.

Neuroscience research indicates that our social needs are almost as powerful as our need for food and water. This type of science has important implications for the workplace, which is a very social situation.

In our work interactions, our brain is hard at work classifying everything that happens with a "reward" or "threat" feeling that converts directly into our behavior. Our brains wants to know...is something happening at work good for me or bad for me?

The SCARF model summarizes these themes in a framework that describes the common factors that can activate a reward or threat response in social or work situations or when people collaborate as part of a group.

The model describes five domains of human social experience: status, certainty, autonomy, relatedness, and fairness.

Status is about where you feel you are in relation to others around you.

Certainty is about your confidence to predict the future.

Autonomy is your sense of control over what is happening around you.

Relatedness is your sense of safety with others, fitting in, or belonging.

Fairness is your perception of whether you are being treated fairly.

Let's consider a situation at work where someone (we'll call them Taylor) is part of a well-established team which has suddenly been given a new, much younger manager to lead them.

No one on the team was expecting this to happen, and in fact, Taylor had assumed that they would probably be promoted to the recently vacated manager position. They are taken by surprise by the announcement of the new manager.

This sudden and unexpected change in how the team will be working from now on actually triggers every one of the model's 5 dimensions in Taylor.

Their status has been called into question. It seems they were not considered for the manager position. Previously, all the team was very comfortable at work - now suddenly what is expected of them may change.

Taylor feels uncertainty. They were not offered any kind of choice, this just all happened one day out of the blue. It's hard for them to know how well they will get on with the new manager or what kind of a team will be wanted.

Taylor feels like this is all unfair. They deserve a promotion! Taylor has many more years of experience than this new person and knows that many people in the team feel something similar.

If you are asked to lead an established team of people, it is worth keeping the SCARF model in mind. If there is a Taylor in the team, it is very likely that your appointment is bringing about conflicting feelings of 'flight' or 'fight' in them. They either want to show everyone that your appointment was a poor decision or to disengage and not be a part of what you are planning.

When you come into a new leadership role, you may feel that there are genuine and tangible feelings of hostility towards you. The key to remember about the SCARF model is that these behaviors are potentially subconscious. People may not even fully realize they are behaving in certain ways as their neurological reflexes have been triggered by the situation and the discomfort it is causing them.

As a leader, the challenge is to work out how to reassure people and show them gradually and tangibly that, for example, their status, certainty, or autonomy is not really under attack. They will probably need to adapt a bit and gradually accept the situation. As their new boss, you must be careful not to deepen their SCARF reactions and give them the time they need to adjust.

It only needs for one or two of the SCARF criteria to be triggered for people to feel unsettled and possibly behave in a slightly aggressive or defensive way—or to become disengaged and distant.

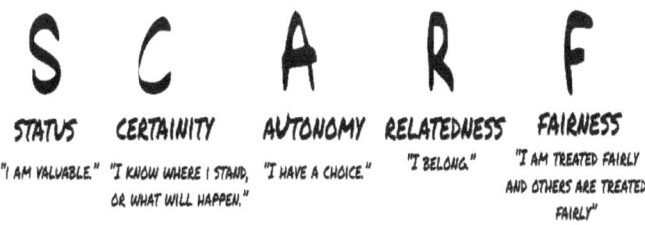

Personality Assessments and "Relational Intelligence"

Our individual personalities underpin our preferences for how we like to work, think, manage information, and communicate with others - or be communicated with by others.

Personality assessments, of which there are many different versions available on the market, can help us to understand more about how we operate, are perceived by others, and how others are similar or different from us. They typically identify us as belonging to a particular group, or a number of overlapping groups, that display certain characteristics.

Whenever I start work with a new client, I ask them to do a DISC assessment. Usually, I end up doing a DISC with all the client's direct reports or key relationships. I use DISC because it is the personality assessment I know the best, and I find it to be accurate and helpful for people and teams.

There are many different assessments available today, although most have a lot in common in terms of what they are based on, albeit with different ways of presenting the data.

Carl Jung (1875-1961), the pioneering Swiss psychologist, proposed that there are essentially four human personality preferences: sensing, intuition, thinking, and feeling, and that these are what influence our personality.

Since the relatively early 1900s, there has been a major interest in personality testing, assessments, and analysis, especially in the work environment. Increased understanding of people's personalities helped companies choose suitable people and helped individuals better know their own drivers and find the career that was the best fit for them.

It all started with the *Woodworth Personal Data Sheet*, also known as the Woodworth Psychoneurotic Inventory. It is considered the first personality test. It was created by Robert S. Woodworth during World War I for the United States Army to help screen recruits for the risk of 'shell shock'.

After the war, it became the basis for the development of many other personality tests. It has been described as the ancestor of all subsequent personality assessments.

Perhaps the most famous of all the assessments is Myers-Briggs - the MBTI (Myers-Briggs Type Indicator). It was created many years ago by Katharine Cook Briggs and her daughter Isabel in the United States, starting as far back as 1917.

Briggs was inspired to dig into personality types when she got to know her daughter Isabel's future husband, Clarence Myers, and noticed he had a totally different way of seeing the world from her.

When Carl Jung published his ideas in his book "Psychological Types" in 1921 (translated into English in

1923), Briggs was impressed but thought his concepts were too complex for practical application to a wider audience.

Despite years of work, the mother and daughter team only truly launched their "indicator" during World War II. They were motivated by a belief that knowledge of personality preferences would help women to identify which sorts of unprecedented wartime jobs would be the "most comfortable and effective" for them. The Briggs Myers Type Indicator Handbook, published in 1944, was re-published as the "Myers–Briggs Type Indicator" in 1956.

The Myers-Briggs Company has published, researched, and updated the MBTI indicator constantly since 1975 and has trained practitioners since 1989. It is estimated that more than 50 million people have taken the MBTI, and more than 1.5 million around the world take it every year.

Nowadays, there is a very large range of options available: *Myers-Briggs MBTI, DISC, 16 Personalities, Hexaco, High 5, Birkman Method, StrengthsFinder*... the list goes on and on, all providing useful information about the drivers of our personalities.

Increasing our awareness of what makes us (and others) 'tick' helps us to communicate more comfortably and effectively with our colleagues.

My own tool of preference, DISC, is also based on Jung's four essential personality types, which actually date back even further to the ancient Greeks. In 1928, William Marston published the book "Emotions of Normal People," describing the four personality traits as Dominance, Influence, Steadiness, and Compliance (DISC). In the late 1940s, Walter Clark built on Marston's ideas and developed the first version of the DISC personality profile.

Like MBTI, it is estimated that over 50 million people have taken a DISC assessment, and it has been translated into more than 50 languages. I find it is remarkably accurate, useful for people, and totally non-judgmental. There is no better or worse way to be.

The four essential styles, which are identified by colors, are broadly as follows. We all have something of each one, but usually one or two are more present in each of us:

- **D:** Extroverted and action-oriented. Likes to move quickly and make decisions. Strong-willed and competitive. Results-oriented.

- **I:** Spontaneous, impulsive, and engaging. Positive, conversational, and people-oriented. Enthusiastic promoter and persuader. Sensitive to criticism.

- **S:** Calm, steady, and friendly. Sees the big picture and gathers information to make decisions. Careful, patient, and thoughtful. Logical and detail-oriented. Supportive. Doesn't like to be rushed.

- **C:** Disciplined, organized, and structured. Systematic, precise, and analytical. Data, fact, and task-oriented with great attention to detail. Desire to "do things right." Can be perceived by some as a little "cold."

DISC only takes 20 minutes to complete and gives you a 50-page report based on your results, providing a wealth of detail and insight.

We all know about the importance of intelligence (IQ), and in recent years, there's been a lot of focus on the importance of emotional intelligence (EQ). With the help of tools like DISC and some healthy discussion, we can also work on developing our "relational intelligence" and, hopefully, improve our working relationships with colleagues.

The most effective teams are made up of a diversity of styles, with different ways of thinking and tackling problems complementing each other.

These assessments are genuinely very useful for people and teams to raise awareness of differences in thinking. They help people to be more aware of themselves and others around them. They provide a new common "language" to describe personalities and preferences.

However, I also believe that DISC (or whichever tool you prefer) is like a lamppost - it is good for throwing some light but not for leaning on it. The most powerful output is not the results themselves but the conversations and discoveries that arise from them. I do not like to think of the results as "science" but rather as a useful and helpful guide.

Indeed, personality assessments are not without their detractors, who call them "pseudoscience" and potentially dangerous or inaccurate. All I can say is that of the hundreds of DISCs I have done with people, very rarely do I feel that someone's essential personality is not well-described.

However, no person should ever be "judged" on the results of a personality assessment. Everyone has their strengths and weaknesses.

Getting What You Want

When we set out to ask for something or maybe explain something, we naturally have a tendency to present it in terms that we ourselves find compelling.

We use language and arguments that we know will win *us* over. However, it may be that the person you are presenting to has a completely different way of seeing the world. What seems obvious to you may seem impenetrable to someone else, and what seems exciting to you may seem extremely uninteresting to others.

Personality assessments are great for reminding us that other people see things and think in totally different ways from us. Once you get used to the particular "language" of whatever colors or terms your chosen tool uses, you can start to consider people you are dealing with in a new light and try to work out how they may think or like to receive information.

Never Stop Working on Your People Skills

As a leader, when can you feel that you have done enough to understand, motivate, and engage your people? I say the answer to that is simple - never.

The complexity of teams and organizations is as diverse and surprising as the individual people who create them. There will always be new ideas and innovations in how to get the very best from people: new ways to make them more efficient, more productive, more engaged, and happier.

Stay engaged with the constant worldwide process of evolution and learning. Being good with people will help them, and usually help you get what you want and need from them.

You may feel that the key to success in your organization is your amazing product, your incredible standout marketing, or maybe your revolutionary just-in-time inventory software.

I'll bet that if you have more than one employee, the key to your success is, in fact, your company culture.

Reflections

Here are a few key questions arising from the themes raised in this chapter:

- Are you a Theory X person? Or Theory Y?
- How does that influence your leadership style?
- When are you at your most productive?
- Where are you operating on Maslow's hierarchy?
- Have you taken a personality assessment?
- If you did, what could you learn about yourself? Or about your team?
- How could that be useful and helpful for you or them?

Chapter 11: Culture Eats Strategy

Along with a lot of other great quotes by him that are scattered throughout this book, Peter Drucker (1909-2005), the legendary Austrian-American writer and management consultant, most famously said, *"Culture eats strategy for breakfast."*

In other words, the prevailing "people culture" in any organization is more powerful than any of the business plans and ambitions that are being put in place. A negative or unhappy culture can derail just about any plan, no matter how much it makes perfect sense on paper.

Your organization is made up of people, and as previously mentioned, people are sometimes unreliable and inflexible.

Are Cultures Created? Or Do They Just 'Happen'?

When any group of people live and work together over a long period of time, they gradually co-create a culture that is often as difficult to define as it is important and powerful.

There can be many fundamental influences at work (national culture, language, history, etc.) that will have a much higher impact on everyday behavior than any amount of leadership efforts to try to make people behave in a certain way.

In the workplace, humans unconsciously create an organizational culture that is as powerful as it is intangible.

It grows naturally from the collective behavior, history, symbols, myths, triumphs, and disasters of the organization over time. It auto-defines its "way of being" and how it sees itself.

Then add in the organization's goals, strategies, structure, and way of handling and communicating with people. Its employees, customers, investors, and the community at large.

If an organization is incredibly focused on profit and regularly fires poor performers, it will have a radically different culture from a non-profit charity. That is not to say one of these extremes will be 'better or worse' than the other. The question is whether you or other people that the organization hopes to attract feel more or less comfortable working in that culture.

Cultures definitely evolve as businesses and organizations grow. Typically, smaller companies will have a stronger, more naturally defined culture as people feel close to each other and have a sense of being part of a "clan."

As the organization grows, new influences (business challenges, new types of people, or just sheer numbers of individuals) will affect the culture.

A larger organization also inevitably needs more bureaucracy to make it run smoothly. As travel policies and holiday allowances become stricter, employees may feel that the company culture they used to enjoy is disappearing.

Leaders can certainly reinforce the culture in their team by working to define it and choosing words or phrases to describe the core elements that make it what it is: the common values, vision, and purpose of the organization.

It is far more effective for leaders to ASK their people to describe their culture and to co-create the agreed way to collectively describe it.

Leaders who TELL their people what the culture should be like are usually disappointed, and the exercise creates more problems and makes people even less engaged than they were before.

If you suddenly announce that the core values of your underperforming team are "quality and excellence" no one will buy into that. Rather, you need to first work out (with the people involved) what the existing values really are and why. Then you can set a collective aspirational goal to turn performance around and shift the culture to something more positive.

What makes a 'good culture'?

Here are seven traits that I feel are usually present in organizations with a strong, defined, and positive culture that actively contributes to success.

1. Well Defined and Co-Created Core Values

Everyone is aligned on what the essential values of the organization are, and these have been put into writing and shared. The process of arriving at these words has been a joint one, and while there may be an element of aspiration, there is also reality and honesty.

It is an inclusive, bottom-up exercise, not a top-down one. It is repeated every few years to ensure that the way of describing your common values is fresh and relevant.

The values are tangible and credible. If you settle on "Excellence, integrity, and best-in-class customer service" as values, then the evidence that this exists should be there for all to see.

If possible, your values should be unique to you and differentiating. Ideas for everyone to be proud of and feel a connection with.

2. Clarity of Vision and Purpose

Your organization has a plan. Everyone in the team knows what the strategy is you are following, what the big aims are, and objectives to be achieved.

Working with your people to jointly create a mission statement can be rewarding and enjoyable for everyone involved. People get a lot of satisfaction from discussing what they do every day and working out what makes your organization special. What makes it 'tick'. You give them a voice.

People like to know why they turn up to work every day and have a stronger sense of purpose than just 'make more money'.

These ideas and statements are the bedrock of your brand, both internally and externally. Everything you do builds upon your essential values, mission, and purpose as a team.

3. Active Alignment Among Senior Leaders

Your senior team or direct reports genuinely and actively buy-in to the vision, purpose, strategy, goals, etc. that you have collectively defined.

If your key lieutenants are in any way out of step with you, or each other, or the overall narrative that has been presented, this will be very obvious to people. It will also rapidly undermine the culture of the organization. Departmental factions can develop, and harmful politics and infighting will follow.

A fully and clearly aligned senior team is vital to maintain a positive and consistent culture.

4. Constant and Useful Communication

There is a consistent and regular program of communicating relevant news about the organization. Internal changes, such as new hires, promotions, and success stories, are efficiently shared. People are encouraged to communicate their own news and wins. Teams know what other teams do and why.

Financial or performance information is shared as openly or as honestly as it can be. People feel that senior leadership is honest and transparent about the challenges facing the company.

As well as effective top-down communication from senior leaders, there is also an information cascade system that makes sure everyone receives the same information and has a chance to discuss it with their immediate boss and colleagues.

4. Demonstrable Accountability

Everybody can see that there is accountability across the organization for both successes and failures. Poor performers are handled fairly and promptly. There are no favorites or relationships based on nepotism or connections.

Clear objectives are negotiated and set, and then there is follow-up and tracking. It is a meritocratic environment.

5. Recognition and Affirmation

When people achieve expectations or go beyond them, they are publicly thanked and recognized. Managers are encouraged to highlight successes and share individual stories of successes and effort. There is an atmosphere of positive and active mutual support among people and teams.

6. Healthy and Fair Environment

You have paid careful attention to the essential "hygiene factors" in the organization. These are the vital bottom parts of Maslow's pyramid.

Compensation is fair and competitive for the jobs people are doing and equitable across the organization. Systems for bonuses, benefits, or promotions are fair, transparent, and well-organized.

People have the equipment and resources they need to do their job properly. The work environment is clean, safe, and a pleasant place to spend time. Everyone is treated equally.

The organization is "kind" and understanding when people need special support due to illness or personal issues.

7. Authentic Leadership

Most powerful of all for the culture of a group of people is the way it is led. Behaviors, ideas, and attitudes at the very top filter down right through all levels, even the largest of organizations.

The culture of a team can change remarkably quickly if a new leader brings new expectations or exhibits different traits from a previous boss.

Leaders are defined by their followers, and if you want to create a winning and positive culture in your team, you will be a massive influence on that. Everyone is watching you, and you set the standards and benchmarks for your people.

Top 30 #20: The 'Family' Myth

How often have you heard business leaders describe their company, organization, or team as being like a 'family'?

It's an attractive idea, certainly, as it conjures up an impression of cohesiveness, permanence, and mutual support. My view is that businesses are not families (in fact, they are nothing at all like them) and that the 'we are a family' idea is a terrible model for the workplace.

We choose which company to work for, and we do not choose our family.

We do not usually get fired or abandoned by our family, with whom we share very complex emotional bonds that mean we stick together even through major trauma.

We are not paid to be part of our family. The reasons we spend time with our families are completely different from why we go to work.

Families are inherently quite dysfunctional and allow people to behave in unacceptable ways. Most families have an equivalent of an uncle who always gets drunk at Christmas or an aunt who buys extravagant gifts that nobody wants. Those people don't get a lecture from HR.

They are accepted and tolerated as part of the complex fabric of the family. In the work environment, we have to be careful to tolerate poor behavior or performance.

Organizations must be much stricter about what is acceptable.

Companies exist for a purpose, and each team member has a part to play in achieving the collective goals that signify success. Families just exist, and they are all the more important and powerful for not being underpinned by objectives, organizational charts, or exit strategies.

A leader's use of the family analogy is lazy, as they are just choosing one aspect that appeals to them of what families usually have - strong social cohesion - and ignoring all the other ways in which the analogy just does not work well.

I worked at the same company for over 15 years and saw how people can buy into the idea that they are part of a work 'family'.

The company also encouraged this by often describing itself in that way. It wasn't a manipulative strategy but rather an idea that everyone liked to engage with, so it gradually became established as a way to describe us all.

Businesses evolve, new ideas and technologies come into play, and people get older, and eventually there comes a time when changes are necessary.

It was at that point that I watched some colleagues become deeply, deeply disappointed to discover that their work 'family' didn't want them anymore.

They had worked incredibly hard and given a tremendous part of their career to this company and could not come to terms with this rejection and disloyalty.

It is easy, and tempting, to fall into a "love" relationship with your job. You love it, and for as long as it is convenient, it pretends to love you - but there comes a time when this relationship becomes unbalanced and to your horror, you discover that not only does your company not love you but doesn't even want you around anymore.

This can certainly happen in marriages - but rarely in families. The family cohesion is typically stronger than anything that tries to break it.

If we have to create an analogy for how businesses are, and are typically run, the professional sports team is much more accurate and honest.

The sports club wants the best players on the field, and they will be paid appropriately and achieve recognition if they play well and win games - and for as long as they are able to do that. Once they no longer perform, they are out.

The club is far more important than any individual. If you think of any famous professional team in any sport, it is only a very few players that manage to hang around for more than a few years at the same club.

There is brutal turnover of talent to keep the club competitive. If you have been supporting the Dallas Cowboys, Real Madrid, Miami Heat, or Boston Red Sox for even a few years, you will now be cheering for a completely different group of players than you were. The club lives on, but the people change constantly.

It is better for companies to be honest and admit that this is also essentially the case in business.

Please don't tell your people "We are a family."

The Small Stuff Matters

As a leader of a team, your way of behaving sets the tone for everyone in your team. How you behave will be observed, judged, and copied. What you do gives permission to the rest of the organization and has a big influence on the overall culture.

If you are often angry and swear a lot, then other people will feel justified in doing the same. If you are kind and thoughtful, others will aim to be also. If you are constantly late, people will turn up late to meetings.

People may be employees and team members, but they are also people, and if you treat others with respect and show genuine interest in them, you will be appreciated for that.

Leaders have great influence over the culture of the teams they lead, more than many realize. Practice me-pathy and be aware of your impact. Often, it is the small details that people remember about you: a kind word, that you remembered the name of their kid, or to wish them a happy birthday.

Not Just Words on the Wall

I have seen companies do a great job of describing their culture and defining their values, creating impressive documents and charts on the wall for all to see every day at the office. Yet sometimes those words can still seem to be just that, empty statements. The description of what you have, or aspire to, does not align with reality.

To drive and foster the positive, productive, and honest culture in your team that you wish for, it is actions, not words, that will have the most powerful effect.

Once you have co-created a statement of your beliefs and made that public, it is essential that everyone actually lives and works in accordance with that. As the leader, you are the torchbearer for that, and if anyone is not aligned with you and those big ideas, you must be seen to do something about that.

Do not permit behavior or actions from anyone (most importantly yourself) that do not fit comfortably with your stated values. Walk the talk, and expect others to as well.

The Challenges of Scaling - and Leading a Growing Team

There's a unique vibe to the culture of a small organization. When your team is just a few people, there's often little structure, discipline, or process. The small group works together to get whatever is needed done. You don't need many internal processes in place because everybody communicates via personal relationships. When you become a bigger organization, things quickly change.

If the startup phase is about creating and proving things, the scale-up phase is about making things repeatable at scale. Scaling up brings a new set of challenges and requires a different set of skills - that to a great extent are about managing and leading people.

You've proven your idea or approach works, so now your focus is on building a bigger team that will allow reliable future growth. Social systems quickly become much more complicated when you add more people, so some processes need to be standardized and rules established.

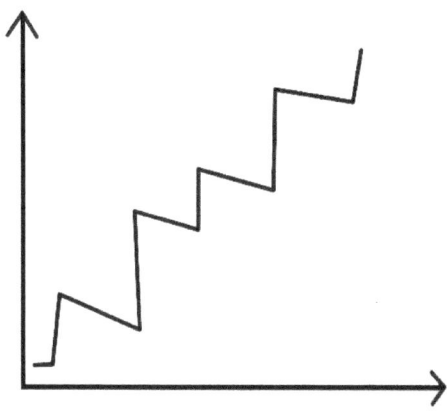

It is often the social systems aspects of scaling up that prove most difficult for leaders, as your job now includes creating rules, imposing unpopular restrictions, or defining boundaries.

You can no longer have various platforms for communication. People can't be paid inconsistently. Culture and norms must become standardized throughout the organization. You need to more carefully manage HR processes like objective setting, giving good feedback, or managing travel and expenses. You have a hierarchy to manage and respect and will need to delegate effectively.

When you are agreeing on something with one person, you must keep in mind what others will think of it.

You cannot scale effectively without rules in place, but imposing rules on a team that has previously thrived on the freedom of a "startup mentality" can create a threat to the successful existing culture.

As a result, you have to watch for pushback and resentful feelings from the team - or even subliminal pushback from yourself. With every new team member, you are less a startup and more a real business that you are responsible for leading.

You're no longer in the process of developing and proving the value of a new product or service. Instead, you're creating and managing the *systems* that deliver that product or service. That's a whole different skill set and creates a different lens through which to view the company.

These changes can catch unprepared founders of startups off guard. More than ever, you must acknowledge your own strengths and preferences as a leader. Your leadership skills will need to grow and evolve as the company grows and evolves.

You have been used to primarily managing and motivating yourself. Now you will increasingly become a role model for the behavior, ideas, and engagement of your growing team..

Seeing With New Eyes

A colleague of mine, Jane, was appointed to be the Managing Director of a national office of a large multinational company. She had around a hundred people on her team.

On her first day of her new job, in early February, she arrived at her new office and was greeted warmly by the receptionist. The new boss had arrived.

In the corner of the small reception area, Jane couldn't help but notice a small, brown, and very dead-looking Christmas tree.

Jane has a good sense of humor and asks the receptionist with a smile, *"So, is that tree left over from last year or are you getting ahead of the game for this Christmas? Please, could we get it thrown away before lunchtime?"*

The receptionist was very embarrassed. She explained that she came in every day and just 'didn't notice' it. Presumably, the other employees who came through reception every day also didn't "see" it or didn't want to say anything for some reason.

When you have an established routine, it is easy to 'stop noticing' things that can be immediately striking to someone newly arriving into your environment.

Sometimes it is a good idea to step back and look at things with "new eyes." Does the office need tidying up? Are people looking happy? Is there anything going on that you should take more note of but have just gotten used to?

'The Client Lens'

Along similar lines, when I was working at a law firm services franchise, we developed a concept we called *"The Client Lens©."* We encouraged law firms to put themselves in the shoes of their clients and really try to understand how it feels to engage them as their lawyer.

We asked them to consider questions such as: Are your people friendly? Is the new client onboarding process too complicated? Do you offer people a cup of coffee? Can clients easily find things on your website? Can they park nearby your offices if necessary? Do you really listen? Do you see your clients as people or as law cases? Is it a good experience to deal with you?

In many cases, we found that due to their great focus on being good lawyers and practicing the law, a lot of firms did not offer an optimum client experience. They just didn't really think about it or notice. The few firms that went out of their way to treat their customers really well were significantly more successful and happier places to work. [21]

We Get Used to Things

Working in an organization with a "toxic culture" is a horrible experience. If you have had any experience of this, you will know how draining, depressing, and demotivating it is to work every day for or with people who don't trust each other or in a climate of fear.

Almost always, this problem is created or made worse by the leader. As the very old proverb (Greek,

---

[21] From *'Driving Success in your Law Firm'* 2016, The Law Society. Co-authored with Sally Holdway

Chinese, Turkish…?) states, *"a fish rots from the head down,"* emphasizing that as well as being a vital contributing factor to the success of an organization, leadership will also be at the root of a culture's failure or dysfunctionality.

It is also a feature of human nature that after a while, we seem to adapt to even the worst of situations and for them to seem "normal" to us, even if objectively, this is not the case.

An extreme example of this was observed in the Japanese prisoner of war camps during the Second World War. Captured soldiers spent months or even years in unspeakable conditions of daily cruelty, with no healthcare and minimal nutrition. Men were forced to hunt and eat rats to survive.

When the US army liberated these camps, they expected the prisoners to rush out and welcome them as conquering heroes. The opposite happened: the prisoners were highly suspicious of, and even hostile towards, their liberators. To them, in their emaciated state, the soldiers swarming into the camp, smiling and laughing, looked grotesquely fat and repulsive.

The prisoners had become so used to their lives of deprivation and misery that it had become their "normal." So much so that now they found it very hard to accept anything else, and for many, it took a very long time to gradually adjust back to their previous lives.

A similar situation can develop in the less extreme circumstances of life in the office. People get used to toxicity, bullying, poor communication, excessive politics, power games, and poor leadership if they are surrounded by it every day. They develop "coping mechanisms" in the absence of any belief that they can expect things to change or get better.

If you are a newly appointed leader of a team that has been living in a regime of toxicity, it will take you a while to fix it. The team will be suspicious of your new ideas and need time to adjust. You will be surprised just how embedded poor behavior has become, and you may even need to make some personnel changes to root out those that seem unwilling or unable to embrace your new approach to doing things.

If a junior manager on your team has been allowed to become adept at hiding information and treating their team with contempt, they will resist becoming an open, thoughtful manager.

Virtual Culture

The pandemic in 2020 dramatically fast-forwarded what was previously a gradual evolution toward increased use of video meeting technology. As all that fades into the past, most organizations now see a partly remote workforce as a great way to save money, avoid travel, and generally increase efficiency. Workers' attitudes will never be the same either.

Companies are radically rethinking their investments in office space. Video meetings are here to stay and have changed everything.

The masks and tests of the pandemic are already history. The impact of drastically changing 50-plus years of 'life in the office' in just a few months will be with us forevermore.

Studies are showing that many office workers overwhelmingly embrace remote work life. People feel more efficient and productive, have more time with the family, enjoy increased independence, and say they generally feel happier.

Some are even moving to exotic locations to take advantage of the new 'work from anywhere' reality. The global pandemic was the catalyst for a massive shift in corporate life in a very short time.

There are some obvious downsides, and indeed, many companies are now insisting that everyone should 'return to the office' for at least some of the time. Good luck with that. People have tasted freedom from the daily commute, and many will tenaciously resist returning to it.

We have learned very fast how to perform many business functions without anyone being in the same room. Brainstorming, knowledge sharing, team building, communication, mentoring, performance evaluation, and data protection are all technical-type challenges being addressed by organizations - with technical-type solutions.

It's the soft stuff, the intangible corporate and learning culture, that remains the great unknown. Long before anyone dreamed of video conferences, companies that underestimated the importance of their culture saw their strategies come to pieces with alarming speed.

Leadership behaviors can indeed nurture a culture by reinforcing it, but nobody really knows yet how that works when everyone is on the other side of a screen. Your organizational culture isn't static, and it can evolve and develop in ways that you may not like and cannot control.

We are humans and have evolved to be naturally social beings. We live in cities, we join clubs, we like hugs, we organize parties to celebrate things. Overwhelmingly, we enjoy being together.

Newcomers to an organization are usually introduced to the culture by formal induction, but more importantly, by informal interaction with colleagues.

Today's new hires, many of them in their first job, may not get to "feel" the environment of their workplace or look their boss or co-worker in the eye, and perhaps never will. As companies reorganize their teams into remote or semi-remote structures, even veteran employees will only have their memories of a past life in the office to maintain the culture.

We should make no mistake – the shift to remote working is a major transformation in the way we work, and it is happening in a very short timeframe. Experience shows that most business transformations fail to achieve their objectives, and this is a massive transformation on a global scale.

In common with every transformation, it will prove to be much harder than we think, require more investment of time and money than we expect, have unforeseen consequences, and require excellent leadership to succeed.

There is a real risk that in our enthusiasm to seek the business benefits of partial or full remote working, we may be rushing things and dangerously underestimating the unforeseeable impacts on company culture.

Along with how to manage AI, navigating the new normal of partial remote work is probably one of the greatest universal leadership challenges of our times.

Leaders of remote teams face all the same challenges as in a traditional office, plus a whole lot of tricky additional ones. Leaders have to work twice as hard in the remote environment.

The Power of Leaders

It's important not to underestimate the impact you have as a leader on the attitudes and actions of the people who work for you. Your everyday behavior as a leader will consciously, or unconsciously, set the tone, standards, and culture of your team.

I feel that leaders very often do not fully realize this, or perhaps do not want to accept it, as it makes them feel uncomfortable.

They downplay the influence they have on the people in the organization that report up to them. Yet everything I have seen tells me that whoever is in charge has tremendous power over what goes on.

If you are slow to decide things, then you 'give permission' to your leaders and managers to be the same. If you are quick to lose your cool and perhaps feared, then a similarly aggressive style of management will thrive in your organization.

If you are a thoughtful leader and take time to greet your team, ask about them and their family and their lives, this will not only leave a great impression on individuals but also set the tone for others.

When I was working in a multinational company with offices all over the world, I noticed how some senior leaders would go out of their way to stop and talk to staff in our far-away offices they were visiting. It was not strictly necessary. Many others just flew in, had their important meeting, and set off again for the airport.

For many of our people working far from the head office, I observed that a few genuine and personal words of enthusiasm and interest from a senior leader would have a positive effect that far outweighed any amount of town halls and carefully scripted videos.

THE
POWER
OF LEADERS

Organizations, whether just a few people or with thousands spread across the world, all have a culture of some sort. There is no doubt that the behavior of leadership has a direct influence on that culture and can allow different styles to flourish or be discouraged.

A change of leadership, even of a very large company, can quickly bring about a change in the culture that may have a profound influence, for better or worse, on the employees that work there and their satisfaction with their employer.

Never underestimate the importance of the culture in your team, office, or company. Or your influence on it as a leader. Do not underestimate how the presence of unhappy or negative culture will undermine your best efforts to create more successful outcomes.

Equally, your hard work to support and foster a positive, team-oriented, and engaging office culture will be rewarded with a happy team that actually wants to work hard and produce great results that they can be proud of achieving.

Reflections

Here are a few key questions arising from the themes raised in this chapter:

- What is the culture like where you work?
- What words would you use to describe it?
- What drives that?
- Would you like to see it change? Why?
- As a leader, what do you do to support or enhance the culture?
- Do you sometimes step back and "see with new eyes?"
- Could you find more time to engage with colleagues?
- How might that make a difference?
- In what ways are leaders powerful?

Chapter 12: Being a Good Boss

Manager or Leader?

"Managers do things right - leaders do the right things[22]"

Good managers are experts at improving processes and guiding people in established tasks that have typically been studied intensely, and so they can be optimized by developing a process to get them done.

Managers deal with tactical, short-term, and known problems. Their job is to work out how to do those things better and to support their team or other resources they may have to make that happen.

Effective leadership, in contrast, is strategic, happens over a longer period, and requires tackling 'novel' problems.

Leaders provide people with guidance or reassurance as they take on unexpected developments, try to work out what will happen in the future, and tackle the challenges of change.

Managers deal with "Déjà Vu" (I've seen this before) and leaders must get used to addressing "Vu Dajé" (I've never seen this before). [23]

Organizations need both good managers and effective leaders to be successful. Of course, many people will be

---

[22] Peter Drucker (1909 - 2005) Educator, author and leadership visionary

[23] *Leadership, A Very Short Introduction* by Keith Grint, Oxford University Press 2010. Page 15

skilled at both, and you don't suddenly one day give up being a manager and become a leader.

Being an effective manager is rational and typically about delivering specific or technical outcomes or results that can often be measured or compared with past efforts. Management is task-centric and focuses on practical outcomes.

Leadership is more emotional and is about convincing and reassuring people that they should believe in you and follow you. You may not have all the answers, but people are sufficiently impressed by you that they will go with you on your journey or follow the path you propose. Leaders are defined by their followers. You need to earn their loyalty, engagement, and trust.

In Chapter 1, we talked about how leadership starts with ourselves and how every one of us needs to be conscious, responsible, and intentional. First with ourselves and with everyone we interact with: colleagues, bosses, and team members.

As a leader, your followers will look to you to provide them with what they need to make a very important decision of their own - to accept you as their leader.

I believe there are three fundamental qualities that you must demonstrate or provide to your followers to engage them. I call them the leader's API: awareness, purpose, and inspiration.

LEADERSHIP

A WARENESS

P URPOSE

I NSPIRATION

Top 30 #21: The Leaders' API

Previously, I talked about how I believe leadership starts with ourselves, and there is far more to it than just the idea of leading others. We need to be conscious, responsible, and intentional to be good leaders.

Building on this, when it comes to being in charge of other people, there are three essential qualities that you need to keep in mind:

1. Awareness

2. Purpose

3. Inspiration

Good leaders think of that responsibility as a separate and complementary skill from their technical skills and invest time and energy to do it well. The first on the list has been mentioned many times already in these pages: Awareness.

Awareness starts with "self-awareness." You will take time to consider your own style, to understand your own strengths and weaknesses, your capacity for empathy, and your me-pathy.

You invest time to be more effective, to find a coach to provide you with honest feedback and an ear to listen. You actively seek out the people you need to advise you to complement your own style and strengths.

You know yourself and also strive to better understand what kind of organization you are leading. The strengths and weaknesses of your team, the situation and culture in your own team and the wider organization.

You need an external viewpoint and never lose track of the wider context in which your team is operating.

When you truly know yourself and understand the makeup and context of your organization, you will also know that to achieve change and success, you need to establish Purpose, the second critical leadership factor.

The establishment of goals, objectives, ideals, a mission, or a vision provide us with a reason for positively engaging with our work every day. If change is happening (as it almost always is), then it is absolutely vital that those living through that change understand why it is important and what success will look like.

With a clear purpose established, your team will choose to embrace, partially engage, reject outright, etc. the plan you put before them, or ideally have created with them. Without a clearly defined purpose, even potential supporters and advocates can be lukewarm and suspicious.

It is your responsibility as the leader to clarify the destination for your team. It is not your responsibility to define that all on your own, although you need to be ready to make decisions that ensure the clarity of the purpose for everyone. If the purpose is agreed upon with input from everyone involved, it has a much greater chance of success.

The commitment, consistency, and support you demonstrate as the team defines its purpose are critical to the commitment of the group and a desire to go on the journey towards a successful outcome – which leads to the third critical leadership factor: Inspiration.

Whether you head a small team or sit at the top of an enormous multinational company, it is your responsibility to inspire every person in the organization. To do this, you will need to be visible and present in all areas of the hierarchy.

You need to see and hear for yourself that the purpose you have developed is understood by everyone. You need to constantly demonstrate your own commitment. You need to be seen to understand what is happening, to be listening, and to fulfill the expectations of the team that they have someone leading them that is worthy of them.

You should not be afraid to engage directly with your people, to be seen, to shake hands, to encourage, to use different channels of communication to reinforce messages and strengthen the understanding of the Purpose. Your energy will empower the whole system.

You set the tone and give permission for everything that happens in your team with your ideas, words, and actions. Never underestimate your power.

Conscious Competence

Developing honest and genuine awareness of your capabilities as a manager or leader is a critical part of being good at it. A good way to think about this is the four types of competence.

Unconscious incompetence is the very worst trait for any kind of leader. You aren't good at something but you just don't realize it, but really believe that you are a star performer, looked up to by one and all. It is very hard to provide feedback to an incompetent boss who firmly believes that they are doing an amazing job. Don't be that person.

Conscious incompetence does not need to be a problem at all if handled well. You know that you have weaknesses and you recognize them and find solutions to address them. People do not expect their leaders to be good at everything. There is great strength in admitting and knowing your weaknesses. Being authentic and honest is much more important than always having the right answer to everything.

Unconscious competence is very likely to be linked to your confidence or self-esteem as a leader. Perhaps you are shy or nervous and do not see yourself as the type of person who will generate followers or motivate a team. However, if you are authentic and honest, it may well be that you will be appreciated for your qualities and people will enjoy being led by you.

Conscious competence is the ideal. Through experience, self-awareness, and feedback from others, you really know what you are good at and how to manage yourself and others. Of course, to be truly consciously competent, you must be very careful not to allow that to develop into complacency or arrogance. You risk ending up among the unconsciously incompetent if you let that happen.

The Three Types of Problems

Do you know when to behave like a manager or act like a leader? Do you sometimes need to just take charge and give orders, or should you always be listening and discussing options with your team?

One way to think about this is to start with what kind of problem you are trying to solve and adapt your approach based on what is needed in that particular situation.

The good news is that, in fact, there are only three types of problems[24] that we face, and once you have a handle on which is which, it becomes quite easy to adapt your style accordingly. I have found that my clients find this simple model extremely useful.

---

[24] Original idea from *Dilemmas in a General Theory of Planning* by H Ritell and M Webber - Policy Sciences , 4 1973 - sourced from *Leadership, A Very Short Introduction* by Keith Grint, Oxford University Press 2010. Pages 15 -21

The three types of problems are:

· Critical

· Tame

· Wicked

We'll start with critical problems. Imagine you are in your office... you're on the seventeenth floor and there is suddenly a smell of burning. You try to focus on your work...

Suddenly, a person wearing a fireproof suit and a yellow helmet, and carrying a fire axe, rushes out of the stairwell into the office. They shout, *"The building is on fire! All of you to the fire escape, now! Leave your things! Run!"*

What do you think happens? Everybody gets up and runs.

You may be a very rational person and renowned for your strategic mind, but you do not say, *"Can you tell us a little more about this fire, please? What floor is it on? How long have you been a firefighter?"*

There's no time for any of that – you just run. This is a critical problem. It is something very urgent and it needs a solution right now.

In business, you will face critical problems that are usually unexpected crises that require a very rapid and focused response. Organizations do scenario planning and create disaster plans to avoid having to deal with critical problems without the benefit of previous planning or response optimization.

Because there is no time for thinking or discussion, critical problems need a "commander" – a person, usually in authority, who provides answers and direction. Military situations are led by commanders, as in the heat of battle, success depends on making fast decisions and everybody doing what they are told.

Critical problems typically require a physical response. You need to do something, and quickly. In a business setting, that might just be answering the phone and making a very quick decision.

The second type of problem is tame problems. All businesses and organizations are constantly dealing with them.

Tame problems are all those situations, challenges, or processes that have happened before and can be studied and improved.

This can be as simple as making a cup of coffee. It's a process... you choose the color of the coffee pod you think you like best, you put it into the machine, you add sugar or milk until you gradually perfect the ideal drink to your taste.

How does it taste? Hmm... a bit bitter, you can add more sugar. It's a process that can be studied and improved.

This also holds true for extremely complicated processes like flying a fighter jet or performing a brain operation. These are also activities that have been done many, many times before, and they have been exhaustively studied and optimized.

Think of medical treatments of 30 or 40 years ago and compare many of those with what we have today. This improvement in capability is because these tame medical problems have been constantly and minutely studied. It doesn't mean that those problems are in any way easy; they can be extremely complicated. The key is that they can be broken down into a process based on past experience to make them work better in the future.

If you think about how businesses work, tame problems are at the heart of what most companies do most of the time. They strive to improve their processes, to optimize their products, services, and factories. To do whatever they do better in order to make more money and be more successful.

Tame problems need "managers". Managers who are going to study the problem ad infinitum. They enable processes and solutions to be improved over the years, and they are wholly focused on that task. Tame problems need a rational and calculated response.

The third kind of problem is a wicked problem. Wicked problems are unique because typically they don't have a solution. They are complex (rather than complicated) and can be worked on, and there can be progress or improvement, but they are rarely solved.

An example of a wicked problem might be the global rise in levels of obesity. Apparently, for example, despite its reputation for the Mediterranean Diet, there are now over 8 million people in Spain considered obese, a fivefold increase in twenty years. [25]

Think of all the myriad different elements that contribute to that obesity problem. There are the individuals themselves, the doctor they are talking to, food cultures in the country, the food and drink companies, schools, governments, diet companies, gyms, NGOs and charities, people in other developing countries who don't have enough to eat...

We all know that obesity will never be completely solved. The best we can hope for is that by getting all these elements to work together with a common plan, we may see some kind of improvement over time. There is no single or simple solution. There may not be a solution at all.

What do politicians do? They campaign like crazy to have sugary drinks banned in schools. And they say, *"We are fighting obesity, we are going to get rid of child obesity."* But what they are actually doing is using a tame type problem approach to attack a wicked problem, and you will never solve a wicked problem with a tame type solution.

In business, the wicked problems are the strategic "unknowns" that must be considered. What will the market do? How will the competition react? How much should we spend on advertising? Should we buy that new factory or not? No one knows the right answers to these questions and

---

[25] Source: Ministerio de Sanidad España 2024
https://www.sanidad.gob.es/en/organizacion/sns/docs/datos.pdf

problems, but they are incredibly important for success in the future.

Wicked problems need "leaders". The leader's role is to ask questions. Effective leaders don't tell you what to do or how to manage something; the good leaders ask you, *"What more do you need to improve your management and optimization of your processes? What equipment do you need down here to make sure that when the place is on fire, everyone can get out quickly?"*

Wicked problems often require something closer to an emotional response. The leader needs to take everybody with them on the journey, providing the inspiration and purpose, without having all the answers.

When you are at work, what kind of problems are you addressing, and what kind of leadership solution do you provide?

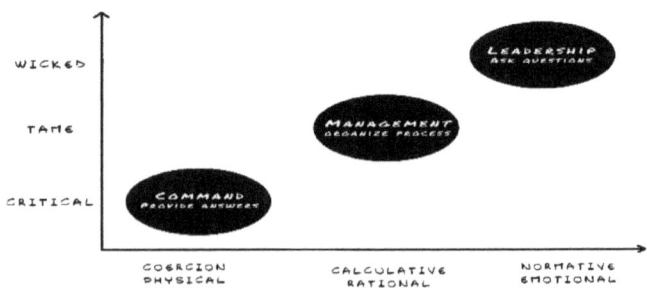

26

[26] Chart adapted from *Leadership, A Very Short Introduction* by Keith Grint, Oxford University Press 2010. Page 21

Are You Addressing the Right Type of Problem?

Bearing in mind the model of the three types of problem, think about what goes on in your office. Leaders should be in their meeting rooms with their top people, doing wicked thinking.

"Where's this company going to be in ten years from now? Who is our competition and what are they going to do, and how's that going to change? How are our products going to work? What should we be doing next? Let's go and talk to one of our managers about what they are doing and find out, listen to them, and take some actions in the future."

But what actually happens in too many offices is that the leaders spend their time irritating their managers by interfering with what they are doing – the tame processes.

"So, what are you doing today? Why do you do this? Tell me about the other… Oh, shouldn't you be…? I think it would be better if you moved Harry across and put him in that department because I think he would be a lot more effective because I like him… he's in my golf club…"

Senior leaders, because wicked problems are so hard, sometimes prefer to stay involved with the tame problems that they can at least understand. Sometimes leaders will even consciously or subconsciously create a critical problem so that they can act like a commander, which makes them feel important.

The boss comes into the office in the morning in a foul mood and says, *"I need that press release on my desk by 11:30."* Everyone runs around… they're writing frantically, they're bringing drafts, making cups of coffee, everyone's totally stressed, they're saying *"The boss is not happy, we need that press release now, stop what you are doing, hurry up."*

It all eventually happens, and the press release arrives on the boss's desk, who looks at it and says, "Hmm, alright, fine, at least someone has done some *work in this office today*," and walks out and goes to lunch thinking, 'Goodness me, haven't I done a fantastic job!'

What, in reality, has happened is that the boss has come to the office, which is a fundamentally tame environment, where people should be managing processes and improving what happens every day, and created a critical problem. The boss should be thinking about the wicked problems and how the company should be moving forward and the right strategies.

In this case, it doesn't cause a life-and-death reaction, but it does require people to leap from their desks and run around to do things they really shouldn't be doing.

20 Traits of Good Bosses

You can take your pick of those thousands of leadership theories you can consider, and books you can read, with the aim of enhancing your performance as a boss. Also, take note of the many people who have given you advice or shared their own experiences with you. All of that is very worthwhile. Definitely do it.

To add to that, I am going to list here some behaviors and ideas that I have observed to be important and effective for good bosses.

I have noticed that they are practiced by people who are successful at engaging and inspiring others. I kept my list to 20, but yours may legitimately have many more.

I. Anticipate

You think ahead and accurately predict outcomes so that your team feels confident that you are one step ahead of any given situation. You are not constantly in reactive mode, but proactively finding solutions. This provides confidence.

II. Be Calm and Collected

Calm bosses do not make a drama out of a crisis and do not waste time and energy on being angry, pointing fingers, and asking, *"whose fault is this?"* when a solution is needed urgently. There will be plenty of time later to discuss what could have been done better. In the heat of the moment, a boss that keeps their cool and helps everyone else to think clearly is highly appreciated.

III. Listen Carefully...

Bosses who do not truly listen to their people will eventually find that no one in the team will bother to try to make their point, however passionately they may believe in it. This is a very dangerous situation for a boss. Your team will see and know things that you cannot and do not, and it is vital that they believe you truly listen to them.

IV. ...And then make a decision

Equally, after genuine listening, your team needs you to be decisive. A boss who can't make up their mind or makes weak choices quickly frustrates a team. The boss may insist that the team work together to reach a decision, but one way or the other, that decision needs to be made. If it is not, the team will blame you.

V. Seek Alignment

You need to ensure that on important matters there is alignment in your team. If there is a genuine disagreement and you let this continue without addressing it, your team members will break into factions that will undermine its effectiveness.

If you are developing a strategy, be sure that everyone truly is buying into it. You may need to "agree to disagree" with some element of the team, but even so, they must undertake to get behind your strategy and show their support for it, despite their misgivings.

Expose disagreements and let everyone talk it out. Don't "take it offline" with individuals. They may agree with you in private but not be truly aligned with the overall team direction.

VI. Find a Solution

Good bosses don't let the team out of the room without finding a solution that works to a degree for everyone. Often, to keep on time with an agenda, a discussion gets closed down as *"we must move on."* If you move on without solving something important, it may never get solved.

VII. Stay True to Values, Be Consistent

Your team should have a good sense of what you believe to be "right" and what behavior you expect or values you hold. Bosses must hold their people accountable and set clear standards that everyone understands and can follow.

Bosses need to be consistent in their views, treatment of individuals, and behavior. Nobody enjoys working for a moody boss or one that treats people unjustly or seems to have favorites.

VIII. Do Your Homework

It is highly demotivating for a team to feel that their boss has not prepared properly. If something needs to be read before a meeting, read it. You are the boss and you need to lead by example. How you behave gives everyone on your team permission to behave like you. If you are late or poorly prepared, they will be too.

IX. Show Your Teeth from Time to Time

You should aim to be a reasonable, caring, thoughtful, and listening boss, but not so reasonable and understanding that your team feels they can get away with anything. You are the boss, and from time to time, you need to "show your teeth." Everyone needs to know that you are capable of getting upset if standards are not met and that poor work will have consequences.

Being a little unreasonable now and again keeps people on their toes.

X. Run Efficient Meetings

Many teams spend a lot of time together in meetings, and if these are not run efficiently and effectively, they can become a real burden for people.

Discuss meeting management with your team. Maybe appoint different team members to chair meetings on a rotating basis. Have a good agenda. Stick to time and don't allow certain people to go over the time they have been allocated to speak.

For a team that meets regularly, like an executive leadership team, it can be useful to have 'labels' for the different sessions and presentations:

·   **Information session:** This is a presentation to inform the team about something.

·   **Discussion session:** Everyone on the team is expected to take part, and the objective is to gather opinions and input on the subject.

·   **Decision session:** This session requires a decision to be made. Until it is, it should not be concluded.

Top 30 #22: Juniors Present

My first real job after graduation was at a London advertising agency. It was a very successful business, and many things that I learned there have stuck with me throughout my career.

Their policy was to push as much responsibility as possible onto more junior team members. It was, to some extent, a 'sink or swim' environment, and not everyone could keep up. But it was not a harsh system; there was a lot of support - but equally, a lot was expected of you.

One corporate behavior, in particular, was both highly effective and a unique practice compared with other competitive agencies. That was to expect junior team members to be able to lead important presentations and to stand up, present ideas, and defend opinions not only in front of clients but also their own bosses.

What happens when the most senior person in the room is leading the pitch and presenting the ideas? All the more junior team members are effectively silenced as they can't speak up over their boss. Realistically, it's an easy ride - turn up and try to look keen and intelligent while the boss does the work.

Our system was totally the opposite. The boss would do the introductions, and then the team (starting with the most junior) would be expected to run the meeting and present the ideas.

Not only was this excellent training (us more junior people had to know exactly what we were talking about), but it also had a curious effect of making the client feel that our senior team was somehow on 'their side'.

Even though we would have previously discussed the details of our pitch, our bosses would fire questions and comments at us: *"Where did you get that figure? Are you sure? Come on, let's get to the point here, please, etc."*

Allowing the most junior members to run the meeting communicated great confidence in the team and allowed clients to feel they could rely on everyone, not just the bosses.

As a pretty inexperienced Account Executive, I was trusted to attend alone a monthly sponsorship meeting of a big client. We shared that client with another big London agency. They used to send their very senior Group Account Director to that meeting. I know how much it annoyed him that our agency sent me along.

What I noticed was that the client treated me and him just the same. I had the confidence and trust of our brand behind me, and bosses backing me up, and as long as my contributions were sensible and informed, the client was perfectly happy.

Many years later, when I was the client, agencies would come to present to me and my team - and the senior person would do all the talking. The rest of the agency team would sit quietly, watching their boss.

Let your team present. Let your team do the work. It makes them better, and it makes you a better leader.

XI. Don't Be a Bottleneck

If you insist on being the only person on the team who can make decisions, there is a good chance that you will become a bottleneck. Your team will gradually realize that many important projects or actions are being delayed because you haven't made up your mind about what should be done.

It is much better to make decisions together with your team in meetings and come to a collective agreement on what is best. You can still have the final say if necessary, but don't hold onto decisions for too long. You just end up blocking progress.

XII. Analysis Paralysis

There is an optimal amount of analysis, data, and discussion needed to make a decision and move forward. It may be tempting to gather more and more information and analysis to support your decisions, but in the end, you just have to make one.

I have seen bosses get stuck in analysis paralysis to the point where they become a serious hindrance to the team's effectiveness.

XIII. Clumsy solutions to messy problems

Sometimes it may seem like there is no good solution to a problem. When issues are complex and messy, it can be really difficult to find a satisfactory way to tackle them. These are wicked problems, and I like the idea that sometimes we need to use 'clumsy solutions' to address 'messy problems.'[27]

In other words, you try things that may seem risky or suboptimal but are creative and might work out well.

Perhaps you can't find a person to fill an urgent role, but you really need the problem to be addressed. Can you come up with a temporary fix by rearranging some people? It's a clumsy solution – but it can work for now. Sometimes the ideal solution is just not feasible, and you would only waste valuable time trying to find it.

Your team wants you to find solutions that help them do their jobs better or more easily. They don't expect a perfect solution; they need something that makes a difference. They need to move forward.

XIV. What You Say, and What You Actually Do

In chapter 1, I talked about 'doing what you say' and how few people actually follow through on their promises. As a boss, it is crucial to align your words with your actions.

Your team will quickly notice if you don't fulfill your promises or fail to get things done on time or as promised. If, for example, you commit to supporting someone for a promotion, then you must follow through.

---

[27] Source: *Leadership, A Very Short Introduction* by Keith Grint, Oxford University Press 2010. Pages 23-24

Trust will erode, and your authority will gradually decline if you become known as a boss who tells people what they want to hear but does not deliver results or take action.

XV. Being a Good Boss vs. Being a Good Person

Being a boss can be challenging because at times you may have to make decisions or take actions that are unpopular or negatively impact people you like. That is why it is crucial to develop the right kind of professional relationships with your employees.

It is important to remember that you are in a leadership position to make the right choices for everyone and for the organization you represent. Delaying tough decisions or choices does not make them any easier.

In hindsight, most of my biggest regrets about my own leadership of people were related to acting too slowly when I realized that change was needed. Others were affected by my choice to delay, even though at the time my intentions seemed right – to lessen or delay the impact on the individual who was not performing.

I was trying to be a good person – but in doing so, I stopped being a good boss.

Top 30 #23: Crisis Response - Regret, Reason, Remedy

Things go wrong, and when they do, as a leader, you will often be tested like never before. You will find yourself under the microscope with people around you demanding explanations, answers, and solutions.

"This is unacceptable. How can this happen? You are to blame? What are you going to do about it?"

It may be customers, investors, the general public, or your own staff that are furious about something - it might even just be your boss.

As head of communication for a publicly listed multinational travel technology enterprise, when things went wrong (as they occasionally did), I would always remind myself and my bosses of a very simple communication formula. I have found it to be invaluable when there is a crisis.

That is "Regret, Reason, Remedy."

Start with an apology: Regret.

Even if you don't feel that whatever has happened is truly your fault, somebody is feeling aggrieved, and it can help a lot for you to show some humility and understanding as a very first step. In business situations, it is often initially unclear who is responsible for a problem as many elements can be at play.

When there was a software outage at an airport, it would sometimes be days before we knew exactly what, or which company or network, had caused the issue - but the passengers were stranded just the same.

"Before all else, we'd like to apologize to all the passengers who cannot board their plane and continue on their journey, and for the impact on their plans."

It may seem counterintuitive to apologize for something for which you may not have been ultimately responsible. But not apologizing, or worse still, trying to pass the blame to someone else, is far worse in the long run.

When companies or individuals point fingers in a crisis, they rarely come out of it well.

In many situations, I have noticed that the apology gets passed over in the desire to get on to describing the reasons and remedies. This is a mistake. Showing humility and empathy when others are unhappy or suffering is the best way to start. It will get you some attention.

Next step: Reason.

"Since 7:30 this evening, we have been experiencing a computer system outage that is impacting all of the airport's normal passenger boarding procedures. As such, until it is resolved, it is not possible to board any passengers on any airlines."

The reason may not sound very good, but it is far better to stick to the truth. Tell them what has happened in simple terms. Don't embellish or try to make it sound better than it is. Don't say it will soon be fixed if you don't yet know if it will.

Finally: Remedy. What are you doing about it.

"Our engineers are working diligently to identify the cause of the outage and to restore all systems as soon as possible. In the meantime, we will provide an update every 30 minutes. The airport is providing free meal vouchers which are available at...."

Even if the remedy does not provide a stranded air traveler with an immediate solution to their problem, at least they will feel informed about what is being done.

Recently, I had the misfortune to be booked on a long-haul flight that was canceled after a 3-hour delay at midnight. The front-line staff obviously did not know what to say to the passengers and just announced that a "technical issue" had affected the plane.

It took a very long time before anyone could tell us where we would stay for the night, when the flight would finally take off, or, let alone, get a decent explanation for what had happened.

I observed how angry and, frankly, rude several passengers became due to this poor handling of the situation.

On the following day, finally airborne, the pilot apologized profusely on behalf of the airline for the inconvenience caused to us. But really, it was far too late.

We needed that apology and those explanations much earlier.

The RRR formula is applicable to any situation where something has gone wrong and you need to offer some kind of explanation and plan to resolve it.

It is just as effective in an individual 1-1 scenario as it is for a corporate communication crisis.

It is useful because it is simple and easy to remember and keeps you on track with the three things that people want in a crisis from whoever is leading them: Someone to say sorry, someone to explain what happened, and someone to say what is being done about it.

REGRET   REASON   REMEDY

XVI. Back Your People

Very early in my career (I had only been properly working in an advertising agency for a matter of months), I was delighted to bring in a great deal for my team.

An ad space salesman from a famous quality daily newspaper suddenly called me out of the blue and offered me a last-minute full page in tomorrow's paper for only £500. I can even remember the salesman's name and carefully double-checked everything with him over the phone.

The normal price was nearly £20,000, so this was an absolute bargain. It wasn't my job to buy ad space, but we all agreed it was too good of an opportunity to pass up, so I hurriedly organized ad copy to fill the space. The advertisement appeared as expected the next day, and I was very pleased with myself. Our client was delighted.

A few weeks later, the invoice arrived from the newspaper—for £5,000.

As you can imagine, there was a crisis. The media buying team was justifiably annoyed that I was buying space at all, and it made us all look foolish.

The newspaper ad space salesman swore blind that it was always offered for £5 thousand, not hundred (he was lying). I felt like I was going to lose my job for incompetence just as my career was starting.

In a bad-tempered meeting with everyone involved, my boss (who had only known me for a few months) asked me a lot of questions and then raised his hand for silence.

He said, *"OK, this has happened, it's unfortunate, but if Eddie says it happened like that, then I believe him."* He refused to discuss it further. He just backed me up, and we took the financial hit.

I have never forgotten it, as it showed me that to be a good boss, you need to make a judgment call on whether to back your person—and if you do, then back them completely.

He also said to me later, *"Next time, get it in writing."* Another good learning point. This happened long before email came into use, and getting things in writing was a lot more complicated than it is now.

XVII. The Truth Is Always the Best Option

When looking to explain something that has happened or maybe is going to happen, it is often tempting to "create a narrative" that may contain some elements of the truth but is not really strictly 100% true. This seems helpful at first and may be more "comfortable" and seem to avoid embarrassment or make things easier for people to accept.

However, just like any other kind of lie (and unfortunately, this is really just a lie), you often find yourself having to tell more lies to keep your storyline intact.

The truth can be painful at times, but as a boss, it really is better to be honest than to try to tell people what you, or someone else, wants to hear.

There can still be many options open to you about how to tell the truth to limit damage or minimize hurt feelings. By basing your narrative on the truth, you will not find yourself caught out by contradictions at a later date.

When faced with the question *"how are we going to explain this?"* start with the truth of what happened, is happening, or will happen - and go from there.

As a boss, the truth may be uncomfortable, but it is always the best place to start.

XVIII. Listen to Your Intuition

If something seems off, it probably is.

In a world of best practices and data overload, it can be hard to listen to your own inner voice when it comes to decisions or choices. Often, we do have intuitive feelings about a situation or a person that later turn out to have been remarkably accurate. We push these feelings away, as they are not proven or scientific, or based on anything more than a "feeling".

As a boss, learn to listen to your feelings and trust your intuition. You may be surprised how powerful that is for you.

XIX. Have Some Fun

Even though your challenges may be great and the situation serious, the people who work for you are still just that – people. Good bosses make sure that there is an element of fun or an opportunity for the team to relax and recharge.

It's not just about organizing dinners or team buildings. Even during the course of a meeting or in the office, it is possible for you, as the boss, to create an atmosphere that allows people to enjoy their work.

Work should be taken seriously, but it doesn't mean everything has to be serious all the time. Allow your team to get to know each other as people and to build some trust and cohesion among themselves.

Show your team that you have a sense of humor and want to enjoy work, as well as collectively doing a good job. Allow people to express their personalities and don't be afraid to show them yours too.

XX. Be You

There is no such thing as the perfect boss. You are a unique individual and you bring certain strengths and weaknesses to your task of leading others.

Celebrate that uniqueness and develop your own style and way of working with your team. As discussed many times in these pages, the "imperfect" and authentic leader is far preferred by people than the person who can never be wrong or never makes a mistake.

Work on your weaknesses, of course, but rely on your natural strengths and do not compare yourself unfavorably to others. Become confident and effective as a boss by building and flexing your own personal, individual leadership muscles. Develop your me-pathy.

And One More

This is an unashamed repetition of Top 30 #12, [28] but it is so important:

"Never stop communicating."

Just because there is nothing specific to say, no real news or announcements to make, doesn't mean there is no need to talk to your team. They want to hear from you, even if it is just for you to confirm that there is nothing new going on.

If you don't communicate enough, the risk is that they will begin to invent ideas for why and suspect that you are not communicating for some specific reason.

People can spend a lot of valuable time speculating on what they think might, or might not be happening. Usually, nothing important is... which is why you aren't communicating!

The communication vacuum will always be filled by something - so it is better to fill it yourself and constantly over-communicate to your team.

---

[28] Page 143 – Never Stop Communicating

Reflections

Here are a few key questions arising from the themes raised in this chapter:

- As a leader, in what ways do you demonstrate awareness?
- And offer purpose and inspiration?
- Are you conscious of your own competencies?
- Do you see yourself as a commander, manager, or leader?
- When was the last time you handled a critical problem?
- What traits would go on your own list of being a 'good boss'?
- Are you tackling wicked problems?
- Do you let your people speak up in meetings?
- What is your approach when things go wrong?

Chapter 13: Your Own Philosophy of Leadership

What Kind of a Leader Are You? Or Do You Aim to Be?

Do a search on Amazon for books about leadership, and it will immediately offer you up to 3,000 titles 'of many'.

Apparently, it has 57,136 books with the word "leadership" in the title. Even more amazingly, it is estimated that several million new leadership books are written every year.

Thousands and thousands of hours of human endeavor have been invested (so far!) to try to help us all be better at leading other people.

Despite all that, you may or may not (probably not) experience your own lightbulb moment about what works for you, or what you think sounds like a good way for you to approach the leadership of others.

It is a wicked problem – it's complex, there is no definite 'right or wrong,' and we just need to keep on trying things, learning, listening, and observing to see how we can gradually be better at it.

Some people seem to find it easier than others, but if you truly work at it, anyone can be a solid leader of themselves at the very least, and why not of others?

Leadership is not a defined discipline like medicine or the law. There is no one leadership 'authority' who is able to pass judgment and deem one person a better leader than another, or dictate leadership do's and don'ts like laws.

The good news about that is that despite all that thinking, writing, and practicing by other people, you can just set your mind to having a go at being a good leader, and how you do that is really up to you.

What I do believe is that it is useful to actively and deeply think about yourself as a boss or leader and invest in yourself to evolve and improve. Your self-awareness of your empathy, me-pathy, impact, weak spots, and strong points will help you enormously.

Deepen your knowledge of what others think about leadership by reading books, going on courses, listening to podcasts, and observing others in action. It is a gradual process, and the more you know about it, the more likely you are to be good at it.

Learn skills like effective speaking, coaching techniques, or meeting management that give you, and others around you, confidence in your leadership capabilities.

Develop your own philosophy of yourself as a leader so that if asked the question "How do you approach leadership?" you can answer it with certainty.

Over the years, I have developed my own ideas about what I feel works for me. It is a combination of my own individual style and personality, which includes natural curiosity about people, combined with absorbing traits of others I have enjoyed being led by. Also, embracing and trying out some thinking and ideas that I have read about or been taught. A mix of trial and error, theory and experience.

Also, I will admit that a rich source of inspiration for me has also been the weak, selfish, toxic, mean, and nasty bosses that I have sometimes come across along the way. You can learn a lot from watching people getting things horribly wrong. You now know what NOT to do.

A key time for me was during my Masters at Oxford SAID/HEC when I really got to understand the "adaptive" approach to leading change (and anything) and felt it made so much sense to me.

As a leader of others, are you more important or special than the people who report to you? Think of a boat cruising through the sea – the prow is "at the front" and parts the waters, and so takes much credit for the progress of the boat with a splendid bow-wave. In reality, it is just one part of a collection of pieces that all need to work together for the boat to function.

Leadership is a role, and an important one, but a leader cannot exist without followers. The real power and energy of an organization is found among the people who make things happen every day. If change is needed, they're the ones who will make it happen...or resist it.

Often, they understand much more than you do about what is happening and what is the best course of action. Ignore them at your peril.

A good leader helps all those people to work better by listening, understanding, and supporting them. Poor leaders can get in the way and make it much harder for people to do their job well.

Think hard about where you fit in, and where, and when you create the most value for others.

The Cruise Ship

A cruise ship is one model for effective leadership, and one in which the leader has a defined role within a complicated organization.

Think of everything that happens on a cruise ship. It is an extraordinarily busy workplace with literally thousands of team members, all with specific tasks to perform to make it all work effectively.

Not only do the crew need to sail the ship safely from port to port, but there are also several thousand other people on board who do nothing useful to help and who need constant attention - the passengers. It is a very intense environment.

It is loaded with individuals who are experts in their particular part of the process. The engineers manage the hi-tech machinery, the navigation team decides on course and destination, the cabin attendants make the beds, the entertainment people rehearse constantly, and someone in the kitchen works on perfecting the breakfast omelets.

Up on the bridge is the captain who sits on top of all those people, responsible for everything. Responsible and accountable for it all working - but not expected to DO any of it, or even ideally to interfere with it.

The key to understanding the captain's role is to realize that it is a specific task like everyone else's with a clearly defined framework and limitations. Yes, to be overall responsible, but also to trust that the system will work and to allow everyone to get on with what they are good at.

Can you imagine how miserable and inefficient the ship would be if the captain felt the need to constantly 'check' that everything was being done properly and no one felt empowered to get on with their own job?

There are established systems and reporting processes that allow the captain to be comfortable that everything is running as it should and to spot problems. It is part of the captain's role to respect and support those systems.

Everyone looks to the captain to tell them where the ship is going next and to be the person they can rely on when needed. Being overall responsible is the captain's individual key task, among all the thousands of others' individual tasks that exist to make the ship run smoothly. If the ship hits a rock, it is the captain's fault, even if they are not even on board at the time.

Due to their great responsibilities, the captain might also believe themselves to be 'superior' to others on the ship and try to interfere directly in the complex running of the ship's routine, showing that they 'know better'.

They may start to speak and order more than they listen. They may override established systems and hierarchies to prove and demonstrate their power. This behavior will quickly create an unhappy and inefficient ship.

The secret of being a great cruise captain is that you know just how much you need to do to allow everyone around you to do their job. And when you are called upon to do yours, you do it well.

Adaptive Leadership

The adaptive approach is based on the premise that most of the solutions to issues or challenges being faced by an organization lie within the people who work in it, who should be encouraged to work together to develop those solutions.

This approach makes a distinction between 'technical' situations and 'adaptive' situations. When the problem to solve is purely technical, it can be handled by the experience of the past, by procedures, and by managers. It will usually be a 'tame' problem. [29]

In the example of the cruise ship, most of what goes on there has been studied and optimized to exhaustive levels. In most situations, a technical leadership style will probably be effective. There will be no great need for analysis of what to do or how to react. Orders will be given, and processes followed.

But what happens if, despite all the experience and the procedures, things just aren't going well on the ship? Passengers are unhappy, staff and crew are demoralized, and clearly change is needed.

You cannot just ask passengers to start being satisfied or order your team to get more engaged. You need to dig in and find out why things are not working and how they can be improved. The best people to help you do that are those directly involved. They will have the answers.

Getting to those ideas and proposals for improvements and change is not a quick or easy process. It involves a lot of listening and creating a 'safe space' for people to express themselves without fear of reprisal.

Ronald Heifetz, Alexander Grashow, and Marty Linsky are considered the preeminent authors on adaptive leadership with their 2009 book *"The Practice of Adaptive Leadership."* Heifetz perhaps is seen as the founding father

---

[29] See page 273 – Three Types of Problems; Critical, Tame, and Wicked

of the ideas in his 1994 book, *"Leadership without Easy Answers."* [30]

The approach outlines six tasks for the leader going about leadership work in this way. [31] You should:

1. Stay on the 'balcony.' Keep a view of the big picture of what is happening, do not get too directly involved or interfere with what the team is doing.

They describe it as being like looking down on a group of people dancing together. Observe who is dancing with whom and what is happening. Only if truly necessary do you go down and dance yourself. Your place is on the balcony observing.

2. Identify the challenge. Work out what the challenge (threat, opportunity, etc.) is that is facing the organization. Your job is to frame it and explain it to others so that they can truly start to work on it together.

3. Regulate stress. Your team must feel truly involved in the problem to be solved and empowered to propose solutions. Your job is to ask questions and get involved in the discussion of options and ideas.

There is a 'productive zone of distress' where people feel motivated to produce solutions but not so stressed as to

---

[30] *Leadership without Easy Answers* by Ronald A Heifetz - Harvard University Press 1994, *The Practice of Adaptive Leadership* by Heifetz, Grashow and Linsky - Harvard Business Press 2009

[31] Adapted from *The Work Of Leadership* by Ronald Heifetz and Donald Laurie HBR Article 2002 (4150)

become exhausted, scared, or blocked. Keep them at it but don't overwhelm them.

4. Maintain discipline. The leader's job is to keep everyone on task, not allowing them to waste energy by blaming each other and to unlock potential solutions, not waste energy on finger-pointing, etc. Do not try to cover up or gloss over disagreement. Expose differences of opinion and push for resolution.

5. 'Give the work back'[32]. Help people to recognize that they have the solutions and allow them to work through their ideas. Do not solve things and make it easy for them by taking unilateral decisions. Make them do the work and let them take both responsibility and credit for it.

6. Protect the voices from below. Take care that more junior people are not ignored or overwhelmed. Allow everyone to get their ideas on the table. Often more junior people have great insights only observable from their perspective.

A challenge faced by bosses wanting to take an adaptive approach is to convince their teams that they do indeed have the answers and can and will be a major part of defining the solution. They are used to having it all done for them.

Heifetz and Laurie say:
"Getting people to assume greater responsibility is not easy. Many lower-level employees are comfortable being told

---

[32] Top 30 # 24, page 311

what to do, and many managers are accustomed to treating employees like machinery that requires control.

Letting people take responsibility in defining and solving problems means that management needs to learn to support rather than control. Workers, for their part, need to learn to take responsibility."

"Exercising leadership from a position of authority in adaptive situations means going against the grain. Rather than fulfilling the expectations for answers, one provides questions. Instead of maintaining norms, one challenges them."[33]

The "traditional" technical leader and the adaptive leader use a different code of engagement with their teams.

You can see how the ideas here create a different role for the leader. It stops being a task of controlling, protecting, and clarifying – and becomes one of challenging, exposing, and questioning.

It pushes responsibility down on people and the organization and demands that everyone gets involved in making things work better or finding solutions.

At its most essential, it is saying that leadership isn't about telling people what to do; it is about creating a situation where every person is enabled to, and wants to, do their very best work.

---

[33] Quoted from *The Work Of Leadership* by Ronald Heifetz and Donald Laurie HBR Article 2002 (4150) page 10

LEADER'S RESPONSIBILITIES	TYPES OF SITUATION	
	TECHNICAL	ADAPTIVE
DIRECTION	PROVIDE SOLUTIONS	ASK QUESTIONS
PROTECTION	SHIELD PEOPLE	LET PEOPLE FEEL PRESSURE
ORIENTATION	CLARIFY ROLES AND RESPONSIBILITIES	CHALLENGE CURRENT ROLES
MANAGING CONFLICT	RESTORE ORDER	EXPOSE CONFLICT OR LET IT EMERGE
SHAPING NORMS	MAINTAIN NORMS	CHALLENGE NORMS

34

---

[34] Chart adapted from Ronald Heifetz - Leadership without Easy Answers (1994) Page 94

Top 30 #24: Don't Do People's Work for Them

It is 6:30 p.m. and you are finishing up some emails, and thinking about going home for the day. There is a knock on your office door.

"Hey boss, got a second? I've almost finished that report you asked for, and I was planning to send it out soon. But of course, I need to get your OK on it before I send it out. I've got a printout here so you can take a look."

"Oh, OK," you reply. *"Er...just leave it on my table."*

"OK boss, good night!"

What just happened?

Your team member just handed you their work. They are now heading off to a bar to meet their friends, happily confident that they have nothing more to worry about tonight.

You, on the other hand, have a long report to read, check, and edit as required. You have taken away all the stress of producing the report from the person accountable for writing it and put it directly onto yourself.

Of course, it's very easy for this to happen as you feel you are responsible for the quality of their work. And it also triggers your ego. You are the boss, so obviously you need to check their work before it gets sent out. Right?

Well, maybe not.

What about if you said, *"Hey, no need for me to check it. I know it will be of first-class quality, and I am looking forward to reading it when you send it out?"*

This leaves all the energy of the situation with your team member. They may not go to the bar after all. The additional pressure you are putting on them also has a strong element of your trust mixed in with it. They will now know that the buck stops with them if there are errors, spelling mistakes, or any other failings in that report.

It is also a higher-risk strategy for you - and one that takes time to establish. You do need to have confidence in your team that they will produce good work - and most importantly, you must be ready to defend them and their work if someone else doesn't like it.

You are still the leader and ultimately responsible. "I didn't read it before it went out" is not an option for you. You will lose everyone's respect if you do that.

Smart leaders will know how much to interfere and support their team during the work process, and you can still have a lot of confidence in that final report without being the final, critical step in the process.

People are constantly (consciously or unconsciously) pushing their work "up" to their bosses, but it works because their bosses allow it to happen. Keep your people engaged, a little stressed, and feeling responsible. Don't do their work for them.

Low Ego Leadership

One reason, perhaps, that the adaptive style of managing and leading people is not better known is that, in essence, it is a low-ego approach to being the boss.

You have worked hard to get to the top, and you feel that your job is to make decisions, hold people accountable, and hopefully be recognized for your work and achievements.

The adaptive approach runs somewhat counterintuitive to this, as it is fundamentally based on the idea of pushing responsibility, decisions, and solutions back down into the organization.

It can feel to the boss that he or she is just asking another question rather than actually doing the real work of being the head honcho.

I decided to truly test it out when I took a new leadership position with a team of 6 or 7 direct reports. In general, I found it to be effective and kept the senior leaders highly attentive, as they could not push their decisions up to me as they had been used to doing.

On occasions, perhaps two leaders would say to me, "We don't agree, so you need to decide what to do." I would respond, "You are both better qualified than me to decide this. Why should I decide? Go away and fix it." And they did.

It is a plank of the approach that conflicts should not be glossed over but actively exposed and resolved. As such, sometimes our meetings went on late into the night…

On occasion, I had to bite my lip when I found I wasn't in full agreement with a decision from the wider team or a team member. I had to follow through and be consistent with the approach.

No leadership methodology will be perfect, but what I learned is that everyone will "push their work up" to their boss if they can get away with it, and if you let them. Traditional leadership styles encourage the boss to make all the decisions and, thus, concentrate power into a single individual.

Adaptive leadership does not diminish the responsibility or authority of the overall leader but actively seeks to lessen the importance to success of that individual by recognizing that the power to solve things truly lies lower in the organization.

The 5% Rule

Great leaders only interfere in the work of their teams 5% of the time. The rest of the time, they allow them to get on with it. Leaders who establish great teams below them can appear to do very little but have enormous success.

The trick is to learn to recognize when it is a '5% moment'.

Your Philosophy

I have only really touched on the ideas of adaptive leadership here. If you'd like to learn more (and there is so much more to learn!), please do look up the articles and books on the subject. It's all easy to find on the internet.

Most importantly, I urge you to develop your own thinking and ideas about what you feel works for YOU as a leader.

Reflections

Here are a few key questions arising from the themes raised in this chapter:

- What kind of leader are you?
- Or do you want to be?
- Have you developed your own philosophy of leadership?
- Where do you think the power of your organization lies?
- Do you let your team give you their work?
- What would happen if you gave it back to them?
- What happens in your team when you go on holiday or are ill?
- Does it still work without you?

Part 3

Leading Business and Change

So far, we've looked at leadership from the perspective of leading yourself, and of the challenges and rewards of leading other people.

Now, let's consider effective business leadership. What makes a good boss, and developing your own philosophy of leadership. In particular, at times of change, or when a specific transformation is needed.

Chapter 14: Everything is Change

We could write a whole book (and there are many thousands already written) about good business practices. I have included a small selection of ideas or items in this chapter that I have found often come up with my clients.

In particular, I think these are likely to be useful if you are starting up a business, or running one that is still quite small, or managing a department or team of people.

In most businesses, there is normally a lot of 'business as usual' - all the stuff that goes on every day: budgets, sales, promotions, office parties, etc. Typically, this is all arranged into departments and teams, and there is a structure and hierarchy that everyone understands (even if you don't love it, you do know how it works).

Modern businesses face such a never-ending cycle of innovation and new challenges that change is never far away. New technologies, new competitors, shifting customer preferences, artificial intelligence, remote working, quiet quitting, shifting government regulations...

They are all lining up to see how they can conspire to make your life more difficult and your business more challenging.

If your structures, processes, and procedures seem satisfactorily established and all working smoothly, I am afraid it almost certainly means you are not looking hard enough at what is about to go wrong.

If managing change requires special skills, then I recommend you start to learn about them, because everything you thought you knew can all suddenly get moved around when you are least expecting it.

Most of the larger companies I have worked for, or more recently worked with as a coach, are in a constant loop of reorganizations and perpetually launching new projects and initiatives.

My proposal is that you treat every day as if you were in the middle of a major change program. Read every book and listen to every podcast on how to manage change effectively.

In essence, much of change management theory is just about making better and brave decisions, setting extremely clear goals, and communicating well and often. What's not to like?

How flexible is your business? How quickly can you adapt? How well do you listen to your customers? How well do you understand what is going on in the marketplace where you operate?

The Boiling Frog

I expect that you have heard of the idea of the boiling frog. Just because it's not a new idea doesn't mean it isn't very relevant still and worth a mention here.

The poor wee froggy is placed in a jar of lukewarm water. It seems fine in there to him; he swims around happily. What can go wrong? Very gradually, the temperature of the water starts to rise, but in such tiny increments that he doesn't notice. He continues to swim and splash unconcerned. He is a very good swimmer. He can handle a bit of warm water. No need for anything drastic.

Suddenly, the water becomes too hot. And it is too late. He is starting to cook; he feels exhausted. His proud swimming prowess built up over his froggy life is suddenly no good, nor is his normally expert jumping good enough to escape from the jar. Confused and panicky, he expires.

He just didn't realize what was happening until it was too late - as he was very confident and not paying attention to his surroundings. He didn't see, or maybe want to see, the increasingly urgent need to change.

The key point of the story for me is that the frog wasn't able to recognize that his environment was becoming hostile. This can, and does, happen in business, and the biggest danger is that we ignore or deny the signs of a threatening change.

I don't mind that the boiling frog story is a well-known metaphor - and that some smart aleck on YouTube has proved that, in the real world, the frog doesn't really get boiled. The essential idea is still important.

When is the best time to ask yourself very seriously how, what, and why things may go wrong? When they are going really well.

Top 30 #25: Analyzing success

"We only learn from our mistakes" and *"Taking risks and learning from our failures is the only way to grow"* are typical modern, or not so modern, business proverbs. And indeed, we usually do learn something important when we get things wrong.

When everything has gone south, most of us are generally very good at picking over the past, seeking moments when we made bad choices and aiming to do better in the future.

But what about when everything is going wonderfully? Sales are booming, the KPIs are all green, and it seems like you can do no wrong. You and your team are very happy with yourselves and certainly don't want to spoil the positive vibe by digging in too much to the details.

You may not know exactly WHY things are going so well, but you don't really care. You do know it is a sign that you are great at what you do, better than your competitors, and generally awesome. The number in the bottom right-hand corner of the spreadsheet is big, and growing - that is what matters.

When we are enjoying success, no one feels much like analyzing it.

When we cycle slightly downhill with the wind behind, we fly along. It's easy to convince ourselves that we are strong and fit. It's only puffing our way back up the hill, on the way home with aching limbs, that we come to terms with reality.

You should be looking very carefully at the reasons for your good performance, and you will be in a much stronger position when an inevitable downturn comes around. If you know exactly where your success is coming from, you may be able to grow it even more - even while it is already growing. You are doing great, but can you do even better?

Success allows weak areas to hide. When the overall business results are strong, it is easy to overlook (by accident or purposefully) parts of your business that are not performing well.

Often, that turning of a blind eye to weak spots is based on your professional relationships and not wanting to create negativity at a time when it isn't strictly necessary. Who wants to talk about cutting costs or resources, or an individual's poor performance when you don't really need to?

Doing a deep dive into your business, your team, your processes, or your cost structures and margins at a time when everything is going well can yield many benefits and unexpected insights.

This is true leadership, as you are expecting your people to show the same level of attention to detail while the sun is shining, as when the storm clouds are gathering. When those clouds do start to gather, you will be very glad you did.

And in the meantime, you will find that by addressing your weaknesses and vulnerabilities at a time of strength, you will just become stronger and even more successful.

Analyze your success while it lasts.

Never Ignore the Context

Just like the poor old frog, you can also get boiled if you allow yourself to ignore the context of wherever you operate and keep track of how it is evolving.

A strong and growing marketplace for whatever you offer can be the greatest and most powerful driver of your growth. Equally, if that market starts to slow or there are new entrants with new innovations, you will have to scramble to remain competitive. Allowing yourself to just ride the wave of market growth can be very risky.

A shifting context has incredible power to create innovation, which may pose a threat to you.

Synthetic Rubber

By the 1930s, the US rubber industry was the largest and most technologically advanced in the world, using up half of the world's supply of natural rubber. Rubber was a key component of many items, not just car tires for the massively expanding US car industry.

For years, scientists had been scratching their heads about how to produce a synthetic alternative to rubber. No real progress had been made, and what was the issue or urgency, really?

The context was that natural rubber was cheap and in plentiful supply. No one was very interested in synthetic rubber, and it was a tiny and largely ignored start-up sector of the wider rubber industry.

Suddenly, in 1942, the USA was at war with Japan. Rubber was a key component of the US war machine. A military plane needed up to half a ton of rubber, a tank consumed a ton, and seventy-five tons were in a warship. Even a foot soldier used 32 pounds of rubber for his boots, clothes, and military equipment. [35]

90% of the natural rubber being used by the US came from Southeast Asia, and suddenly the context had dramatically shifted as Japan totally cut off the supply.

This urgent situation resulted in the creation of a truly impressive transformation program. A team was quickly created of government officials, key scientists, and rubber companies, and working together, they cracked the

---

[35] "United States Synthetic Rubber Program, 1939-1945" commemorative booklet produced by the National Historic Chemical Landmarks program of the American Chemical Society in 1998 (PDF)

previously intractable synthetic rubber problem in no time at all. They reviewed the science, created patents, converted and created new rubber factories across the USA, all in a matter of weeks.

In 1941, the USA produced only 231 tons of synthetic rubber. By 1945, that had risen to 920,000 tons, and there was no longer any need for natural rubber. The industry never looked back after that. Today, the global synthetic rubber market is worth over $31 billion dollars. [36]

Wars and other times of crisis tend to be catalysts for advances in medicine and technology as the urgency of the need for innovation pushes aside the normal barriers to quick decision-making.

Always pay close attention to the wider context of whatever you are doing, as if it changes, even slowly, it can change everything for you.

Do You Have a Plan?

Often I am surprised that leaders of businesses or departments do not have a written plan. I once listened patiently in a coffee shop while a young entrepreneur explained to me all his ideas for his business and how it was going to change the world. His enthusiasm was compelling.

When he finished, I asked him whether he had all that written down. Did he have a plan? Nope. So the only way to

---

[36] Forbes Business Insights - Synthetic Rubber Market Report 2023

understand his ambitions and vision was to book a meeting with him over a coffee.

Having a written plan is helpful in so many ways. It forces you to clarify and simplify your thinking, it gives you a tool to help explain to others, it drives alignment with teams or partners, and it is professional. It can always be changed later if the situation evolves.

Just because no one (your boss, your investors, your co-founders, your colleagues...) has asked you to show them a plan is not a good reason not to make one. You will find the process very useful.

10-Point Basic Business Plan

These are the ten elements that I recommend to build a concise but comprehensive business plan. This can be used for a small business or a startup idea or a plan for a department or team. You might want to interpret some of the elements a bit differently, but the essence will be the same.

Your first step is usually to write down all your ideas in a more detailed Word document and then convert that into a presentation that can be easily shared and presented

1. How we got here: History, timeline of achievements, and important moments in the evolution of the business.

2. The business today: Current status, resources, portfolio, locations, clients, etc.

3. The context - Where do we sit in our marketplace? Who are our competitors? Is the underlying market positive? What is the potential for growth? How big is the prize?

4. High-level strategic vision for the year ahead - explaining the core elements of the plan and its 'big picture' objectives. This is your 'destination'. What you want to achieve.

5. Strategy rationale - Why we are doing this, why it makes sense, how it will benefit us/differentiate us. Be unique. Be powerful for clients.

6. Tactics - specific business objectives and plans to achieve them. Get into detail of the 5 to 10 things you plan to make happen to move the strategy forward in the coming

weeks/months. How we will make the strategy become reality.

7. KPIs and Milestones - what will happen, and what gets measured, by when. Possibly divided into projects in some cases. To measure progress as we go along.

8. Resources and capabilities - a chart showing the existing organization and a second showing how the team is planned to grow, functions to be covered, capacity increased, any partnerships with other companies, etc.

9. Finances - a version of a P&L, or whatever helps to best explain the financial situation/plans of the business. Historic, current, and forecast financial performance. Mention issues such as cost control, compensation approach, bonus plans, plans to seek investment/loan if applicable. For confidentiality, you can also explain the finance situation without using actual numbers - with growth percentages, graphs, etc. There should be a consistent format for tracking and reporting finances/results.

10. Risks - what might slow us down or obstruct our plans? How will we overcome those obstacles? Planning for setbacks in the plan. Scenarios.

A key is to differentiate between the strategy you will follow and the supporting tactics (actions, projects, etc.) that you will employ to realize the strategy.

Strategy Versus Tactics

"Strategy without tactics is the slowest route to victory. Tactics without strategy is the noise before defeat." [37]

It is very important to differentiate between your strategy (why you are doing things, why they will make a difference) and tactics (what you will do, how you will do it, and when).

It is easy to get totally absorbed in the daily activities of your business or responsibilities and to lose sight of the bigger picture. As the leader, you must keep a vigilant eye open to ensure that all your tactical activities are truly aligned with your strategic ambitions. Your strategy is your map that shows you where you need to get to.

Working in the Business, Working on the Business

As a leader of a team, it is very easy to be extremely busy but also to be busy doing the wrong things. It can be satisfying and reassuring to "get your hands dirty" and be highly involved in the daily, tactical activities of your business.

Just as in the critical, tame, wicked model of problem types described in Chapter 12, it can be a lot easier to tackle

---

[37] Sun Tzu, Art of War. 5th century BC

tame and critical problems than wrestle with the frustrating wicked problems that are the real task of leaders.

Many leaders feel they are so busy they just don't have time to think strategically or plan for the future. This is dangerous, as the future is most certainly coming, and if you aren't thinking about it, then who is?

I recommend that busy leaders keep a record of their activities to see how much time they spend actively working in the business, rather than focusing on the business and its wider needs and opportunities.

A good test of this is whether you can take time off, and the essential activities of your business, team, or department continue to work without you. If your teams need you to be there to operate the day-to-day work, then you have a problem. Your goal must be to make yourself redundant from the tactical work so that you can work on the strategy.

Creating the Right Structure

One of the great challenges of any growing team is how to create the right structure to deliver whatever is needed for success.

As per point 8 of the basic business plan, I recommend that you draw out your organization chart and think about how it can or should develop. With one client, I was convinced that his organization was not what he needed. He had no written plans.

I asked him to draw his organization on a whiteboard and then to step back and tell me what he thought about it. It was the easiest coaching session of my life, as I didn't have to say a word. Just the act of writing it up there was enough for him to realize he needed to rethink the structure.

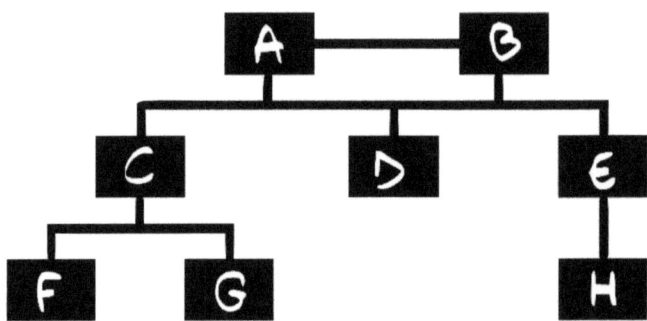

When planning the evolution of your team, first draw the future organization without any names. In each box of the chart, just put the functions/roles that you will need.

Later, you can add in names of your existing team and ask yourself whether they are truly right or ready for the role. I have found that this simple exercise is very powerful and helps you to focus on what you really need, rather than what you currently have.

Top 30 #26: Strategy, Structure, Story

Whenever you are setting out to do something new, remembering these three words can be useful. Many different, and often apparently highly complex, challenges, both big and small, can be clarified by starting out with a bit of simple thinking.

Strategy - This is what you are setting out to achieve. Your desired outcome, your objective. It is what you are aiming to achieve and why.

Structure - The resources, people, and tools you will need to do it. We overcomplicate our challenges by overcomplicating the structures we put in place. Don't start with what you have, but rather focus on what you really need. Keep it simple.

If you have people already on your team, it's tempting to create a new structure around them, building around the individuals you already know.

Instead, start with just the roles, skills, and functions that are essential to achieve the task. Leave the people and their individualities, or relationships with you, out of it. Once you have the structure clear, you can add in the names afterwards.

Story - This is the narrative that you construct around whatever it is you are doing. It should be consistent for all the stakeholders involved: external, internal, investors, commentators, influencers... It must be coherent, engaging, and dynamic. It is what will convince everyone the strategy is achievable with the structure you have put in place.

This approach may seem overly simplistic, but often very straightforward thinking can be helpful, even in a massive complex multimillion project.

So often I have seen organizations getting themselves tied in knots as they wrestle with their existing hierarchies, departments, budgets, corporate history, and people politics.

If you find yourself leading a team in a situation like that - blank it all out and ask what is the "strategy, structure, and story" you need to succeed.

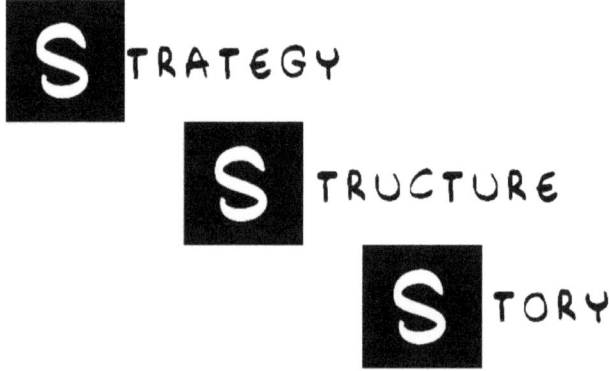

Keep It Simple

Running a business and leading people is challenging, frustrating, and exhausting. Just about anything that can go wrong will go wrong. Every founder of a successful business has their stories of terrible mistakes they made or the dark days when they nearly gave it all up.

My observation is that the most effective and successful business leaders are the ones that keep things as simple as possible.

SIMPLE = BEST

Here are five basic ideas of what I mean by this:

1. Have Your Story Clear and Aligned: Whatever you are doing, you will have a history of how you got here, what you are doing now, and an ambition for where you want to get to.

Make sure you can describe all these elements very comfortably. If you are working in a team or have colleagues (like co-founders or peers), make sure that everyone is in agreement with this storyline.

2. Use Simple Language: It's all too easy to get into the habit of using jargon, corporate-speak, or acronyms in your everyday communication. This doesn't impress anyone but it does confuse people. Use plain language that is easy to understand and self-explanatory.

3. Watch Out for Analysis Paralysis: We all want to make good decisions and, of course, want to back them up with sound data. Sometimes you can have too much data and be too slow to make a decision through a fear of getting it wrong.

Not knowing the answer is a big part of leading a business or project, and you will need to listen to your instincts at times. In a 2020 study of over 200 executives, 99% said they felt their bosses suffered from some level of analysis paralysis, and were slow to make decisions because of it.[38]

4. Know Why You are Doing What You Are Doing: When someone is explaining their incredible new business idea to me, I always ask them the same two questions:

- **What problem are you solving?**
- **How will you make money out of it?**

Usually, I find leaders are good at answering the first question (although not nearly succinctly enough) and vague about the second question. Aim to pare down your thinking

---

[38] EMC Leader Report 2020 (https://www.emcresearch.com)

to the essential bones of what you are trying to do. Stay focused on the vital stuff.

5. Never Stop Simplifying: As your business, project, or department grows in size or importance, it will also grow in complexity. As a leader, it is easy to get caught up in all that, and as a result, you can lose focus on what truly matters.

If people bring you a 35-page deck full of numbers and graphs, ask them to distill it down to 3 or 4 and to clarify the key questions or decisions that need to be made.

Very often in business leadership, the core questions to be solved are actually very simple (not easy), and we do not help ourselves by overcomplicating them and overwhelming ourselves with data and detail.

Change ...or a Transformation?

Change is happening all the time, whether we like it or not. How well you manage it and adapt to it is probably intrinsically correlated with how successful you are likely to be.

We respond to change and we change things as we go along. It is often an almost imperceptible process of evolution.

Sometimes we have a very clear vision of a change that needs to happen. It is not just going to happen on its own. It needs a plan and a lot of effort. There are going to be obstacles and possibly resistance from people who feel that the proposed change is not good for them.

Deliberate, organized change with a defined objective. A transformation.

Reflections

Here are a few key questions arising from the themes raised in this chapter:

- What do you do to stay aware of the evolving context around you?
- When things go well, how closely do you analyze why?
- Do you have a written plan?
- How much time do you spend on tactics versus strategy?
- Is your structure fully supporting your ambitions?
- Can you "tell the story" of what you are doing?
- Do you feel that you overcomplicate things?
- How could you make things simpler?

Chapter 15: You Want, or Need, to Transform…So Where Are You Going?

"The best way to predict the future is to create it" [39]

Being a good leader is hard enough in any situation. When you find yourself in charge of a specific "change process," it gets even harder.

Most of us dislike change, especially if it is being forced upon us by someone else or by a circumstance beyond our control.

"I don't mind change, but I don't like being changed."

As I have said, I believe that most modern businesses are typically in a constant state of change. New technology and market forces bring about significant day-to-day challenges in how to make or keep them successful. So just being a business leader means you must also be a good leader of change.

Sometimes we realize that we have to accept that a very specific change is required. This may be personal, in which case you need to lead yourself through it. It may be a business or organizational challenge that must be achieved to stay relevant, competitive, profitable…whatever it may be. You know that how you do things now just isn't going to work in the future. So, change is a necessity.

---

[39] Peter Drucker (1909 - 2005) Educator, author and leadership visionary

Currently, there is a massive and ever-evolving shift towards the digitalization of businesses. According to research by Gartner, [40] the consulting group, the worldwide expenditure by companies on radical digital transformations will reach $3.4 trillion by 2026.

91% of companies are engaged in a digital rethink of their business, and 87% of leaders say that digital transformation is a priority. That's an awful lot of major radical change going on.

It is often the case that some things need to change significantly to tackle a new opportunity or threat, while others need to be kept the same to keep existing revenues flowing. When the same people must do both of those things at once, it is especially challenging.

Just recognizing that change is needed is difficult in itself.

Recognizing the Need for Change - The 'Why' Question?

A good starting point for thinking about the need for change is to ask yourself, "why" do you do certain things. Sometimes we just get stuck in a rut, doing the same things year after year, and we have to step back and question more deeply, not just "what" we do or "how" we do it, but "why" we do it.

---

[40] Gartner research results quoted by quixy.com "90+ Digital Transformation Statistics and Trends To Help You Navigate it in 2024"

The business leadership pioneer Chris Argyris (1923-2013) carried out groundbreaking thinking and study in the 1970s and published a highly regarded book about individual and organizational learning, and the extent to which human reasoning influences behavior and action. [41]

He described "single-loop" and "double-loop" thinking. The single loop relies on established decision-making rules, while the double loop challenges those rules, and potentially modifies them in the light of experience. Double-loop thinking brings about real change.

Double-loop thinking recognizes that the way a problem is defined and solved can itself be a source of the problem. Double-loop thinking will drive creativity and innovation, going beyond just adapting to change, but rather anticipating or being ahead of that change. The single loop

[41] *Reasons and Rationalizations - The limits to Organizational Knowledge* by Chris Argyris published by Oxford University Press 2004

identifies the goal, and then the double loop questions that goal.

Single-loop learning asks, *"This is what we do. How can we do it better?"* while the double loop asks, *"Why do we do this? Should we do something else?"*

Single-loop thinking is based on established, accepted, safe--and sometimes entrenched or defensive--ways of thinking or acting. *"We've always done it like this..."* The second loop challenges that accepted thinking.

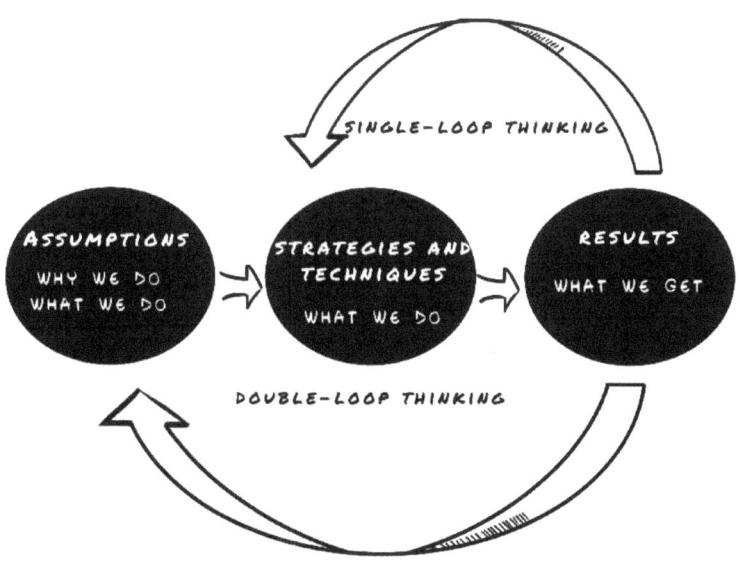

The double loop is the "why?" question. Often the hardest to answer but also the most powerful. If we don't know why we do something, we probably shouldn't be doing it.

More recently, inspirational speaker and author Simon Sinek has further championed a focus on "why" we do things - his most famous book being *"Start with Why."* He argues that really successful leaders and businesses understand and communicate why they do things, not just what or how they do it. [42] As such, they are more compelling for both employees and customers.

Individuals and organizations consciously or subconsciously may resist double-loop thinking, as it exposes ideas, doubts, questions, thoughts, and feelings about established practices that make you uncomfortable and vulnerable to the reaction of others.

It can be invaluable to think in this way as you set out to create a vision for change or transformation.

When you consciously set out to change something specific, you can justifiably call that a "transformation" project. Most transformations in the business world like mergers, acquisitions, and digital transformations seem to fail. In various studies, it was found that 85% of digital transformation processes and 70% of mergers did not deliver the value that had been expected.

Transformation projects are hard. Very hard.

---

[42] Start with Why - by Simon Senik published in 2009 by Penguin Books

The Journey, and the Destination

When you, as an individual or perhaps you and your team, come to the realization that you need to engage in a process of real transformation, the first step is to be clear about where you are hoping to get to. That is not to say that you don't need to think very hard about the best way to get there as well; both are very important.

Ralph Waldo Emerson (1802-1883), the American philosopher and poet, is credited with saying, *"Life is a journey, not a destination."* And the Greek poet Homer said, *"The journey is the thing,"* right back in the 8th century BC. We've been thinking about this stuff for a long time.

On the other hand, also a couple of thousand years ago, it was Lucius Annaeus Seneca (4 BC - 65 AD), the Roman philosopher and statesman, who wagged a warning finger while he declaimed, *"If you don't know to which port you are sailing, no wind is favorable."*

I think all of them are right in their own way, and that you must have a good sense of where you are going and also aim to get the absolute best from the journey.

Getting the most out of the learning and experience as you gradually move forward will bring you satisfaction, confidence, and the energy to continue. When you arrive at one destination, you will probably already be thinking about where you are going next.

You Are Definitely Going Somewhere

None of us knows exactly where we will end up or how our business will look in the future. Even our most carefully laid plans often do not work out as we expect. Setbacks, surprises, and even new opportunities force us to adjust.

Along the stages of our life, most of us set goals or ambitions that give us a sense of direction and purpose and hopefully move us forward in some way.

If you don't have any idea where you think you are going, how do you even know when you have arrived? If you don't pay attention, you may end up somewhere that you'd rather not be.

One chilly Italian October night, after a long day of meetings in Milan, Italy, I had been waiting some time at the airport to board my very delayed plane back to Madrid. Finally, the flight was called. I went wearily to the gate, climbed aboard a bus, and then up the stairs onto the plane.

I went to my seat, 12D, only to find someone sitting in it. I pointed out confidently (and I hope quite politely) to this person that they were in my seat. To my great surprise, they then produced their own 12D boarding card. The air hostess came over to see what was happening.

It turned out I was on the plane about to take off for Barcelona, not Madrid. If, by chance, the seat with my number on it had been empty, I would almost certainly have spent the night in a hurriedly-booked hotel in Barcelona, not in my bed at home. Everyone then seemed to become very cross with me, and eventually, after a lot of fuss, I was transferred on a bus to the correct plane.

It was an unnerving experience to realize how close I had been to ending up somewhere totally different from where I was confidently expecting to be. I thought I had done everything right – but I had somehow missed important signs. As much as I tried to convince myself that someone else was to blame for what happened, the truth is that it was my fault.

I've noticed that many people and businesses, especially smaller ones or departments of larger ones, and even sometimes big ones, are often surprisingly unsure about exactly where they are going. And that is despite often appearing outwardly to be successful, well-functioning, and busy every day. They also sometimes get on the wrong bus. They too are missing signs and signals.

It is said that athletes who win a gold medal at the Olympics all have something in common. That they can truly imagine themselves on the podium having that medal hung around their neck. They believe that they can do it. They can see themselves up there.

These people have the clearest sense of their direction. Tangible and measurable for themselves and all to see.

The hours and hours of training and dedication are probably only possible thanks to that clarity of vision and the narrow focus of the chosen goal - the podium and the medal. Could an athlete maintain the discipline and rigor of that training program if it were just to 'get fit'?

The journey is all the work they have to do to be competitive, and their destination is to hang that medal around their neck.

Athletes do not win medals on their own; without exception, they have a coach. Probably several coaches, and a support team. Sportspeople have known for decades what the rest of us seem to have only realized more recently – having a coach is really useful if you want to get something done, or improve at something, or change something.

Most of us aren't Olympic athletes, and our goals and ambitions may seem more mundane in comparison. But that doesn't make them less important for us or any easier to achieve.

Life is indeed a journey, and the achievement of goals along the way can bring us a great deal of satisfaction. With a bit of thinking about your destination, or a series of destinations, the journey will be more fruitful and enjoyable.

We all have experiences, make mistakes, observations, and discoveries on our personal and professional journeys. Often a bit of common sense is our very best traveling companion.

Where do YOU want to go? Or want your business to go?

If you are embarking on a genuine personal, organizational, or business transformation, then it really is critical to have your ideas very clear before you begin. Often it is also not even an option just to keep things as they are.

As my favorite saying about change goes, *"If you don't change direction, you might end up where you are going."*

By really focusing on your future, you can improve it. As with any journey, a map of where you want to go, and what you may meet along the way, can be very helpful. I call that map the A to B model.

Your A to B Vision

Regardless of the details of what business you are in, or what you do every day, my transformation coaching work always starts with the same exercise: to first work out where you think you are now (A), and then to imagine where you would like to be at some point in the future (B).

This A to B can present itself in many different forms. A might be today, and B is ten minutes after a really important presentation you have tomorrow. You want it to be a big success, and you need to work on a range of things to do yourself justice. Defining what you are trying to achieve at this moment, and how to measure that, can be as simple as working on how to make an important presentation really impactful.

Or your A to B can be much more complex, long-term, and existential. In six months, you want to be in a different job, or to get promoted, move to a new company, or to become much better at something that currently you feel you are bad at. Maybe you want to completely rethink your life.

Or maybe you need to make changes to your organization, your top team...and that means hard conversations with people who you like. They've contributed years of good work, but you just don't need them anymore in your direct report group. Those are tough decisions and mean unpleasant tasks - and you will need all your resolve to do it.

If you are very clear about what, how, and why you need to change things, it helps you enormously to stay the course and do what needs to be done.

Imagine yourself fast-forwarded by six months. When you look back, what will be different? What will you have changed or achieved?

Without at least an idea of a basic A to B plan to make specific things happen, it is likely that not very much will change at all. And perhaps you are fine with that - it is your choice. Nobody can force you to be a driver of change, to be a great leader, or a respected manager.

You want to be able to look back from whenever or whatever 'B' may be, and say "I did it" - or at least "I have made significant progress, "and I am ready to redefine and create a new, adjusted "B."

Identifying Your 'A' State - Step 1

The first step before going anywhere is to identify where you are now - your "A state." This can be surprisingly difficult at times. To make a plan to go forward on a journey in a new direction, you need to be realistic and honest with yourself about where you are starting from.

You may be pessimistic about the current state of things, or more optimistic, perhaps even unrealistic. You may think nothing much needs to change, but others you work with may see you and the situation quite differently from how you see it yourself.

You need some clarity on where you feel you are now before trying to make any plans to go forward. Creating and agreeing that starting point is the first step in the coaching and transformation process. It just isn't a good idea to rush ahead and discuss how the future should ideally look before being comfortable and honest about how things are today, and why.

At a personal level, there can be misunderstandings or even self-delusion about your A state. For an individual, an HR department or a boss may provide your coach with a briefing. This may include assessments and reviews from other bosses and colleagues.

You need to know if your perception of yourself matches how others see you. It's a test of your me-pathy. If not, it's important to make sure you understand their perception before trying to advance.

Sometimes that briefing includes opinions about how you should change. That means someone else is trying to define your A to B. It's important that you take on board what they think about you, and why, and decide if you willingly accept the challenge of trying to get to the B state they have suggested.

Someone else may be prompting you to make changes, but it is still *your* journey and your new direction. And if you don't want to do it, or don't see the need, or believe you can change, you won't.

People who have issues with alcohol or drugs are often urged by others to give it up. That is achievable, and while the encouragement of others will certainly help, only if the individual decides for themselves to kick the habit will it happen. Real personal change comes from within and looks for outside help.

Top 30 #27: Imagining the Future

Find a quiet place. Sit down, get comfortable, and close your eyes.

Can you imagine yourself in 30 years from now? What are you like? Are you a better or disappointing version of yourself? Are you feeling satisfied and enjoying a sense of achievement? Have you turned out to be the person who you dreamed of being? Or are you just the same as now, but older? How does imagining your future self make you feel about who you are today?

Perhaps it is not such a personal exercise, and the task is to paint a future picture of a business or organizational situation that is different from today.

This exercise of imagination may seem trivial, but it is at the very heart of the A-B model and so achieving change or transformation in your life or business. If you can imagine it, you can do it.

Shorten the timelines on the exercise to a few months or weeks from now. You have a list of things, professional or personal, that you want or need to achieve. Fast forward to that point and what do you see when you look back to today? What has changed? What did you get done? What didn't happen as you hoped? What got in the way? What did you learn?

When you consider your objectives, do you honestly believe you can achieve them? Do you maybe feel you could achieve them, but realistically probably won't? If so, why not?

What is the difference between your success or failure?

The A-B model has five vital elements to consider in order to make real progress with your ambitions and make genuine changes or take relevant actions to achieve them.

1. Being very clear about where you are now, where you are starting out from (A). Don't try to start imagining B before you are comfortable and honest with yourself about your starting point - your A.

2. Your vision for what will be different in the future with the relevant milestones, timings, and measurements of success (B).

3. What is your plan to get from A to B? What resources do you need? Who do you need to support you? Will you need specialist skills or help? How long will it take? How much money will it cost?

4. What can go wrong? An intentional focus on the obstacles that you may face and the plans you have to mitigate them.

5. How will you communicate your plan and progress? To yourself and to your stakeholders, or people you need to support you or go on the journey with you. Who needs to support you to ensure success, and how will you keep them well informed?

The A-B model can help you convert your vision for the future into reality.

To lead a team forward or just lead yourself, you need to be able to imagine your own future, want it, and believe in it.

Alignment of Teams

Agreeing that A state is even more challenging for groups of people or teams. Some may feel that much needs to change, others not so much. People may be protecting their power base, department, or people, and may not be fully honest about what they believe or recommend.

To effectively lead a transformation, you and all your team must be aligned behind the "why" of the changes on the table and united about the desired outcome in the future.

"Going along with it" will never work. If you are a leader of change, the most negative situation you can face is if everyone around is telling you they support you and your new ideas when, in fact, they are not being honest—maybe to please you or to distract or confuse you. That lack of alignment will undermine you and the transformation.

If you are leading (or part of) a team that is setting out to better manage, change, or develop something new together, then you must get to alignment. Does everyone agree on where we are now? Where to go? What to change? Don't attempt to set off for B before you all agree on your A.

A creative exercise can be used to demonstrate leadership alignment. I worked with a group of six partners at a law firm that had recently been formed by merging two smaller firms. I handed out sheets of paper and asked the partners each to draw a picture of the firm today. There was plenty of backchat and jokes about lawyers being bad at art, etc., but eventually, we had six drawings.

I asked each of them to present their drawing to the group. Each person had a totally unique way of trying to describe what they were all doing every day.

I then asked them all to draw another picture or to change their current one to show how things would ideally be in three years from now. Total chaos. No alignment at all.

How could they hope to lead 200 staff forward to a successful merger and a better business when they could not even agree on the basics of what they do now or why they do it? And even less about what they wanted for the future?

The "A" State SWOT

An effective way to demonstrate alignment, or lack of alignment, among a team is to co-create a good old-fashioned SWOT[43] together, describing the current status.

If you can reach genuine agreement over these fundamental elements of whatever situation you are facing, then you are pretty aligned. I have found that in strategy meetings, rarely is enough time allocated to create the "A" state SWOT as opinions on the future plan run hot and discussions quickly develop - as they should.

Leave enough time to get to an agreed output on where you are now before you start to tackle the future.

Differences of opinion are important and should be exposed and properly discussed - and ideally resolved. If you shut them down and try to move on without resolution, they

---

[43] SWOT = Strengths, Weaknesses, Opportunities, Threats

will resurface later and significantly impede, and possibly derail, your transformation plan.

The essential point here is that it is a mistake to set out to try to make changes before knowing where you are starting out from. Once we are feeling confident about the "A" state, you can begin to work on the exciting part - your new direction, where you want to go, what you want to change, and the "B" state you aspire to achieve.

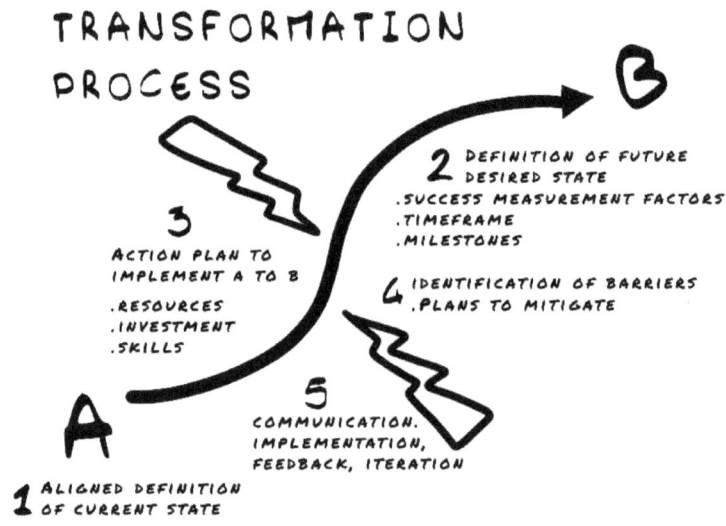

Imagining Your "B" State - Step 2

With a good sense of where you are now, you can begin to work on how you would like things to look in the future. You decide what you want to change, and by when. Of course, this may be a very complex analysis or relatively simple if you are already very clear about your ambitions.

Essentially, the basic model is the same for a large company or organization as it is for an individual - what will differ is the complexity of the plan and all the elements impacted. (See Figure 1 above).

It's just the same for a business challenge, but thinking of it from your individual perspective, imagine yourself transported to a future point in time. Looking back to today, in your mind, what has changed? What has stayed the same? In what way have you successfully transformed yourself?

You will construct a detailed picture of your own transformation and how you will know when you have achieved it. It is your vision for the future.

You need to work out your realistic timeframe, your success measurement criteria, and what the milestones will look like along the way for you to know you are making progress.

Let's use an analogy. Your A state is that you are sitting at your desk, hard at work in your home office. You haven't had a vacation in far too long, and you have a headache.

Your B state is that you are able to imagine that you are on a white-sand beach on a beautiful tropical island. There is a warm breeze, somebody is bringing you a delicious cocktail from the luxury hotel that you are staying at for a few days. Your phone is turned off.

Defining your desired B state will no doubt be more difficult than this - but in essence, this is the easy part. What do you want to be different then compared with now? What does the outcome look like?

In six months, *"I will speak Spanish. Profits will double. Costs will be reduced by 20%. I will have a new marketing manager in place. I will be divorced. I will be promoted to Partner."*

Setting these well-defined, time-bound ambitions is the first step in the transformation process. They should be as precise as possible. Goals such as 'make some improvements' or 'reduce costs' will not be effective because they are not concrete enough to drive towards, and are not supported by defined success criteria.

"Take a holiday" is not precise enough to work with. It might mean skiing, sightseeing in Paris, or camping in the local woods.

Creating Your Transformation Plan - Step 3

Once you have that essential vision of what success looks like, you need a plan to make it happen. Returning to the analogy – you need to identify the island you want to go to, the hotel you will stay at, how you will get there, how long you will stay for, check if you can take the time off, and ensure that you have the funds to pay for the trip. And then reserve it.

Without the necessary level of detail, you aren't ever going to get out of your office. Your ambition will remain an idea rather than an achievable goal.

What are the actions, decisions, resources, investments, or skills that you will need to create the transformation that you want to make happen?

Identifying those measurable milestones is key to success. Your transformation is a process and will take time. Having a measured sense of progress will encourage you to keep going to your goal and warn you if you are falling behind.

The more detailed your plan, the more likely it is that you will succeed. A transformation coach can help you build that plan, challenge you to stretch yourself, and point out if you are being unrealistic or over-ambitious. It should all be written down, and you should be able to explain it easily to anyone who is involved in making it happen.

If this is a plan for a team or a business, then many people will need to contribute to it, and once again alignment and genuine engagement with the future vision are key. The essential principles for all transformation plans, whether big or small, individual or organizational, are the same.

Identifying Obstacles That May Get in the Way - Step 4

As part of your planning process for getting from A to B, it is vital to specifically identify and hopefully prepare to mitigate, what can go wrong. Overly optimistic ambitions and plans are very likely to fail.

Spend time thinking honestly about the barriers you will face and how to tackle them.

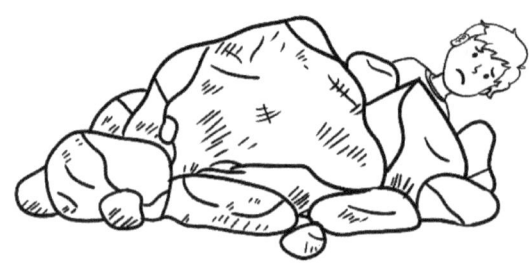

As mentioned, in major corporate transformation projects, it is known that most of them fail to deliver the expected value identified at the start.

Usually, this is because potential obstacles are ignored or underestimated as everyone is caught up in the enthusiasm of how great everything is going to be. Also, it has been shown that it is often the less tangible "soft" human factors that get in the way of achieving the numbers in the plan.

We underestimate "feelings" and "emotional factors". Whether it be the challenges of merging two teams or finding the personal motivation and time needed to effect an ambitious transformation.

According to a 2020 study of all the people who sign up for a new gym membership in a typical new year rush of enthusiasm, nearly 50% have canceled it by February. Less than 20% are still going to the gym in October[44]. Everybody absolutely wants to get fitter, slimmer, etc., but there are many barriers to doing so.

You need to be realistic and realize that achieving real transformation is very hard for companies, teams, and individuals. It's important to be realistic as well as ambitious and to create an A to B plan that has a real chance of success.

Socializing, Communicating, Managing Implementation, Tracking...and Feedback - Step 5

The final element of the A to B model is the communication part. Perhaps this is the most important part of all. In business transformation projects, there is a tendency for there to be a lot of upfront enthusiastic communication work from leaders that all too quickly dies away. Similar to that short-term enthusiasm to go to the gym.

---

[44] 2020 study by Elsevier 'Psychology of Sport and Culture' - https://www.sciencedirect.com/science/article/pii/S14690292203027 9X

Transformations take many months - how will you keep everyone informed, enthused, and on-target?

There is a lot to consider to effectively take everyone with you on a business transformation journey. And, of course, you will have to adjust as you go along. Sometimes your transformation plan will evolve into a collection of smaller iterating transformations, or some unexpected development will mean a complete rethink.

You may arrive at your beautiful desert island only to discover that there is a plague of malodorous seaweed that is clogging up the beach and making a day splashing in the surf totally out of the question. Your swimming plans will have to change. I know this can happen because it has happened to me.

Even as an individual, it is essential to communicate and socialize your "B" target. It can be important to share your ambitions with colleagues, friends, or family.

If you really want to achieve something, then stating those intentions clearly to others brings you the pressure, and creates the expectation, that may be the difference between success and disappointment. In the next chapter, we will look at communication in a change process in more detail.

Transformation Work is Different and Needs Special Focus

You have your A-to-B plan. You have created your vision for the future and have some idea of the journey ahead. Now you need to execute it. This is the hard part. As Napoleon is supposed to have said to his officers:

"Strategy is easy – execution is the hard part."

Reflections

Here are a few key questions arising from the themes raised in this chapter:

- Do you regularly work to optimize how and what you/your team do?
- And do you also ask 'why' do I/we do it?
- Can you imagine your future?
- Do you like what you see ahead of you?
- Do you want or need to change something?
- Do you have a plan for how to change it?
- What is stopping you from making those changes?

Chapter 16: Executing a Transformation

Making Time, and Room, for Transformation

To bring about a genuine transformation, you will have to do things differently. You cannot treat it as just another project.

The biggest enemy of transformation work is whatever it is you currently do every day. You are already extremely busy, and it really is a significant challenge to find the time to tackle new ideas and projects - even if you know they are good ones, or maybe even vitally necessary.

"If you want something new, you have to stop doing something old"[45]

Your transformation work needs to be carved out and focused on in a different way from your everyday stuff. This is true whether you are embarking on an individual, personal transformation or a massive corporate one.

In large organizations, special transformation teams will need to be set up and must work together in a specific way separate from their normal everyday jobs.

Transformation work often threatens people's existing power base or familiar routine. Your plan to change is much more likely to fail than it is to succeed. So it needs special attention.

---

[45] Peter Drucker (1909 - 2005) Educator, author and leadership visionary

In addition to focus, effort, and a detailed plan, every transformation needs a leader. If you are that leader, you must show total commitment to the transformation plan.

Many people on your team may be lukewarm at best about what is being proposed, and if they sense you have doubts, they will exploit those. A transformation project can be easily undermined.

A strategic transformation cannot march to the tune of all the tactical issues and priorities that must still be addressed on a day-to-day basis.

Dedicated Transformation Teams

You and your people probably have more work than you can handle just trying to manage the "business-as-usual," but these are usually the same people who (at the same time) will somehow also have to deliver a transformation.

Normally, your work may be divided up and handled by specialist departments or teams (marketing, sales, etc.), but even if the transformation is sales or marketing-related, these are not the best people to take it on. It will just become another project among many others.

To create the right team for a transformation, you must look beyond the traditional corporate structures and select the best individuals on merit for their potential to bring about the change.

The transformation team may end up being a haphazard gathering of people with cross-functional experience from different departments (product, legal, marketing, operations, etc.) that collectively can focus on the specific problem.

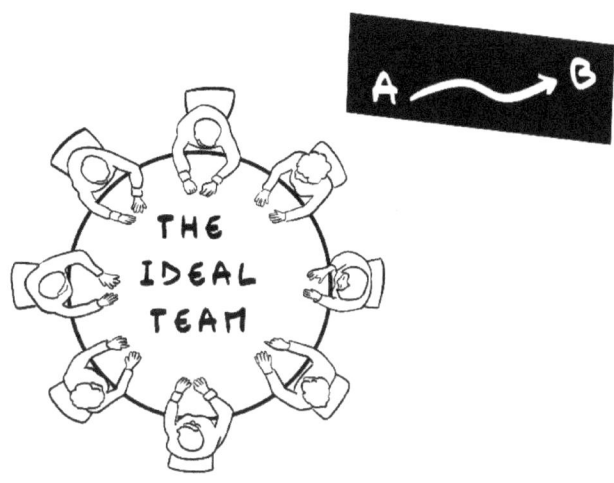

You will need to create the space for these people to work together outside of their normal jobs. This may create issues with their normal line managers, who may not even like the sound of the transformation project, which may threaten them in some way.

Some transformations are complicated and multi-faceted and may need several of these transformation groups (or streams) to be created to deliver different aspects of the transformation.

Each group will need an accountable leader. That person is responsible for delivering against the agreed milestones and outcomes.

Keep That Outcome Focus

Transformation streams must stay focused on the outcomes needed to move the transformation forward. The way to measure progress is to closely track whether outcomes are truly being achieved. To eventually reach your destination, you must be honest and clear about reaching the necessary milestones along the way.

As the overall leader of the transformation, you will need to establish a cadence of regular reporting with the individual stream leaders to track whether the streams are making the required progress. Usually, this means weekly meetings. In a transformation, it is vital to maintain the energy levels of everyone involved to achieve real change.

For this reason, transformation programs need to have an end date by which you plan to reach B. They cannot be open-ended or they risk becoming a version of business-as-usual.

Transformations signify special, intense work by one-off teams brought together over a planned period of time to achieve a specific outcome. Transformations need an end date to work towards.

The Transformation Officer and Office

Companies that are serious about transformation may create a "transformation office." This leads the transformation process, starting with the overall transformation design.

It will manage the many distinct initiatives, identifying the desired outcomes, and will be no-nonsense, data-driven, and focused on value.

It is important to clearly explain the mission of the office to everyone, highlighting the reporting structure (which should be direct to the most senior executive/CEO), and define the competencies, roles, and responsibilities of the transformation office leader and team.

The appointment of a specific transformation officer is a strong sign to everyone that you mean business and that the transformation is a real thing. You can appoint any senior leader to this role who is respected, knows the business well, and has a lot of energy and enthusiasm for the transformation. He or she literally embodies the ambition to change.

The transformation office pushes for outcomes and results through standardized, regular, action-oriented meetings. Attendees include the accountable leader of each workstream, plus usually an appointed representative from finance to keep track of the numbers. The agenda is strict and action items are rigorously tracked.

The best transformation meetings are not like the usual leadership meetings with presentations, debates, and discussions. They are rapid and focused sessions led by the transformation officer and designed to create action and remove obstacles.

The transformation office needs a mandate from the CEO to challenge upwards as well as downward; even the

CEO must get things done on time to make sure the transformation keeps on track.

The transformation office becomes the "single source of truth" and is critical to the creation of a transformation culture in the organization.

Most Transformations Fail

The harsh reality is that transformations fail much more often than they succeed. According to the Harvard Business Review, if you define success as meeting or exceeding the expectations originally defined, then as few as one out of every eight transformations will be considered a success.

Research by Bain & Company consultants among 300 companies shows that between 2013 and 2023, gradually fewer transformations failed completely, but the number that truly succeeded is stuck obstinately at 12%, and that rate remained constant over the ten-year study. [46]

Of the CEOs that were interviewed by HBR, more than half said that their companies had at least two major change projects underway. So, there is plenty of it going on, but creating real change is really hard, and despite more practice at it, we still fail over and over.

There can be many reasons for that. I like a list proposed by John Kotter, the leadership guru and Harvard

---

[46]Transformations That Work - Lessons from companies that are defying the odds by Michael Mankins and Patrick Litre HBR Magazine (May–June 2024)

Business School professor, in a now quite ancient 1995 HBR article. [47]

Kotter lists eight errors that organizations make that lead to the failure of their transformation efforts.

1. Not creating a strong enough sense of urgency. Kotter suggests that more than half of transformation programs never get past this stage. There needs to be brutal honesty about the need for change and the consequences of staying the same. To shift people out of their comfort zones, they have to feel that the only way forward is to embrace change.

---

[47] Source: adapted from John P Kotter HBR article "Leading Change: Why Transformation Efforts Fail" 1995

2. Not creating a strong enough "guiding coalition." Kotter describes the critical group of senior leaders who inspire the need for change and, for example, the creation of a transformation office. If these people are not fully committed, failure will result.

3. A weak or confusing vision. The "B" state you are aiming for must be clearly defined, accepted, and understood by everyone involved.

4. Not removing obstacles that hinder change. This may be individuals who are working against the changes that they don't like or established processes or ideas that make change more difficult. You have to be strong. These are the "obstacles that may get in the way" identified in step 4 of the A to B model.

5. Not planning for short-term wins. Change can be exhausting and take a long time, perhaps years, to truly come about. People need to see progress on the journey and to celebrate that. They can easily become exhausted and disillusioned.

6. Announcing victory too soon. It will be tempting to declare a transformation over, and a success. If you do that before it is really the case, you risk catastrophically undermining the whole project.

7. Not anchoring the change in the corporate culture. It is important that everyone can see that certain behaviors or individuals are rewarded and valued as the transformation starts to give results. It's no good leaving old systems and values in place if they are not consistent with the change.

8. Under-communicating by a factor of ten. Most leaders simply do not put enough effort into communication of the vision for change, the progress being made, or publicly recognizing people who are making important contributions.

The Human Factor, Communicating a Transformation

Over and over again, a transformation plan that looks great on paper fails to deliver due to an underestimation of the "human factor" and how much encouragement, support, and communication people really need.

You will need to rethink how and what you communicate, and how often. You and your team are going into a metaphorical battle to get this change done, and what works for "every day" won't be good enough for the transformation.

Clear for Action

On a wooden sailing warship 200 years ago, wooden walls (called bulkheads) separated the living quarters, cabins, sick bay, cooking areas, etc. Below decks, the ship was a warren of dark, confined, and crowded spaces.

The crew ate, slept, and socialized in all these spaces, which they made as comfortable as possible, and they developed close-knit relationships with those nearest to them. Factions developed.

But the ship was a weapon of war, and when there was a battle, everything changed. The ship was "cleared for action."

The ship's carpenters used wooden mallets to smash down the bulkhead walls, removing all the partitions and cabins and throwing them down into the hold. The whole process could be done in less than 10 minutes, and one can imagine the noise and disruption.

This meant that across the gun deck, suddenly everyone could see each other and communicate effectively, as they worked together to fire the guns in coordination.

The officers in charge could be seen and heard by everyone as they shouted orders. In that moment of crisis, the normal organization and structure weren't fit for purpose, and barriers had to be (literally) broken down for things to work effectively.

When a major change is needed in an organization, the situation is similar. The comfortable departmental silos and teams of marketing, sales, or product development that may have worked for years need to be replaced by task-focused cross-team groups.

Leaders need to communicate with each other, and to the wider organization, in a totally aligned and straightforward way. Every employee needs to know their task, and divisions must be broken down so everyone can see exactly what is happening.

When you sail into the battle of radical change - to succeed, you must take out your metaphorical mallet, smash down barriers, and "clear for action."

Top 30 #28: Advocates and Detractors

The world of humans is made up of bell curves. In any given situation involving people, there will always be a bell curve lurking.

Take soccer players, for example: there are very good ones, very bad ones, and most people in the middle who are neither very good nor very bad at soccer. This applies to everything you can think of: salespeople, jugglers, cooks, drivers, dancers, or marathon runners.

When it comes to a situation where people are being asked to change, to accept something new and put the old way of doing it in the past, there is another bell curve at play.

At one end of the scale, you have the true "advocates" of the change that is required or proposed. These people can see all the advantages of going about things in a new way and are vocally supportive. Often, as a change leader, you will ask them to become "change champions" to actively promote the new ideas or processes to others.

You do that because a key task of the change leader is to move the vast majority of the people who are to be found in the middle of the bell curve towards the advocate end.

Those people in the middle are watching. They want to see whether the advocates of this new way of working are going to win. If they can see that they are, they will gradually become advocates themselves, albeit cautiously and with some reservations. Certainly, they will decide not to join the other team, the "detractors."

The detractors, for a range of possible reasons, are against the change being proposed. They will vocally oppose it, and they will sabotage it whenever they see the chance.

The motivation to be a detractor may lie in a perceived loss of power or influence or maybe from loyalty to a previous leadership that has been supplanted. Whatever the reason, those detractors are a real threat to you bringing about the change you need.

The people in the middle may decide to join the detractors if it is perceived that they are getting traction in their bid to resist the change. Most people don't enjoy "change," and so will consciously or subconsciously avoid it if they can. Never underestimate the power or appeal of the detractors.

What should you do about the detractors? Sometimes they may be colleagues that you appreciate and have worked with for many years. You want to give them a chance to be supportive. You may convince yourself that they are trying to adjust or will come around.

The most dangerous type of detractor is the one who tells you in public that they support you and the changes you propose - but then works against you in private. It is so easy to agree to things in meetings and then...do nothing.

The answer, I am sorry to say on many occasions, is that you have to get rid of them. There really is no other way. You have to move them away from the change process by finding them a new role or, if it comes to it, removing them altogether.

A true detractor will never become a true advocate, and one with influence can massively undermine or even destroy your efforts to do something different.

When you are leading a change process, always work out who is where on the advocate vs. detractor bell curve. Do not allow yourself to be convinced that there aren't really any real detractors - there are.

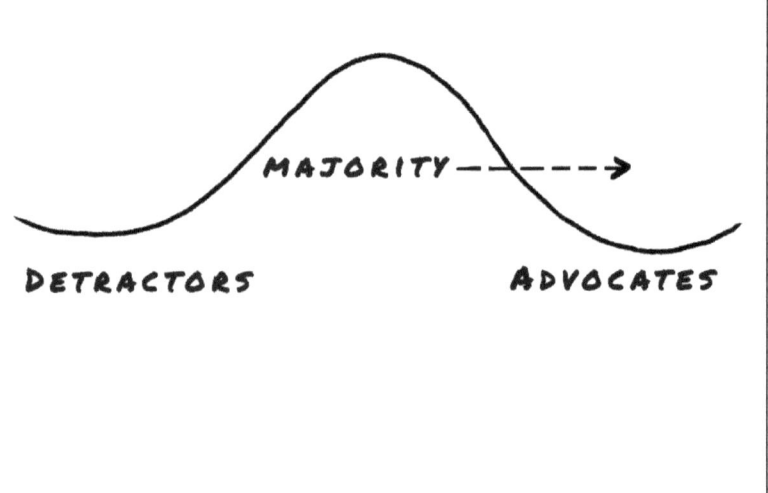

Impact of Change/Stages of Grief

Do not underestimate how challenging change is for people. It is not an exaggeration to say that people literally grieve for their past situation, now lost forever to a program of change that they never wanted.

Perhaps the most famous model for analyzing emotional response to change is the Kübler-Ross Model, first proposed by Elisabeth Kübler-Ross in 1969 in her book *"On Death and Dying."*[48] She studied grief and the emotional stages people pass through as they come to terms with it.

The emotional transition process of grief described by Kübler-Ross has been widely accepted as also applicable for people going through a significant change. They grieve for the old way of doing things.

Living through a transformation, you will probably have to tackle new and alien ways of working. This can be traumatic and may involve a perceived or real loss of confidence, power, autonomy, or prestige. Perhaps you are thinking, "This is all very dramatic, nobody has died," and of course, you are right. Hopefully, no people will perish in the transformation process you are leading.

---

[48] Elisabeth Kübler-Ross, *'On Death & Dying'*, (Simon & Schuster/Touchstone), 1969

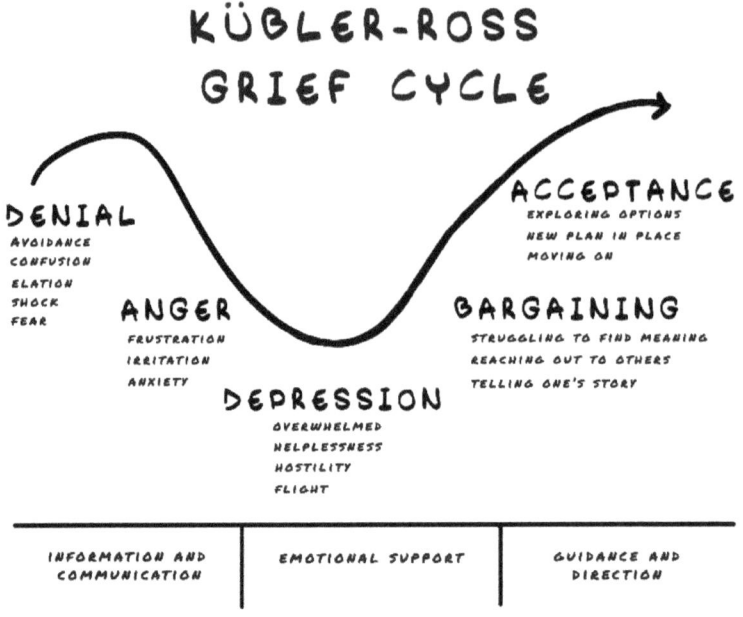

KÜBLER-ROSS GRIEF CYCLE

DENIAL
AVOIDANCE
CONFUSION
ELATION
SHOCK
FEAR

ANGER
FRUSTRATION
IRRITATION
ANXIETY

DEPRESSION
OVERWHELMED
HELPLESSNESS
HOSTILITY
FLIGHT

BARGAINING
STRUGGLING TO FIND MEANING
REACHING OUT TO OTHERS
TELLING ONE'S STORY

ACCEPTANCE
EXPLORING OPTIONS
NEW PLAN IN PLACE
MOVING ON

INFORMATION AND COMMUNICATION | EMOTIONAL SUPPORT | GUIDANCE AND DIRECTION

Nevertheless, to compete and thrive in the time ahead of genuine change, some or many long-held beliefs, ways of behaving, and established practices may have to die, or frankly be killed off. Probably by you.

Segment Your Audience

The more you communicate, and keep communicating, with people affected by a transformation, the more likely you are to succeed in making it happen. Everyone needs to get a consistent message so that there cannot be any suggestion of a lack of alignment among leadership.

Not everyone needs to get the same amount of information. Consider who is directly affected by the changes taking place. They need the most support and information. Others may be only indirectly affected or just vaguely interested, so be careful not to overdo the information they receive, or they may switch off or be irritated by too much detail.

COMMUNICATION TO STAKEHOLDER GROUPS

EACH GROUP NEEDS A SEPARATE PLAN

WHY ARE WE DOING THIS? WHAT ARE WE DOING?

HOW AM I IMPLICATED? WHAT IS EXPECTED OF ME?

GUIDING COALITION	DIRECTLY AFFECTED	INDIRECTLY AFFECTED	REST OF ORGANIZATION	EXTERNAL INFLUENCERS	MARKETPLACE

STAKEHOLDERS
REPORTING

Be Consistent and Keep It Going

Often, a transformation project will begin with an impressive trumpeting of information and speeches, compelling videos, and handshaking by senior leaders. Then, as time passes, less is heard from those leaders who seem to have moved on to other things.

In reality, the start of the change program may even be when less senior support is needed, as hopefully there may be enthusiasm for new ideas and a sense of a new start. As reality bites and the challenge of truly doing things differently becomes constantly harder - that is when people need constant encouragement, recognition, and support.

Just as the communication trails off, so does the chance of a truly successful outcome.

Who Should Be Communicating?

Your team want to hear from two important people: The big leader (CEO, managing director, or whoever they perceive as being overall in charge) and also (very importantly) their own immediate boss (you).

Once the big speech and launch event is over, people want to be able to sit with their direct boss and get the local perspective. If it turns out that the person you report to feels just as in the dark as you do, it is a very bad feeling.

It is vital that an "information cascade" is put in place to allow absolutely everyone in the organization to get the same essential information from all possible different sources. Junior managers need to be provided with talking points and regular updates that allow them to talk with confidence to their teams.

In my experience, this is the part that most organizations get wrong. The top person may be an excellent communicator and an inspirational leader, but too often the whole job of reassuring and engaging is left up to them.

It is time very well spent to work out how to ensure that your messages are disseminated effectively and consistently throughout the organization.

A 2020 study[49] by *Training Industry Magazine* interviewed 2,100 people from different industries and found that there was a consistent response of what was most wanted from leaders at times of change — being a really good communicator was the number one item on the list.

If you can ensure that not only are you an effective communicator but that also the whole team communicates well, then you are onto a winning strategy. You want consistent, supportive, and regular communication to be constantly swirling around the organization.

A Two Way Street

The second most important item surfaced by that study was for people to have a voice and "be heard," as well as to be talked to and informed. Good communication is a two-way street.

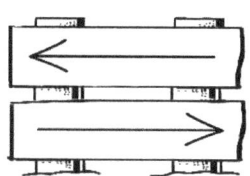

---

[49] Training Industry Magazine, 2002, March-April edition

You may be leading the overall communication of the transformation, but in what way are you empowering the people who are living through it to share their experiences, ask questions, and give their opinions?

This can be achieved through workshops, team meetings, via video conferencing tools, etc., and by inviting others to talk and share. The real power to make change happen lies with the people of the organization. Do everything you can to harness that power and make sure people have a voice and feel listened to.

Own the Story

Above all, as the leader of a major change, you are responsible for owning and consistently telling the high-level, big picture "story" of what is happening.

This is the compelling "why" of everything that you are doing and asking your team to do. You must never lose sight of that or allow the transformation work to become "just one more project."

People become very tired and disillusioned with the "how" and "what" of the challenges they face as they tackle change. You must keep them engaged and motivated by reinforcing the vision and reminding them constantly of the "why."

Remember, as a leader, you are looking to create an emotional connection with your team and for them to trust you to take them somewhere better, or at least help them understand very well why change is needed. It is less about a process and more about their belief.

Get a Coach to Help You

Whether you are a leader of a giant corporate transformation or managing a small team, or just managing yourself to get somewhere new, executing a successful transformation is extremely challenging.

A lot of this chapter has been about bigger, corporate transformations but I hope you can see that most of the basic ideas are similar for an individual.

To give yourself the best chance of success, I recommend that you find yourself a coach to work with you. And not just because I am one.

The list of things that a coach may be able to help with, as you set out on a journey of evolution and change, is long, varied - and totally up to you.

As a start, you can get some help in building your A to B plan to get you clearer about wherever you want, or need, to go.

Your coach should be your valued companion on your journey of transformation. Someone independent that you can trust to go on your journey with you, to be your ally, and tell you the truth.

Reflections

Here are a few key questions arising from the themes raised in this chapter

- Are you involved in a transformation?
- What is your vision for the future state?
- How does your "day to day" work get in the way of your ambitions to change?
- Do you have the right structures and people in place to make a transformation happen?
- Do you have buy-in from the most senior leaders at the top of your organization?
- Why do you think most transformations fail?
- In your organization do you know who might be the likely detractors of change?
- And the advocates?
- Are you communicating enough?
- Is there a way for information to cascade to everyone?

Chapter 17: About Coaching

What Coaching is and What Coaching isn't?

Coaching is all about YOUR ideas. The ambitions of an individual, team, or an organization and the desire to improve, change, or achieve more. You create the vision and decide where you want to go.

Your coach should not be telling you where to head for or how to get there. Coaches support your ideas; consultants bring you theirs.

Consultants are popular with executives because they take things away and work on them and provide suggestions, options, and choices. They will do a lot of the work for you and probably, as part of that process, play back a lot of things to you that you already told them. And they will tell you what, in their opinion, should be done; they may even offer to do it for you.

In contrast, good coaches will constantly push accountability for action and decisions back to you or your team.

The coach's job is to help you think and draw out your own solutions and ideas. Those solutions are more powerful for being created and owned by you. Coaches ask questions. They want to know your answers and why you believe or feel something. The job of the coach is to help you achieve something on your own.

Consultants are often criticized for having 'power without accountability.' They come into your business and generate all sorts of amazing ideas that work brilliantly on paper. They often provide a promise of a financial upside that helps to justify their enormous fee.

A good coach will never take power from you; they will hold you accountable to recognize your own power and your own accountability for your ideas and actions.

If you are looking for ideas, get a consultant. But if you know you need to change and recognize that the energy to bring that about will come from within you or within your team, then engaging with a coach can be transformative.

You Drive the Coaching Agenda/Relationship

Although your coach should help to define or express opportunities or obstacles, you should always feel full ownership of what is being discussed, planned, or actioned.

Some coaching programs bring a series of "modules" to work through—that is fine if it works for you, but it is really teaching. If you have nothing to bring to the coaching process, you probably don't need or want a coach.

You should feel personal responsibility and genuine ownership for what is being discussed and worked on. It is your transformation plan, nobody else's. You need to believe it and want to do it.

Henry Ford famously said, *"Whether you think you can or you think you can't – you're right,"* and certainly attitude and belief massively influence our success or failure.

But just as important is to feel ownership. If it's someone else's idea, it's easy to put the blame elsewhere when real change doesn't happen.

Confidentiality, the 'Coaching Alliance'

Coaching is personal, whether with an individual or with a team. To achieve powerful outcomes, it is highly likely that you will need to share and discuss your fears, perceived weaknesses, or doubts.

Like any professional relationship with a doctor, lawyer, or therapist, absolute confidentiality is needed for both the client and the coach. Issues discussed may start as a business challenge but quickly turn personal. Helping people deal with intensely personal issues is often the path to solving business problems.

You must build trust. Your coach should proactively request and promise total confidentiality at the very start of the relationship. I use the metaphor of sitting in a private, sound-proofed room with the door closed, phones off, blinds shut - a totally safe space.

Business leaders are often lonely. They have many challenges and problems to work on, many times involving delicate issues with people.

They cannot comfortably talk about these to their boss, colleagues, or team without potentially exposing themselves in some way. The coach offers a unique possibility to share concerns and have a good rant without risk. You need to feel that your coach 'has your back.'

Confidentiality extends to the HR team, who may be paying the coach and expect feedback on progress. The coach needs to agree with the client what to share with others. The HR team needs to know and accept that if the coach/client conversations are not confidential, coaching will not get results.

Honesty

Almost as important as confidentiality is honesty. At the start of the coaching relationship, your coach needs to ask your permission to be totally honest. They should say what they see and not hold back in case of causing offense or hurting your feelings or ego.

The coach should be the one person who can really speak their mind to you, not bringing any agenda or being subject to corporate politics.

Equally, the coach should expect and request honesty from their clients. If coaching isn't working for you, you must say so.

If you are having a miserable day and feel like having a good grumble about your infuriating and annoying colleagues, then your coach is the ideal person to 'vent' to.

The 'Laboratory' Mindset

Just as in a brainstorming session, in coaching, there are no bad ideas. The more creative and original, the better. The client and coach should agree that 'anything goes' when it comes to disruptive or controversial proposals and solutions.

Once again, with your coach, you have someone to try out crazy ideas or radical changes. Those ideas might seem politically dangerous or irresponsible if shared with colleagues.

The coach should help you take the best of those experimental ideas out of the laboratory... into your world[50].

Coaching v. Therapy

Due to the often personal nature of discussions, where clients are encouraged to talk about their feelings and experiences, coaching can feel a bit like therapy. Coaches

---

[50] Term first heard by the author in a leadership session in 2009 run by Michelle Kempton (https://kct.es)

shouldn't be afraid of this—it is vital to connect with genuine emotions for people to make real progress.

The vital difference between therapy and coaching is that therapy delves into the past, seeking reasons or events that may influence the present. Therapy clients are looking to come to terms with past experiences and surface feelings. This hopefully can help them feel better about themselves and better manage the present.

Coaching is all about the future, and taking action to make changes or achieve something specific.

It may look at past events to make a better-informed plan, but essentially it is focused on the situation now and how to go forward from there. It is all about bringing out the ambition and energy to make changes or do things better.

What is Coaching Good For?

If people are struggling or unhappy in their job or underperforming, so that remedial action is needed, then coaching is not usually the right approach.

Coaching is about drawing out energy, ideas, and solutions from an individual—to help them envision and plan an optimal future. Therefore, it is most effective when you are already motivated and successful and want to be even better.

A coach should not be used as a convenient solution to give tough feedback or warnings to underperformers. That is the job of management or possibly HR.

Being offered a coach should be positioned as a benefit and seen as a sign of potential and an investment in the individual. Naturally, a coach will want to identify and work on the areas that a person wants or needs to improve, such as being a better speaker, a more confident leader, or better at giving feedback. But these are development areas building up skills for someone who is already working well.

Coaching Strategy

Ideally, an organization will have a coaching strategy developed so that working with a coach is 'normalized' and well understood by everyone.

Coaching is great for people who have just been promoted and are facing new challenges. However, exciting and motivating as it may be, it can also be very daunting to suddenly have an increased scope and responsibilities.

When I was promoted from running a cozy team of 4 to a big-budget worldwide responsibility with a team of 85, I was offered a coach.

It was a game-changer for me as I felt a lot of new pressure. I was able to discuss all sorts of stuff to do with people, structure, and execution with my coach that I could never comfortably discuss with my boss or team. I was also able to discuss my boss.

Many organizations use coaches to help their executives get ready for promotion or achieve promotion hurdles, which is fine. But sometimes I find that my coaching mission comes to an end just when my client needs me most - after that promotion.

Coaching is just one tool in the developmental toolbox available to managers and HR teams and is highly effective if used well. It is most effective for stars on their way up or people who have already achieved significant responsibility. It is not just another type of training.

Can It Be Embarrassing to Have a Coach?

Unfortunately, when someone is not performing well, a coach is often drafted in to try to help. This means that in some organizations, working with a coach is seen as a sign of "problems to be addressed."

If it is felt that having a coach is a sign that you have 'issues,' then executives will naturally shy away from accepting one. I have occasionally had to overcome initial hostility from a client who felt that a coach had been imposed on them.

A useful first step when starting with a coach is to reach out for informal 360-style feedback from colleagues and team members. If you feel that letting people know you have a coach is a sign of failure, then naturally you may be unwilling to broadcast that. Nevertheless, getting the input of your peers and colleagues is a great way to start your coaching journey.

In the best organizations, the very senior leaders all have their own coaches, and it is well understood that having a coach is normal, a positive sign, and encouraged from the top.

If the CEO swears by his or her coach and is open about the benefits of coaching, then everyone will want one!

The CAO

If you are a CEO, business owner, or team leader, you rely on your team to keep you informed, deliver results, and execute your strategy. Despite having all these people around you, it can feel very lonely at the top.

Your coach makes sure that you deliver your part in the success of the business and should have the guts to tell you straight about the things you aren't seeing or maybe don't want to see or hear.

A coach is a powerful addition to your team and ideally will bring significant and relevant experience from their own past or career, and be able to quickly grasp the challenges you face.

Not being a full-time part of your everyday team gives your coach a uniquely big-picture perspective that will be invaluable to you. Your coach is not 'in the politics' and has nothing to lose by being honest with you.

Most importantly of all, your coach will agree with you on what actions you need to take to achieve your goals and ambitions and, by mutual agreement, hold you accountable to make those actions happen.

Your coach is your personal *Chief Accountability Officer.*

<u>Top 30 #29: Coaching is About You</u>

Coaching supports individuals or teams to define their ambitions and then make a plan to achieve them. It is 'you'-centric.

You are the question, the answer, and the plan.

In sports, the coach does not come onto the field and take the kick for you.

Your coach is there to hold you accountable, not to make your decisions for you. To help you think, not to do your thinking for you.

Reflections

Here are a few key questions arising from the themes raised in this chapter.

- Would you like to get a coach?
- Why?
- Or why not?
- How could a coach change things for you?
- Might you feel embarrassed to admit you have a coach? Why?
- What kind of coach are you looking for?
- What are your next steps to find the coach you want or need?

Part 4

The Big Picture

Whatever you are doing in your life at the moment, there will always be an intersection of your inner personal thoughts and ideas with those visible to others in your professional or more public life.

Who you are, what you believe, and why.

You may be a highly-paid and successful business leader (or maybe not) but you are still a person, and you will certainly have some of your own personal philosophy underlying your professional persona.

In this last section I am sharing some of my own more personal thoughts and musings. Some of my own philosophy, to finish off the book.

Chapter 18: No Such Thing as a Free Lunch

Are You Happy?

Is there anything more powerful as an ambition than to be happy? If you achieve contentment, you have got life nailed.

Audrey Hepburn, despite all her beauty and fame, said that, *"The most important thing is to enjoy your life, to be happy, it's all that matters."* She also said, *"Remember, if you ever need a helping hand, it's at the end of your arm,"* implying that it's up to us to fix our own problems and manage ourselves. This is a recurring theme of this book.

You may equate happiness with possessions, money, power, professional achievements, etc., but many 'successful' and financially well-off people are not as happy as you might expect.

Research studies seem to indicate that there is a threshold of financial wealth that we need to reach to not be worried or made unhappy by being short of money. This is in line with Maslow's ideas discussed in Chapter 10.

As you earn more money (up to about $100,000 a year in the USA, for example), you gradually get happier, but studies show that when you pass that point and you have 'enough,' then your happiness level does not increase much even though you may earn a lot more.

Having more money is also likely to make you more isolated from others, which may make you feel less happy overall. Being wealthy sets us apart from others; for example, you may buy a big house with security gates and a long driveway, which will be very luxurious but also potentially lonely.

As you get richer, you don't rely on others like you did in your poorer past. As you get wealthier, you value independence more and being socially connected less. [51]

When you were a poor student, you shared a noisy house with three other equally poor students and probably were quite happy with your life, even though you didn't have much money or many possessions and little privacy.

In his entertaining 2011 TED talk, author and researcher Shawn Achor lays out his theory that rather than success making us happy, it is, in fact, being happy that makes us successful.

His thesis is that happiness and optimism fuel our performance and achievement in life. So, the happier we are, the more successful we're likely to be. He calls this "The Happiness Advantage" and wrote a book about it with the same name. [52]

You need to work on understanding what really makes you happy and content - and if necessary, make adjustments in terms of focus or effort. If you do achieve happiness with what you have, what you are, how you are

---

[51] Studies by Patricia Greenfield of UCLA and Dacher Keltner of Berkeley

[52] "The Happiness Advantage" by Shawn Achor- published 2010 by Crown Currency

perceived by others, and where you are going, everything else is easy by comparison.

The Humanists

Humanistic psychology came about in the 1960s and was something of a rebellion against the two established schools of psychology: "behaviorist" and "psychodynamic."

Carl Rogers (1907 - 1987) is credited with being its founder, although it is also strongly rooted in the ideas of Maslow and his hierarchy of needs.

Behaviorism is all about human behavior being driven through conditioning and how we are influenced by reward or punishment. Appropriate or desired behavior is encouraged through positive reinforcement, and undesirable behavior is limited or eliminated through negative reinforcement. It is only concerned with behaviors that can be observed or measured and does not include the consideration of emotions or motives.

So if you do your homework, you get a prize, and if you don't do your homework, you get punished. You gradually get the idea and adjust your actions accordingly. Behaviorism believes this exchange of reward and punishment is what governs all our actions.

Psychodynamic psychology focuses on the unconscious forces that motivate what we do - especially events from childhood that theoretically have a big effect on us as adults. So the psychodynamic approach delves into our past to try to explain our present.

Both the behaviorist and psychodynamic approaches were regarded as "dehumanizing" by the mold-breaking humanistic psychologists of the 1960s.

Humanistic psychology emphasizes the consideration of the "whole person" and every individual's uniqueness. It assumes that people have free will and are motivated to achieve their potential through their own actions and decisions.

You decide to give your life meaning by actively seeking happiness and helping others to do the same.

Some core concepts of humanism are that you are conscious and aware of your ability to understand yourself. That you have responsibility because of your ability to choose. That you search for meaning, value, and creativity, as well as aiming for goals and being intentional in influencing your own future.

Humanism urges you to acknowledge your basic needs before trying to address your higher needs and ultimately self-actualization.

Humanistic psychology believes that you possess the inner resources to grow and heal yourself if necessary - and that the idea of therapy (if you choose to have some) is to help you remove obstacles that are blocking you.

Your present functioning is what is important, with a big emphasis on your "now" rather than examining your past or attempting to predict your future.

The part I like best about the humanist approach is the belief that to be mentally healthy, you must take personal responsibility for your actions, both positive or negative. You need to grab hold of your own steering wheel and start to drive. You only control yourself.

The ultimate point of being alive is for you to achieve personal growth and understanding. Only through self-improvement and self-understanding can you be truly "happy."

The humanistic approach may be interesting for you if you tend to see the positive side of humanity and believe in your own free will.

Carl Rogers said that for you to be a fully functioning and healthy person, you should be open, present, trusting, creative, and fulfilled.

Personally, I think that is a powerful list.

Creativity

Thanks to creativity, the world moves forward. It's amazing how even over the course of your life, which really isn't very long at all in the greater scheme of humanity, you have seen and will continue to see significant changes in the world and how we live in it.

When I look at photos of myself and my friends in the 1980s, it is fascinating to notice how out of date and old-fashioned we all look. At the time, we thought we were just great. Our hair, clothes, the cars we drove, the TV programs or films we watched, or the music we listened to were all the latest thing.

That is a constant and imperceptible process of change that is going on every minute of our lives, and it is driven by human creativity. We are all part of it.

To be creative requires you to have the courage to let go of certainty and to be able to imagine doing something differently. You've always done something this way, and so to do it a new way can feel uncomfortable and unsettling. You may not be personally designing new things or developing new ideas directly, but by embracing them and buying into them, you also form part of them becoming a reality.

You can't use up creativity; the more you use, the more you have. Albert Einstein said that *"creativity is contagious."*

Enhancing and focusing on the creativity in your life and work is also about embracing change and being ready to take risks.

Taking Risks

There is a thin line between genius and stupidity.

Bubba Watson is possibly the most controversial professional golfer of all time. The left-hander from Florida claims to have 'never had a golf lesson'. He is also rather unpopular among his fellow golf professionals who find him inconsistent and temperamental.

He has an unorthodox swing style that golf commentators love to chortle about when he is playing badly. Despite all this, he has won 10 PGA titles and twice won the US Masters tournament - arguably the number one thing to win in golf.

In the 2012 US Masters, he was in a 'sudden death' play-off with South African player Louis Oosthizen. They hit off at the tenth hole, and Oosthizen was nicely placed in sight of the green (and victory). Bubba hit a long drive but it went deep into the trees on the right-hand side and came to rest on a pathway, at right angles to the fairway, and with no view at all of the green.

The only sensible thing to do to get a clean shot was to chip out along this pathway onto the short grass of the fairway. But also, that probably meant losing the Masters. But there was no other choice ...or so it seemed.

Still 164 yards from the hole, Bubba took aim straight down the tree-lined pathway, perpendicular to where he needed the ball to go, and gave it everything he had. The ball sailed out from the trees, low at first but gaining height, and then suddenly, due to the way Bubba had hit the ball, started to hook dramatically right. He ran out of the woods to see where it had landed as he had no sight of the green or the flight of the ball.

Miraculously, the ball turned through a 90-degree arc and landed just a few feet from the hole to the uproarious approval of the crowd. He made a par and won the Masters. It has gone down as one of the most brilliant golf shots ever played. Genius.

But hang on - let's imagine a different scenario. The maverick Bubba takes out his club, plays the shot, and it skids across the fairway and lands in a pond.

Now he's not a genius, he's an idiot. We can just imagine all the pundits and commentators having a great time talking about his unwise decision and how really he wasn't at the right level, has a poor attitude, didn't have the right technique in the first place, etc., etc.

He took a risk, and it paid off. In leadership situations, risk-taking is not usually so urgent or with such immediate consequences. 'Who dares wins' is often the case, and by definition, every start-up business only starts at all because someone takes a risk.

The people who create incredibly successful businesses are geniuses, and all the many, many others who fail are stupid? I don't think so.

"People who don't take risks generally make about two big mistakes a year. People who do take risks generally make about two big mistakes a year." [53]

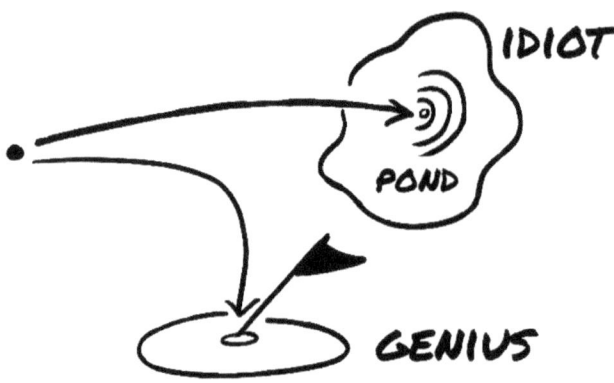

As businesses become more established, the temptation is for their leaders to also become risk-averse as there is more and more to lose. It makes sense. Unfortunately, with risk-taking, it does tend to expose you to that oversimplified binary judgment of 'genius v. stupid'. Managed risk-taking has to become part of every leader's golf bag of tools.

The trick is to find the balance between the right amount of analysis and good management of what you have

---

[53] Peter Drucker (1909 - 2005) Educator, author and leadership visionary

- your skills, resources, leverage, etc. - and being ready to take some risks when needed.

Finding the right balance of risk that works for you, or for your business, is a fundamental element of success. Finding the right balance is fundamental for everything.

Balance

Have you ever been in love? Not for nothing is it called being 'madly in love.' When we seriously fall for someone, everything else becomes less important and we can indeed become a little crazy. You don't call your friends or family, you can't concentrate on work, you forget to eat, your whole life becomes about when you can next see that special someone who has entered your life and turned it on its head.

I hope you have had that experience because it is an amazing and unique feeling. But is it sustainable?

It would be exhausting to live for years in a state of distraction and obsession with the object of your desire. You would never get anything done, and probably no one would even get married or get organized to buy a house together if that were the case.

Falling in love is a key part of the process of finding a partner to share your life with, but there are many other less exciting but still highly important parts to that too, if that is going to work out well. Being crazy in love puts you out of balance, and that is not a sustainable way to live.

We can and will go out of balance at different points in our lives and work, and very often that is a necessary step

413

to achieve success. To pass important exams, we need to study for hours every day (and night), but we can't keep that up for months at a time.

For our lives to work well over an extended period, we need eventually to be in balance. Being out of balance is manageable for a while, and may even be enjoyable or exciting, but it is not sustainable.

When we are working 15 hours a day, ill, distracted by being madly in love, drunk, taking drugs, depressed, or ecstatic, it means we are out of balance - and it is good to recognize that.

Every one of us is different, and you may be one of those lucky people who can live on only 4 hours of sleep every night - known as 'short sleepers'. Most of us cannot do that. If you try, it will have consequences.

In the short term, not getting enough sleep will affect your cognitive functioning, mood, coordination, motor skills, and anxiety. Over the long term, it increases your risk of diabetes, serious depression, heart issues, and even psychosis. Just as night follows day, you were designed to work, rest, and play. You just have to find the time and the ways to make that happen.

Getting enough sleep is just one example. We have to be conscious of what is 'just enough' for each one of us. Too much or too little of anything will eventually have negative consequences.

A respected mentor of mine used to say to me, 'a little of what you fancy does you good'. In other words, we don't have to deprive ourselves of things or activities we enjoy in order to be successful. We do have to aim for moderation. One glass of wine is good, two glasses is probably great, six glasses is too many for most of us.

The idea that balance is important is nothing new, in fact, it is extremely ancient. The familiar symbol of yin and yang is from Chinese philosophy dating from around 650 BC, which describes opposing but connected forces that interact to affect our lives and well-being.

The philosophy says that these balanced forces are complementary and present in all aspects of our lives. In some circumstances, one force may become more dominant and push you out of balance.

Yin is described as negative and passive energy from the Earth and the moon. It is receptive, dark, cool, soft, still, and contemplative. Introverted.

Yang, on the other hand, is positive and active. It comes from the energy of the sun. Energetic, expansive, and warm. Extroverted.

While these forces may often oppose one another, they coexist in harmony. They are equal and dependent upon one another. The constant state of flux between these life forces helps create a balance, which benefits individuals, societies, and cultures.

Underpinning the Yin and Yang philosophy are three important essential ideas or philosophies about how life works:

1. **Change** - everything is always in a state of flux, which means that we might emphasize the

positive or negative depending on the demands of any given moment or situation. We never stand still.

2. **Contradiction** - everything is made up of opposing, simultaneously existing elements or forces.

3. **Holism** - all things are connected, and nothing exists in isolation. We cannot understand what is truly happening without looking at the big picture of experiences, people, and events.

The yin-yang philosophy views mental well-being as achieving a balance between the positive and negative forces in your life. This emphasizes not just the importance of equilibrium but also the inherent interconnectedness of everything.

We need to build up our awareness of our own limits and limitations and, when we feel we are going out of balance, recognize that. Depending on the situation, you may need days, months, or even years to achieve a balanced life as well as achieve your chosen goals - but that must be your eventual ambition.

To do that, you will need to make choices.

Choices

We have control over our own choices, and they have a direct effect on what happens to us. It is a myth that we are "forced" in certain directions by other people, and trying to make others responsible for choices we make is not honest or constructive.

Circumstances can force us to make difficult decisions, and it is tempting to say that our lives are out of control. However, how we choose to deal with setbacks and challenges is, in itself, a choice.

Life is a long series of choices, and how well we manage each one is directly linked to our success and, ultimately, our happiness. You can do anything you want, but not everything you want.

Focus on the Good Stuff

I find it useful to step back and think about the situations of life and leadership as being like a house observed from a distance after dark. There are many windows in the house, and from some of them, light is shining brightly. It looks warm and cozy in those rooms.

Other windows only show a weaker light, and it is hard to see what is happening in there. Some rooms are dark and look totally closed off. Cold and unwelcoming.

It is natural that not everything is going to be perfect, but in general, we might expect light at all the windows, shouldn't we? Why is there no light shining from some rooms? It may well be worthwhile to investigate and try to improve the situation. It is terrible that those rooms are dark, right? What is happening? Who is to blame?

But hang on, there is strong, warm light coming from some of the house. Whatever is going on in there seems to be working. How about investigating that and finding out the secret to success rather than focusing on what obviously isn't going well?

We have a tendency to focus on what is going wrong when sometimes the clues to how to improve things can be found by looking more carefully at what is going right.

If we pay too much attention to the rooms where there is little or no light, we can start to feel like the whole house is unwelcoming and depressing. We can soon develop negative feelings about it even though some areas are working well.

This is also a good metaphor for relationships - whether personal or professional. Not everything is going to be ideal. Perhaps there are reasons why someone doesn't want to enter those dark rooms with you. Maybe that will take some time and some work for you to go in together and try to generate some light together.

Focus on the good stuff, what is working well and creating light. Perhaps the reasons for the dark rooms will naturally emerge and some ideas for shedding some extra light too.

You Can Do It

Whatever you set your mind to, within practical reason, you can do it.

My mother was quite an inspirational woman. She dealt with a lot of setbacks in her life and never gave up or gave in to negativity. She never criticized other people or blamed others for things that happened to her, and relentlessly looked for a positive outcome. Typically, she found one.

She died at 94 after a long and interesting life.

When she was about 75, she announced to her family that, despite no previous experience, she was going to write a novel.

Perhaps you can imagine our reaction? "Sure! Great idea, Mum. Of course, a novel...! On you go."

We couldn't possibly imagine that she could make it happen. But she could imagine it. She sat down one day in front of her typewriter and started to write and kept at it.

In the end, not just one, but four of her novels were published. You can buy all of them on Amazon if you'd like to have a read. [54] When she was asked on national television why she chose to start writing at such an age, she just said that she "felt like doing it" and enjoyed it.

The point of this story is that if you set your mind to it, you can do just about anything you want. The obstacles may seem daunting, the reasons for giving up or not starting many, and the naysayers will be all around you.

But if YOU decide you can achieve something, then you probably can. You need to be able to see yourself up on the podium getting a medal. You have to focus on the reasons why you can, not on all the reasons why you can't.

You Can Do Anything You Want, Just Not Everything

There are so many possibilities in life, and usually the main thing holding us back from achieving just about anything is our own self-limiting feeling of our capabilities, limitations, and what is possible for us.

Others may tell us that we cannot do something, and we have to be careful not to let others limit us or give us an excuse for not believing in ourselves.

If we truly set out to do something, really, it can almost always be achieved. But if we believe it cannot be done, we will most certainly prove ourselves right.

---

[54] Novels by Nancy Ross published by Poolbeg Press Ltd. *Still Waters Run Deep* (2003), *The Enchanted Island* (2004), *Love & Friendship* (2004), *Alice* (2006)

Also, we need to accept that we cannot achieve or obtain everything we want all of the time. There are 24 hours in a day, and achieving one thing will logically have the opportunity cost of giving up on other things.

It is helpful to have this clear and to be conscious of what we are doing at this moment, what we are leaving for later, and what we accept we are never likely to do.

This also means that we need to be decisive. After we have chosen one path, it is nothing but a waste of time and focus to be constantly doubting our decision. If we dither too long, we may lose a good opportunity.

No Such Thing as a Free Lunch

You don't get something for nothing in this world. We can choose not to get on the train, but then we must accept that we are not going anywhere new.

Typically, success in anything (work, relationships, family, projects, sport, life) is a function of the effort, time, and mental commitment we are ready to put into it.

If you do not feel you are successful or satisfied, it is likely that you will need to choose to change direction or work harder at it to expect improvement.

The more we face up to our fears, challenges, and weaknesses and address them, the sooner we will get nearer to what we truly want.

Equally, our success or achievements will almost certainly come with some kind of price that must be paid.

This is the essence of Yin and Yang philosophy. It is, in itself, part of life's balance.

If you want a big salary, a nice office, and a shiny car, you will have to pay for it with your energy and your time. Many successful people talk about how they regret that their success has come at the cost of something else that they value. Time spent with family or loved ones being the most typical price of success.

An Australian palliative caregiver named Bronnie Ware recorded the final sentiments of the people she cared for in their very last moments of life. [55] What did people regret most about their lives? This is the list:

- I wish I'd had the courage to live a life true to myself, not the life others expected of me
- I wish I hadn't worked so hard
- I wish I'd had the courage to express my feelings
- I wish I had stayed in touch with my friends
- I wish I had let myself be happier

It seems like at the moment of dying, you don't tend to say, *"I wish I'd made more money and been more successful,"* or *"I wish I had gotten that promotion,"* or *"I wish I had a bigger office."*

Notice how all of the regrets expressed were of a personal and emotional nature. How life turned out to be about doing things that got in the way of family, friendship,

---

[55] *The Top Five Regrets of the Dying: A Life Transformed by the Dearly Departing* by Bronnie Ware - Hay House, Inc., 2012.

and ultimately, happiness. So, is success, in the end, the opportunity cost of happiness? I don't believe so.

It's all very well to realize all this when you are at death's door, but in your life, you are under tremendous pressure to work hard, compete, and succeed at whatever it is you do.

What I do think is important is to always remember that we are truly only responsible for our own lives and for the choices we make for ourselves.

If anything is going to change, we have to change it. We blame others or situations we find ourselves in for our inability to make changes, and often there is truth in that. There are many obstacles. Change is hard.

In the end, those choices you make, your state of balance, and your level of acceptance that nothing comes for free are all exclusively yours, and yours alone. We only control ourselves; we don't control others, and nobody controls us.

If in your final moments you have regrets, then really you have only yourself to blame. If you want to change something, then work out how to change it. Be a leader of yourself.

Three Elements at Work

Some years ago, I went through a divorce. It wasn't a terrible one, and in many ways, it was a successful process of transformation without any great damage being done to anyone involved.

Spending more time on my own than I was used to, I found that it was a time of reflection. I thought a lot about how the world works and what forces are at work to make things happen to us, as well as how we react.

To sum up these last pages, my own personal model, which came to me during that time, combines the three elements of choices, balance, and how nothing comes to us for free.

The context (and context must never be ignored) is that we must remember that in all things, you only control yourself.

When you accept this, it makes everything clearer, not necessarily easier. You have sole responsibility for your decisions and actions. Things may "happen" to you, but how you choose to react is your choice.

- Your **personal choices** are fundamental to what happens to you. If you feel like you are being "forced" to make a choice you don't want by someone or some situation, you must be honest with yourself about what is happening. Deciding to accept it is a choice.

- **Balance** is essential for a happy and successful life. Your idea of balance may be totally different from other people's, and there is no magic formula. You can be out of balance for a while, but it just isn't sustainable. You need to decide what balance means for you.

- **You don't get anything for nothing.** Whatever it is you want, you will have to work hard for it and sacrifice other things to get it.

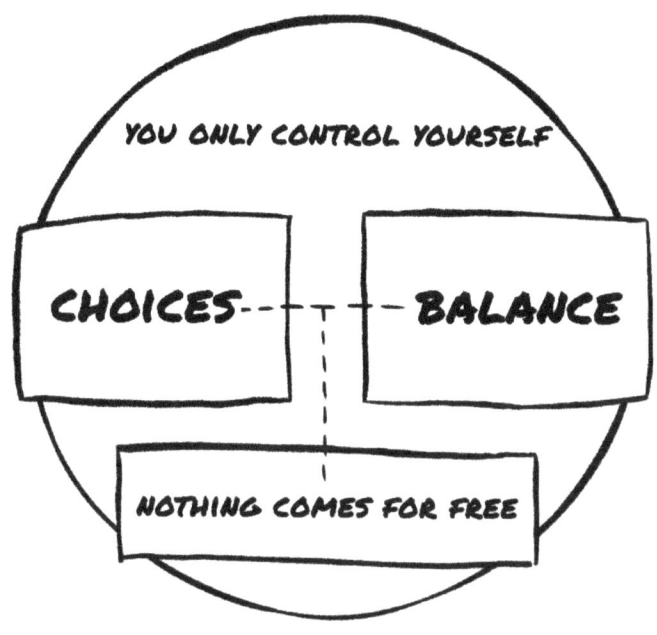

The Only Constant Is Change

Life is a never-ending process of change. King Cnut was a popular king and ruled England from 1016 to 1035. He was fed up with his fawning courtiers and followers telling him he was all-powerful and could do anything he wanted.

He had his throne (perhaps with him on it, who knows?) carried down to the beach and commanded the tide not to come in.

Once he had gotten his feet thoroughly wet, he admonished his team, reminding them that some things are just not in our control. Legend has it that he then hung up his crown and never wore it again.

This story is also interesting as it has been wrongly recorded by history as an anecdote about an arrogant leader, that the king believed he could stop the tide and was then made to look a fool. (See how important good communication is to make sure the real story is not replaced by a more interesting one?)

Trying to hold the 'tide of life' back from its destined course and being in denial and hoping that you can control the natural evolution of things does not help you to cope with it..

Unexpected, and often bad, stuff happens to us in life and it is tempting to ask 'why me?' A better question is 'What am I going to do about it?'

It is not the things that happen that you can control; it is how you manage them that is in your hands.

As leaders of ourselves or of others, the extent to which you take responsibility for your actions in the face of the inevitable process of change has a direct impact on the likelihood of a positive evolution or outcome.

Life and leadership will constantly throw us curveballs on our personal journey. We can certainly influence to a great extent what happens along the way by how we approach and accept the challenges, opportunities, and setbacks we meet.

Nothing stands still. Change is the only constant.

Embrace it.

Top 30 #30: Embrace!

Nothing is permanent. Embrace change, don't fight it.

Recently, I was on the beach in Spain with my daughter, who is 9. Together, we built an impressive sandcastle with various towers—a larger one for the Queen to live in—an outer defensive wall with more towers, and various ditches and moats. It looked pretty impressive, and we were proud of our work.

Then, it began to dawn on her that the tide was coming in. Every few minutes, the lapping waves became more threatening. Sections of the outer walls were breached, a tower collapsed, and the moat filled with water. She fought a frantic battle of digging and reinforcing to stave off annihilation, even enlisting her big brother to help.

Eventually, much to her frustration, tinged with a little bit of excitement, our magnificent castle was overwhelmed by a wave. The water sloshed in the moat, the walls collapsed, and the Queen's tower was suddenly leaning at a critical angle. It was all over. A few hours later, when we walked along the same stretch of beach, nothing at all remained of our previous efforts.

Is this a sad story? Certainly, it is not a bad metaphor for life itself.

However impressive our life works or achievements may be, in the end, the eternal process of nature is as insurmountable as the incoming tide.

The life cycle of a sandcastle is not long, nor its impact on the world significant. Its success is measured only by the transient enjoyment of making it and the satisfaction it brings while it is still there.

If we take the attitude that it is a pointless exercise as we know how it inevitably ends, then we will never build any sandcastles. And many people never do.

We can experience great satisfaction from mowing our front lawn, both from the act of doing it and seeing how it looks once we've done it; even though we know that in a matter of days, it will need mowing again.

Returning to a theme that has recurred throughout this book, there are many things in life that we cannot control—but we can control how we choose to deal with them, react to them, and interpret them.

Life and business will throw triumphs and opportunities into our path, as well as disappointments and setbacks. Frequently, we find ourselves in situations that we did not expect, and for which we have had no time to prepare ourselves. Change is forced upon us, and our natural reaction is often to reject it, fight it, and try to get back 'on track'.

What if we consciously decide to accept that life is indeed temporary by its very nature, and that its very lack of permanence is what makes it so extraordinary?

What if we actively recognize that constant change and dealing with the unexpected is, in fact, what makes life worth living? What if we intentionally face up to the reality that we actually control nothing at all?

Does any of that in any way detract from the value of our efforts to make the absolute best of everything that comes our way? To take every opportunity. To tackle every challenge.

We can make a conscious choice to focus on the job well done, or the feeling of satisfaction, or the realization that we have done something that has helped in some way.

We can take away that when we were tested, we chose to accept the test, and when questioned, we did our best to answer the question.

Life itself is a constant, if gradual, change process. Birth, growth, learning, aging, decline, and eventually death... Despite this, and maybe because of it, every one of us is innately resistant to change.

Change is around us every single day of our lives, and how well we cope with it can be a measure of our success and happiness.

We can resist change but we can never stop it. We can influence it by choosing to accept it, rather than reject it.

Whatever we achieve in life will come at some kind of cost, and getting on with the new will inevitably mean letting go of the old. Whatever we do will always inevitably come with a price of some sort. Sorry, there really is no free lunch.

I was once asked what image or phrase I would choose to be written up on a billboard at the side of a busy highway, as a message to everyone who passed it on their personal journey through life.

I said I'd like to see just one word filling the whole space:

'Embrace!'

Whatever life throws at you, embrace it. Work out what you can do to influence it and manage it, and make it work for you. Own it.

The End

Index **Page**